Contents

Introduction

Introduction to the first edition

This book is for that marvellous person: 'the average reader'. It is not for academic linguists, or advanced students of language. Rather it is aimed at those generations of readers who have passed through the British school systems without being able to say quite what a verb, or a preposition, or a clause, is. Those generations now extend – unbelievably perhaps – to include a generation of schoolteachers of English, many of whom cannot themselves say exactly what a verb, or a preposition, or a clause, is; and who are now rightly being asked to inform their pupils about such basic aspects of the language.

It is not that we do not know what grammar is; we have all been using language, in all its complexity, from early childhood. It is merely that we have not for several generations of British schooling felt its articulation to be worth while.

What is grammar? Grammar is the study of a language. Students of grammar are interested in dismantling language – and putting it together again – to see how it works. So grammar is the study of the mechanics and dynamics of language. In a way, we are all students of language from the cradle to the grave. Five-year-old children are particularly keen students of grammar, and can pronounce authoritatively and often correctly: 'That's wrong,' or 'That isn't how you say it.' We all know grammar therefore, but we are not all able to describe its nuts and bolts. This book tries to help us with these nuts and bolts. Technical terms are therefore included, but I try to keep them to a minimum and to define them along the way in clear and consistent terms.

As part of our general knowledge, grammar should of course be taught in schools. A good knowledge of grammar should help us use language more effectively, both in our writing and in our speaking. It should encourage us to be precise and measured in our utterances. And, of course, knowledge of our own grammar will be especially helpful to us when we come to study foreign languages and their grammars. Much of the grammar we study in our own language turns out to be useful with foreign languages – they too have verbs, tenses and clauses. And surely one of the reasons for Britain's appalling record in foreign-language provision has something to do with our refusal over several generations to teach the basics of our own language. That, after all, is where everything starts.

How to use this book
In setting out to prepare this project, I was reminded of the oriental wisdom that there are sixty-three different ways to climb a mountain. So it is with grammar. Where to begin?

I have begun with **words** in Part 1 of the book, because we all know – or think we know – what a word is. From there I have gone to **phrases**, as the next building block in the hierarchy. Part 2 deals with **clauses** and **sentences**. I realise that there are those who believe that grammar should be approached the other way about. But I felt that to start with the sentence would offer a harder route to the summit – the North Wall of the Eiger rather than the Cook's Tour of the Alps. And as part of my aim was to make the approach as simple as possible, this route seemed less appropriate for me.

I have tried in Part 1 to avoid using terms that are not defined till Part 2, so in that sense I assume the book will be used consecutively. But I hope it will also be used for reference, and to that end a detailed index is provided.

Parts 3–6 of the book are autonomous and may be read in any order. Part 7 offers a few simple exercises, where readers may check up on how much they know.

January 1993

Introduction to the second edition

Since the first edition of this book was published in 1993, it has become standard practice for British universities to offer special classes in English for their new undergraduates. The decline in standards of written English – widely remarked – means that the written work of many if not most students today is littered with grammatical errors, spelling mistakes and erratic (or absent) punctuation. There has been a significant, measured and settled decline in the ability of students to construct coherent, well organised and grammatically correct essays. Many students don't know the difference between *its* and *it's*, *whose* and *who's*, or *there* and *their*. They may use commas too often or not at all. Some of them randomly, erratically and inconsistently sprinkle their punctuation marks through their essays at the end of their exam (rather like confetti): or that is the impression given, especially perhaps with apostrophes or hyphens.

It wasn't always thus. British universities didn't used to offer 'remedial' English classes. They viewed it as the job of the schools to turn out literate students with basic writing skills. They thought it was the job of the schools to teach children the nuts and bolts, such as the difference between a noun and a verb.

They assumed that their students had learned the functions of sentences and paragraphing before they left school. But the proof of the pudding tells them otherwise. Many of their undergraduates arrive at university unable to write a coherent essay (let alone a stylish one); they don't know what a verb is; and for most of them the rules of sentence-building and paragraphing are a complete mystery. Common errors listed by one professor of English include skewed tenses and failure to make verbs agree with nouns, and paragraphs that roll along for ever like Ole Man River. He listed common spelling errors such as *rembers* for *remembers, refference, single-handidly, computor, comission, absense, godess* (everyone has their favourite examples), and a wide range of versions of *contemporary, procedure, parallel* and *necessary*.

For some time there have been complaints (from higher education as well as from employers' agencies like the CBI) about standards of literacy, whether among first-year undergraduates or graduates entering employment. In many ways the current generation must comprise the most knowledgeable and articulate students in our history, but far too many of them cannot express their ideas in clear and fluent writing. The problem exists across the entire spectrum of study: whether they are law students, historians, scientists or linguists, they all need classes in basic writing skills. They all need to learn about the overall design and unity of coherent writing; and how to lead from one thought into another with appropriate sentence linkages and sensible paragraphing.

Perhaps the best way to learn to write well is by reading well. Good writing skills can be absorbed by many people – but not all – through a diet of good reading; by a sort of osmosis. But many schoolchildren and students read less today, and the reading diet is often substandard; so nowadays we have to depend less on this route to good writing.

That brings us to things like grammar. Sadly, too many people regard grammar as boring; and it has been allowed to remain as unpopular as ever in schools, despite lip-service – political window-dressing! – that suggests otherwise. But a knowledge of grammar and punctuation give us the rules and structures necessary for effective and competent communication in writing. In order for students to become proficient in the skill of good writing, they need to familiarise themselves with the rules and language of language. That is why universities now offer classes in the art of writing for students; because too often the schools have failed to provide it.

The problem has been most dramatic in the teaching of foreign languages in British schools and universities. How do you teach foreign languages to students who lack any knowledge of the workings of their own? How do students acquire the grammar of French or Japanese when they don't know their own? This problem, more than any other, is behind the collapse in the numbers of students of foreign languages in Britain: this in a country that is light years behind other EU countries in the learning of foreign languages.

In the first edition of this book, I said it was for that marvellous person, 'the average reader'. This second edition is also for all those students – of whatever subject – who have problems with their writing. They know who they are, and they know that 'the system' has let them down in this basic skill. This book is a reference tool for them. It should provide them with the necessary vocabulary and examples to develop their own writing strategies. There are also a few exercises (with answers), particularly of punctuation.

Editing, writing and modern technology

It is easier than ever nowadays to write an essay. No longer are we faced with the laborious job of physically rewriting it. We have built-in spell-checks, and an online thesaurus to proffer a ready supply of synonyms. But the paradox of the computer has been to reinforce our obsessions with speed and quantity, and not our aspirations to raising the quality of our writing. The World Wide Web contains vast amounts of accessible information, much of it slickly produced but appallingly written. E-mail has likewise encouraged sloppiness: anything goes in terms of grammar, punctuation or spelling (and the thinking behind it) in order to send a message *now*.

So, in a funny way, the computer exacerbates the decline in standards of writing (and thinking). Basic skills and standards have had to make way for the instant response. And the easiest way to do that is to feed off other instant responses; and goodness knows, there's more than enough to choose from when accessing infinity online. But problems like relevance quickly arise: often a selected source is only tangentially relevant to the students' essay topics. So do they 'fillet' it for the relevant bits, and then build these into their essay? Have they the skills to do this? Or do they lift the entire piece? In either case, do they acknowledge their sources? (Plagiarism is a separate matter, but is now quite a serious problem.)

Where, in all this, is the *process* of writing? If their writing is actively to aid students' understanding – and help them react to and interact with their essay topics and unravel the complexities of their thought processes – they are going to need the time and space to take their ideas back to the drawing board and develop them from scratch. This means paper and pencils; it means second thoughts (and often third and fourth); it means building up their own coherent and well argued responses. And only then does it mean committing a draft of their writing to the electronic keyboard (and then editing it, as often as necessary). Otherwise what is to stop them making do with semi-relevant sound-bites and sequences of clumsy sentences that may have taken their fancy, trawled and plagiarised from who-knows-where on the Internet?

The current wisdom is that IT is sexy, grammar is boring . . . This nonsense has gone on too long and it's high time it was challenged, head on if necessary. Such a formidable technological resource in the hands of students who have not been taught how to write at school? Is that not a formula for serious communication breakdown? Panacea it certainly aint.

A note on style

In the sense that style is affectation, it is to be avoided in writing. It's as simple as that. Student writers of English should aim above all for clarity of thought and expression: the right word in the right place, to paraphrase Jonathan Swift. If you can manage that, it is then worth thinking about a sense of rhythm. A series of one-sentence paragraphs is not advisable, for example, even if you plan a career working for the *Sun* newspaper: that is the equivalent of machine-gun fire, and lacks variety.

The following definitions and descriptions of style are from the dictionaries of quotations:

'True ease in writing comes from art, not chance,
As those move easiest who have learned to dance.
'Tis not enough no harshness gives offence,
The sound must seem an echo to the sense.'
(Alexander Pope, in An Essay on Criticism, 1711)

'Proper words in proper places, make the true definition of a style.'
(Jonathan Swift, 1720)

'Whoever wishes to attain an English style, familiar but not coarse, and elegant but not ostentatious, must give his days and nights to the volumes of Addison.'
(Dr Johnson, in Lives of the English Poets, 1779–81)

'People think that I can teach them style. What stuff it all is! Have something to say, and say it as clearly as you can. That is the only secret of style.'
(Matthew Arnold, attrib. 1898)

'The web, then, or the pattern; a web at once sensuous and logical, an elegant and pregnant texture; that is style, that is the foundation of the art of literature.'
(R L Stevenson, in The Art of Writing, 1905)

Dr Johnson is right to recommend we study the classics in order to achieve a decent style of writing; for Addison, we might today substitute some slightly more modern exemplars – whether from children's writing or adult. Good examples of modern classics might include work by writers such as Winston Churchill, E M Forster, Muriel Spark, Joseph Conrad, D H Lawrence, George Orwell, Evelyn Waugh, Laurie Lee, Anthony Powell, Kingsley Amis, V S Naipaul, Doris Lessing, Chinua Achebe, N'gugi wa Thiongo, Harper Lee, Ernest Hemingway, Truman Capote or John Updike. The R L Stevenson quotation is perhaps a little high-flown for our purposes, but we can see what he is getting at. We may not all aim to write literature, but we should all aim to write well.

Acknowledgements
A second edition of a book is often harder to put together than the first. This book has been no exception, and bears out all those people who tell us that it is easier to start work from scratch than to revisit past work. Whatever the truth of

this, I would like to acknowledge two particular sources of help without whom this new edition would never have come about: Betty Kirkpatrick for kick-starting me into revisiting the project, and Vivienne McDonald for much practical electronic assistance in nailing it to the floor.

May 2007

One

Words and phrases

words

nouns
pronouns
adjectives
determiners
verbs
adverbs
prepositions
conjunctions
interjections

phrases

The investigation of words is the beginning of education.

Antisthenes the Sophist

Every name is called a NOUN,
As field *and* fountain, street *and* town;
In place of noun the PRONOUN
stands,
As he *and* she *can clap their hands;*
The ADJECTIVE *describes a thing,*
As magic *wand or* bridal *ring;*
The VERB *means action, something
done—*
To read *and* write, *to* jump *and* run;
How things are done the ADVERBS
tell,
As quickly, slowly, badly, well;
The PREPOSITION *shows relation,*
As in *the street or* at *the station;*
CONJUNCTIONS *join, in many ways,*
Sentences, words, or phrase *and
phrase;*
The INTERJECTION *cries out,* 'Hark!
I need an exclamation mark!'

An old children's rhyme for
remembering the parts of speech

Why words?

Wisely or unwisely, this book begins with words. Why? Because words are the building bricks. Without them there is no language, and no grammar is feasible. Also, it is likely that words came first historically, after grunts. Later on came the mortar of grammar to give structure to the building bricks; or so one might imagine. Over time, the rules of grammar evolved, and continue evolving. Many of our grammar rules are traceable to ancient Greek, and to the Latin of the Romans. We are reminded of this every time we speak or hear another Indo-European language: the grammar of English is very like that of French, German, Spanish, Italian or even Russian. And not just the grammar; often the words too derive from the same family of roots.

Among other things, words give us the language of language. That is perhaps another reason for starting with them. If we start with the eight or nine traditional parts of speech, we give ourselves a basic vocabulary for thinking or talking about language.

The nine parts of speech (see the foregoing list) were once taught in every British school, albeit in a rather prescriptive way. Then in the 1960s and 70s we threw out the baby with the bath water, and there are many people who would add that it's been downhill all the way ever since. I don't take that view; but I do take the view that we need as a society to become more adept at and comfortable with using the language of language. It is not acceptable nowadays for educated people (whether lawyers, teachers, town planners, civil servants, farmers or whatever) to ask the question, 'What is a noun?' This is especially true if they have a good set of public examination passes that include English; and quintespecially true if they have acquired a university degree (which takes us back to the introduction to the new edition of this book).

So: parts of speech, as we once called them. They are easy to understand. They unlock the door into grammar and the vocabulary of language. We should all be familiar with them. For these reasons they are worth learning, and no apology for teaching them is required.

Nouns

There are far more nouns in the dictionary than all the other parts of speech put together. That is why, when learning foreign languages, we have to learn reams and reams of nouns before we even begin to acquire a working vocabulary in that language.

Traditionally, **nouns** are defined as 'naming words', or the names of persons, animals, places or things. This is still a useful definition, as far as it goes. But modern grammarians are interested in describing the function of a word, as well as defining its meaning. They like to clarify what a word does in a sentence before assigning a part of speech to it. For example, look at the nouns (italicised) in these:

Stop the *watch*!   **Watch the *stop*!**
They threw out the *rubbish*.   **They rubbished his *throw*.**

Stop, watch, throw and *rubbish* may be verbs and they may also be nouns – their function in the sentence dictates their part of speech. It is important to remember that the same word can do different things in different places.

Types of noun – proper or common

The words *city* and *country* are called **common nouns**; there are lots of cities and countries in the world. But words like *Moscow* and *Russia* are called **proper nouns**, because there is only one particular country called *Russia* and only one *Moscow*. Similarly, *woman* and *man* are common nouns; there are lots of them too. But *Eliza* and *Augustus* are proper nouns (and also proper names), and *Eliza Doolittle* and *Augustus Montague Toplady* are proper names too, because they refer to very particular individuals. They are specific, or proper, to them alone. Proper nouns require the use of an initial capital letter, common nouns do not.

Sometimes proper nouns find their way into the language as common nouns:

He is a proper *Scrooge*.
This isn't the *Paris* I used to know.
I used to know three different *John Smiths*.

Types of nouns – abstract or concrete

Nouns may be either **concrete**, when they refer to things you can touch (*nails, cabbage, chocolate, table, tyres*), or they may be **abstract**, when they refer to ideas or concepts (*beauty, truth, Marxism, theology*).

Types of nouns – singular or plural

Most English noun endings indicate a difference between 'one' (**singular**) and 'more than one' (**plural**). The vast majority of them add -*s* or -*es* to show the plural form. If they end in a consonant + *y*, they change that to -*ies*:

Singular	Plural
book	book**s**
dog	dog**s**
banana	banana**s**
tree	tree**s**
bush	bush**es**
kiss	kiss**es**
berry	berr**ies**
fairy	fair**ies**

A few English nouns are **irregular**, and form their plurals in other ways, by changing their vowel, by adding *-en*, or by following a foreign rule:

Singular	Plural
man	m**e**n
woman	wom**e**n
child	child**ren**
ox	ox**en**
foot	f**ee**t
tooth	t**ee**th
goose	g**ee**se
mouse	m**i**ce
stimulus	stimul**i**
bacillus	bacill**i**
larva	larva**e**
criterion	criteri**a**
automaton	automat**a**

A few nouns ending with *-f* form plurals with *-ves*:

Singular	Plural
loaf	loa**ves**
wolf	wol**ves**

Similarly with words like *leaf, thief, scarf, hoof*.

Some nouns have two plural forms. *Brother* has *brothers* or the older form *brethren*. The latter form is now used only in a special (mainly religious) context. Other words with two plural forms are:

Singular	Plural
appendix	{ appendi**xes** (anatomical) { appendi**ces** (literary)
formula	{ formula**s** { formula**e**
focus	{ focus**es** { foc**i**

Some nouns are used only in the singular:

news	**chemistry**	**music**
snooker	**mathematics**	**physics**

and other scientific subjects. Other nouns are used only in the plural:

scissors	**trousers**	**cattle**	**vermin**
jeans	**thanks**	**congratulations**	**police**

To refer to any of the latter in the singular, use constructions such as:

a pair of scissors/jeans/trousers
a police*woman*

Types of noun – countable or uncountable

> Nouns are **countable** if:
they can be preceded by *a*: *a car*
they can be both singular and plural: *a dog, dogs*
they can be counted: *one taxi, two taxis, twenty taxis*

> Nouns are **uncountable** if:
they are preceded by *some* rather than *a*: *some salt, some marmalade*
they are not normally counted or pluralised: *two butters, eleven flours*

Most uncountable nouns denote commodities or notions that tend not to be counted out as individual objects. We say *two oranges* or *six apples* (countable), but we don't normally say *two butters* or *six breads* (so *butter* and *bread* are uncountable). For uncountable commodities we have to bring in other forms of measurement, such as:

a *bag*/*spoonful*/*ton* of flour   a *slice* of bread/cake/beef
one/two/three *grains* of sand   a *ton* of rice/cement/rubbish
a *piece* of information/music   an *ounce* of curry powder

Occasionally, nouns may be either countable or uncountable, depending on the context. Look at these:

I need *a pound of sugar.* (uncountable)
One sugar or two? (countable)
I never eat *cake.* (uncountable)
Here are *two nice chocolate cakes.* (countable)
Light travels faster than *sound.* (uncountable)
Please switch off *the lights.* (countable)

Noun gender

Unlike many other languages (such as French or German or Latin), the English language makes little use of grammatical **gender**. English nouns are grouped according to the three 'natural' genders, and classified accordingly. So *a man* is classified as **masculine**, *a woman* as **feminine**, and *a table* as **neuter**.
    The gender of the noun demands the use of the appropriate pronoun:

The man was wounded. *He* had been shot.
The woman was unhurt. *She* had a lucky escape.
The car was a write-off. *It* had crashed into a large beech tree.

Some nouns have **dual gender**. They refer to categories of people or animals without indicating gender. Nouns like *actor, artist, singer, cousin, baby, adult,* *child, parent, dog, student, teacher, engineer, secretary* are all in this category. Without additional context clues, it is difficult to know which singular pronoun should accompany these nouns.

Traditionally, *he* was an acceptable pronoun for both sexes, but nowadays many people label this as **sexist language**. So now it is best not to say:

Each passenger must ensure that *he* has all *his* hand luggage with *him*.
Each applicant must sign *his* name at the bottom of the page.
Each student must check that *he* has answered three questions.

Writers nowadays either put these kinds of sentence in the plural, and use *they/their* instead of *he/his;* or they use a rather clumsy but non-sexist construction which is now widespread:

Passengers must ensure that *they* have all *their* hand luggage with *them*.
Each passenger must ensure that *s/he* has all *her/his* hand luggage with
   ***her/him*.**

It is also increasingly common to meet this kind of blatant change from singular noun to plural pronoun:

Each passenger must ensure that they have all their hand luggage with them.

This is not recommended. It is far better to rephrase your statements completely.

There is more on this subject under **pronouns**, p. 12, and **syllepsis**, p. 168.

Noun case

The **case system** of noun endings comes from Latin grammar, where nouns were described as having six cases: **nominative**, **vocative**, **accusative**, **genitive**, **dative** and **ablative**. Latin noun endings were very important, because it was these which showed the noun's relationship to the other words in the Latin sentence.

English nouns can of course do everything that Latin nouns could do, but in English it is mainly word order and prepositions which signal a noun's function in the sentence. Unlike Latin, therefore, there is no need in English to learn case tables like the following:

Case	English	Latin	Latin
Nom.	girl/boy	puell**a**	puer
Voc.	O, girl/boy	puell**a**	puer
Acc.	girl/boy	puell**am**	puer**um**
Gen.	girl**'s**/boy**'s**	puell**ae**	puer**i**
Dat.	to/for a girl/boy	puell**ae**	puer**o**
Abl.	by/with/from a girl/boy	puell**a**	puer**o**

English, as the table shows, has only two case endings: the **common** case ending and the **genitive**.

The genitive case signals possession or ownership. In most singular nouns, it is made by adding *s* preceded by an apostrophe. For plural nouns already ending with *s*, it is made by the addition of an apostrophe:

Barbara's bike
the boys' bikes

The alternative genitive construction is to use *of*:

the ship's crew
the crew *of* the ship

The choice between using the genitive case or the *of* construction is based on factors of gender and personal style. Proper names and animate beings tend to take the genitive ending, and inanimate objects the *of* construction. Usually, you would not say *the bike of Fred* or *the book's pages*; *Fred's bike* and *the pages of the book* would be commoner. In a case like *the ship's crew* versus *the crew of the ship*, you can grammatically distinguish a stronger emphasis on *crew* in the former, on *ship* in the latter.

There is more on case under **possessive pronouns**, p. 11.

Collective or mass nouns

Collective nouns refer to groups of animate beings, such as *class*, *committee*, *council*, *government* or *herd*. They are singular nouns, but they carry a plural connotation. They are used when the whole group or gathering is being considered (rather than individual members of the group).

Being singular, collective nouns usually take singular verbs or pronouns:

The team played *its* heart out. *It was* magnificent.
The jury reached *its* verdict, and pronounced *its* view.

This agreement should be consistent, and singulars and plurals should not be mixed. Avoid, for example:

The team played *their* heart out . . .
The jury reached *its* decision, and pronounced *their* view.

Mass nouns such as *grass*, *hair*, *timber* are like collective nouns, but they refer to inanimate entities.

There is a large stock of collective nouns specific to certain animals and groups. Some of the best known include:

A drove of ponies
A flock of sheep
A herd of cattle, pigs
A gaggle of geese (when they are on the ground)
A skein of geese (when flying)
A nest of vipers, ants, rabbits

A troop of lions, monkeys, cavalry, fairies
A pack of wolves, hounds, submarines
A team of oxen, mules, horses
A shoal of herring, mackerel
A school of whales, porpoises
A brood of chickens
A litter of puppies, kittens, piglets
A congregation of church-people
An audience of concert-goers
A crowd of spectators
A horde of savages
A company of actors, artists
A gang of workmen, prisoners
A carillon of bells

Suffixes that indicate a noun

Certain word endings, or **suffixes**, are often used to form nouns, with some of
the commonest being the following:

-age mile*age*, us*age*, wast*age*
-al arriv*al*, committ*al*, dismiss*al*, rebutt*al*, remov*al*
-ant combat*ant*, contest*ant*, entr*ant*
-ation admir*ation*, connot*ation*, explan*ation*, irrig*ation*
-dom bore*dom*, duke*dom*, king*dom*, star*dom*, wis*dom*
-eer mutin*eer*, profit*eer*, racket*eer*
-ency complac*ency*, insolv*ency*
-er explor*er*, foreign*er*, New York*er*, runn*er*, speak*er*
-ery green*ery*, knav*ery*, slav*ery*
-ese Chin*ese*, Japan*ese*, Vietnam*ese*
-ess enchantr*ess*, host*ess*, waitr*ess*
-ette kitchen*ette*, laundr*ette*, usher*ette*
-ful belly*ful*, jug*ful*, spoon*ful*
-hood child*hood*, father*hood*, spinster*hood*
-ian Arcad*ian*, Canad*ian*, Orcad*ian*
-ion act*ion*, express*ion*, suggest*ion*
-ing carpet*ing*, floor*ing*, moor*ing*
-ism ideal*ism*, loyal*ism*, national*ism*
-ist commun*ist*, Mao*ist*, social*ist*, union*ist*
-ite Ludd*ite*, social*ite*, Stalin*ite*, Thatcher*ite*, Trotsky*ite*
-ity advers*ity*, hostil*ity*, pervers*ity*, stupid*ity*
-let book*let*, flat*let*, pig*let*
-ling duck*ling*, gos*ling*, under*ling*
-ment employ*ment*, enjoy*ment*, excite*ment*, pay*ment*

-ness cleanli*ness*, good*ness*, happi*ness*, wicked*ness*
-ocrat bureau*crat*, demo*crat*, Euro*crat*, merit*ocrat*, plut*ocrat*
-or object*or*, prospect*or*, surviv*or*
-ship friend*ship*, owner*ship*, steward*ship*
-ster gang*ster*, trick*ster*, young*ster*
-ty beau*ty*, cruel*ty*, pover*ty*

For **suffix spelling rules**, see pp. 96–7.

Compound nouns

One of the commonest types of word formation occurs with the joining together of two words to make a **compound noun**. These may be:

> pairs of words:

biscuit tin	**beer bottle**	**fairy tale**
face towel	**breakfast time**	**bear cub**
coffee jug	**shoe polish**	**plant pot**

> hyphenated words:

passer-by	**knuckle-duster**	**holiday-maker**
engine-driver	**bull's-eye**	**mid-air**
spin-off	**tin-opener**	**hanger-on**
fire-eater		

> single words:

babysitter	**doorstep**	**battlefield**
housewife	**bearskin**	**seaweed**
clergyman	**teapot**	

All these words are at different stages in the process by which *ground sheet* becomes *ground-sheet* and finally *groundsheet*. Even dictionaries disagree about which of these words require a hyphen and which do not, with Americans slightly less keen on hyphens than UK writers. Generally, hyphens are favoured for longer words, or to avoid an odd spelling like *fire-eater*. Single, hyphenless words tend to indicate a well-established, frequently used word often made up of two short one-syllable words (*bedroom, bloodshed, teaspoon*).

Perhaps the best advice to give with compound nouns in these circumstances is to check their spellings with a dictionary, to be consistent in one's own practice, and to be watchful of other writers' practices.

Other compounds are:

> combinations of two or more words into longer **noun phrases** (see below):

down-and-out	**colonel-in-chief**
mother-in-law	**Berwick-upon-Tweed**
man-of-war	**Stow-on-the-Wold**
whisky-and-soda	

> combinations of letters and words:

S-bend	**U-turn**	**T-junction**
X-ray	**T-square**	**e-mail**

For more on compounding, see p. 87 and **hyphenation**, pp. 130–34.

Noun phrases

A group of words centring on a noun is called a **noun phrase**. It can appear at the beginning, the middle or the end of a sentence, and as **subject**, **object** or **complement** (see p. 72). Noun phrases consist of the noun on its own or accompanied by other words that modify its meaning.

Headword	Rest of sentence
<u>Trees</u>	live a long time.
<u>Many trees</u>	live a long time.
<u>Most of those pine trees</u>	live a long time.
<u>All the coniferous trees in that gully</u>	live a long time.

The noun phrases in the above examples are underlined. It will be noted that they can be extremely varied in their make-up. In the following extract, all the noun phrases are underlined:

> When <u>the rains</u> stopped at <u>Wimbledon yesterday evening</u>, <u>the grunting</u> began, and <u>Monika Seles</u>, <u>who reached the women's semi-finals here for the first time</u>, was accused by <u>her beaten opponent</u> of putting <u>her fellow players at a disadvantage</u> when <u>her grunting</u> reaches <u>a crescendo</u>. <u>Seles</u> was called over by <u>the umpire after the eighth game of the second set</u>, and asked to keep the noise down. <u>The crowd behind the umpire's chair</u> cheered when <u>the warning</u> was issued.

There is more on phrases, including noun phrases, on pp.57–63.

Pronouns

John Brown is very tall. *He* is a big lad now.
Sally has arrived. *She* is here at last.
The house is very old. *It* is falling down.

A **pronoun** substitutes for a noun. It is usually defined as a word that stands for a noun, or a noun phrase, or something relating to one. The meaning expressed by a sentence containing pronouns tends to be less specific than the meaning of a sentence containing nouns.

Personal and possessive pronouns

John took the stone and threw *it*.
Then *he* phoned Sally and invited *her* to supper.
'Where shall *we* meet?' *he* asked.
Here are the drinks. *This* is *mine*. *Hers* is the sherry.
Theirs is the third house on the left.

These are **personal pronouns**. Of all the different types of pronouns they occur most frequently. You use personal pronouns to refer back to something or someone that has already been mentioned. You also use them to refer to people and things directly. They are called 'personal' because they refer to the people or things involved in the text.

There are three types of personal pronouns: **subject pronouns**, **object pronouns** and **possessive pronouns**. As the names imply, subject pronouns are used as the subject of a sentence; object pronouns as the object of a sentence; and possessive pronouns are used to say that a person or thing belongs to or is connected with another person or thing:

	Singular			*Plural*		
subject pronouns	I	you	he/she/it	we	you	they
object pronouns	me	you	him/her/it	us	you	them
possessive pronouns:						
used with nouns	my	your	his/her/its	our	your	their
used instead of nouns	mine	yours	his/hers	ours	yours	theirs

Pronouns indicate **person**. The **first person** in the sentence is, or includes, the speaker/writer referring to himself or herself. Thus *I, me, my, mine, we, us, ours,* are the **first-person pronouns**.

You and *yours* are the **second-person pronouns**. The second person in the sentence is the person or thing being addressed, and excludes the speaker/writer.

He, she and *it* are the **third-person pronouns**. The third person in the sentence includes all third parties and excludes speaker and addressee. (Note that 'person' in this context can refer to things as well as persons.)

Pronouns can also reflect the possessive case, as the table above shows. The **possessive pronouns** are *mine, yours, his, hers, its, ours* and *theirs*. Note that no apostrophe is used in writing a possessive pronoun: *it's* is not a pronoun, but an abbreviation of 'it is'. (*Her's* and *your's* are also very common spelling errors.) The only exception to this no-apostrophe rule is the formal pronoun *one,* meaning 'people in general':

One should listen to *one's* conscience, shouldn't *one*?

Pronoun gender, sexist language and generic 'he'

he/she	his/hers
him/her	himself/herself

Two of the third-person pronouns reflect **gender**. This is not normally a problem area unless a writer refers to *he* or *him* when in fact the reference should be to men and women both. As we have seen, in certain contexts gender-specific pronouns are avoided nowadays:

The applicant must pay *his* own travelling expenses.
If a pupil fails the test, *he* will receive extra tuition.
Everyone must do *his* best.

Unless it is known that all the applicants and pupils and people referred to in the above sentences are indeed male, these sentences would nowadays tend to be re-phrased. The easiest way to do this may be to render the sentences in the plural, to rephrase, or to say 'his or her':

Applicants must pay *their* own travelling expenses.
Pupils failing the test will receive extra tuition.
Everyone must do *his or her* best.

But idiomatic sayings like 'Everything comes to him who waits', 'He who hesitates is lost', 'He laughs best who laughs last' (and many others) should perhaps remind us that the generic pronoun *he* was an acceptable English usage for several hundreds of years – and that it cannot simply be expunged retrospectively from the language.

Reflexive pronouns

Tell me all about *yourself*.
He should be ashamed of *himself*.
John told the boy to get *himself* a haircut.
She has just bought *herself* a new computer.
They are making fools of *themselves*.

These are all **reflexive pronouns**. They refer back to a noun or pronoun elsewhere in the sentence. The complete list of reflexive pronouns is:

Singular	*Plural*
myself	ourselves
yourself	yourselves
himself/herself/itself	themselves

Sometimes a reflexive pronoun is used for emphasis:

The house *itself* was little more than a shack.
The prime minister *himself* is going to pay us a visit.
I saw him *myself*, with my own eyes.

Sometimes a reflexive pronoun is used to show that someone has done something alone and/or without any help:

He cooked the meal *himself*.

Did you build it *yourself?*
She was sitting in a quiet corner *all by herself.*

Reciprocal pronouns

They accused *each other* of the betrayal.
The Browns and the Smiths were always getting at *one another.*

These pronouns are used to convey a two-way relationship.

Demonstrative pronouns

***This* looks like an interesting book.**
***Those* are John's shoes. *These* are mine.**
Where on earth did you get *that?*

The **demonstrative pronouns** are *this*, *that*, *these* and *those*. They are used mainly to point to things. *This* and *these* usually refer to something nearby; *that* and *those* to something farther away.

Remember that these words can also function as **determiners** (see pp. 23–5):

Where did you get *that* hat?

Demonstrative pronouns are also frequently used to introduce or refer to particular people:

Who's *this?*
***These* are my daughters, Judith and Joan.**
Was *that* Elizabeth on the telephone just now?

Demonstrative pronouns may refer back or forward in a conversation:

***These* are some of the topics I hope to cover next week . . .**
***That* was an interesting comment John made just now.**

The one or *this one* are used to stand in for a subject or object and function as a sort of demonstrative pronoun:

I'd like *this one/This one* will do.
Take *this one* here, not *that one* over there.
His car is *the old green one.*

Indefinite pronouns

He waited an hour before *anybody* came.
Is *anything* the matter?
Is *anyone* there?
***Someone*'s been sitting in my chair.**
Would you care for *something* to eat?
There was *nothing anyone* could do.

Indefinite pronouns refer to people or things without specifying exactly who or what they are. The list of indefinite pronouns is:

anybody	everybody	nobody	somebody
anyone	everyone	no one	someone
anything	everything	nothing	something

Note that *no one* is usually written as two words. All the others are compound words.

Occasionally words like *so* and *such* function as indefinite pronouns:

I hope *so*.
Such is life!

Interrogative pronouns

Who said that? (subject)
What happened to you? (subject)
Whose are those filthy shoes? (possessive)
Which of these books did you most enjoy? (object)
To *whom* did you give that book? (indirect object)

These are the main **interrogative pronouns**. They are used interrogatively, to ask questions, and are sometimes called *wh*-words.

Who, whom

The subject pronoun is *who* and the object pronoun is *whom*:

Who is there?
I can't see *who* is there.
To *whom* did you speak?
There's the man to *whom* I spoke.

The object pronoun rule is breaking down in informal spoken English, where we often hear:

Who did you speak to?
There's the man *who* I spoke to.

Whose, who's

These forms are confused because they sound the same. *Who's* is the contracted form of *who is*:

Who's afraid of the big bad wolf?
I sent a fax to my boss *who's* abroad.

Whose is a pronoun, or a possessive adjective:

Here's the man *whose* house was burgled.
If that hat is yours, *whose* is this?

What, which

What and *which* are used to ask questions about things:

What on earth was he talking about?
Which of the two cars do you prefer?

If *what* or *which* are immediately linked to a noun, they become **interrogative adjectives**:

Which car did he prefer?
What topics were on yesterday's agenda?

Relative pronouns

There was an old woman *who* lived in a shoe.
The shoe *that* she inhabited was, fortunately, enormous.
Here's the boy *whose* bicycle was stolen.
She destroyed all the letters *which* she had been sent.
She was the only person in *whom* I could confide.

The five **relative pronouns** are used to introduce **subordinate clauses** (see p. 75).

Distributive pronouns

These refer to members of a group or class:

All (of them) went to the pop concert.
Both of you should go along too.
Each of us received a reward.
Either of them might fall off the rock.
Neither of them will forget that climbing experience.

The distributive pronouns are usually followed by *of* + *pronoun*.

I and me [the first-person pronouns]

There is uncertainty in many speakers about when to use *I* (subject) and when to use *me* (object). This probably stems from the childhood recollection of being corrected for answering the question *Who is there?* with the words *It's me.* Strictly speaking, we should say *It is I.* This rule has broken down in spoken English, but not in the written form.

It is correct to say *John gave it to me,* and so it is also correct to say *John gave it to Sally and me.*

It is correct to say *I have been playing tennis,* and so it is also correct to say *Sally and I have been playing tennis.*

To decide which is right in the following, leave the other person(s) out of the sentence and imagine it in the singular. Then you will know whether to use *I* or *me*:

John, Tom, Wajid and ___ were all born in September.
You and ___ are the only ones who can speak French.
Can Sally and ____ sit here?
Joan and Maureen are playing against Pam and _____.
In front of my wife and ____ sat the Browns.
This go-cart was made by Andrew and____; Tom and ____ are going to make
another one.

Pronouns misplaced

Writers often fail to check what they have written. One of the commonest errors
they make is to fail to put the pronoun in the correct place – as near as possible to
the noun to which it refers. The results can be quite ludicrous:

We met an old man and a little boy whose beard was long and white.
Complete the form with the required information about your house, which
should then be sent to the town clerk.
We have a cupboard for storing bread that was made a hundred years ago.
Norfolk has many quiet and unfrequented villages to which thousands of
visitors go each year.
Nelson was greatly feared by the French, in whose honour Trafalgar Day is
still celebrated.

How should these sentences be written? Here are some alternatives, which make
the sense clearer:

We met an old man, whose beard was long and white, and a little boy.
Send the form to the town clerk after completing it with the required
information about your house.
We have a cupboard – for storing bread – that was made a hundred years ago.
Each year thousands of visitors go to Norfolk, which has many quiet and
unfrequented villages.
Nelson, in whose honour Trafalgar Day is still celebrated, was greatly feared
by the French.

Suitable punctuation, in addition to well-placed pronouns, helps get the meaning
across. See also the sections on the **comma** (p. 119) and **dash** (p. 125) to mark off
parentheses; also **dangling modifiers** (p. 77).

Adjectives

Adjectives are words that describe or give information about nouns or pronouns.
They are therefore often said to **modify**, or limit, nouns and pronouns. Adjectives
are usually easy to recognise in a sentence, often describing or modifying an
object's size, colour or amount, as in:

Size: a *huge* ship, a *tiny* flower, a *narrow* window
Colour: a *blue* balloon, *white* bread, a *red* alert
Amount or number: *twelve* months, *one* year, *second* prize, *many* problems,
   few assets (these last examples are also called determiners; see p. 26 for
   more on this)

A second feature of adjectives is that they can have **comparative** and **super-lative** forms, formed in one of two different ways:

Adjective	Comparative form	Superlative form
fat	fatt**er**	fatt**est**
black	black**er**	black**est**
fattening	**more** fattening	**most** fattening
intelligent	**more** intelligent	**most** intelligent

There is more on this in **Comparison of adjectives**, overleaf.

Thirdly, adjectives can be modified by an adverb, as in:

a *very* old man
He is *extremely* old.

Position of adjectives

Adjectives can occur in various positions. They can be placed immediately before
a noun:

a *delightful* evening
an *endless* journey through a *darkened* landscape
a *long* drink of *cool* water for a *thirsty* camel

These are called **attributive adjectives**.

Adjectives can also be joined to their nouns by a verb:

The dogs were *noisy*.
They seemed *hungry*.
The result of the game looks *doubtful*.

These are called **predicative adjectives**, so called because they help the verb to
form the predicate of a sentence (the predicate being everything but the subject;
for more on **predicates**, see p. 70).

Less frequently, adjectives can go directly after the noun:

The people *concerned* should notify the police.
the president-*elect*
'The River Weser, *deep* and *wide* . . .' (Browning)
'Something *old*, something *new*, something *borrowed*, something
   blue . . .'

These are called **post-modifiers**.

Certain fixed terms and technical designations also have adjectives following their noun:

letters patent	**body politic**
heir apparent	**time immemorial**
poet laureate	**lords temporal and spiritual**

These fixed terms tend to be **borrowings** (see p. 84) from other languages, but they have extended to certain other fixed phrases:

Friday next/last	**for the time being**
the sum outstanding	**motivated by greed pure and simple**
the amount accruing	**whisky galore**

Very occasionally a plural is required for one of these forms, and it is the noun – not the adjective – which pluralises, as in *court**s*** martial.

Comparison of adjectives

Most adjectives can be used comparatively in one of three ways. The qualities they describe may be compared to a higher degree, to the same degree, or to a lower degree.

Comparison of adjectives to a higher degree is shown by adding *-er* and *-est*, or *more* and *most*, to the absolute or base form of the adjective. The **comparative** form is used to compare two items (e.g. *older, more beautiful*), and the **superlative** form compares three or more items (e.g. *oldest, most beautiful*):

Andrew has an *old* car.
It is *older* than John's. (comparative)
It is the *oldest* car in the rally. (superlative)
It was a *beautiful* day.
It was a *more beautiful* day than Monday. (comparative)
It was the *most beautiful* day of the holiday. (superlative)

Comparison of adjectives to the same degree is shown by using the phrase *as . . . as*, or *so . . . as*:

His car is not *as* old *as* all that. It's not *so* old.

Comparison to a lower degree is indicated by the use of *less* and *least:*

Her contribution was *useful*.
John's contribution was *less useful* than Joan's.
Neil's was the *least useful* contribution to the whole debate.

Most adjectives are regular when it comes to forming comparatives and super-latives, and the choice between *-er/-est* and *more/most* is dictated by how long the adjective is. For example, one-syllable adjectives *(slim, bold, shy, black)* tend to take *-er/-est*. Two-syllable adjectives may appear in either form, with some preferring the *-er/-est* form: *clever, gentle, narrow, happy,* etc. Three-syllable adjectives (or longer) almost always use *more/most;* only if they begin with *un-* (*unlikely, unhappy*) do they sometimes take *-er/-est.*

Remember that some adjectives are irregular, including *good/better/best, bad/worse/worst, little/less/least,* and *much* or *many/more/most.*

Some adjectives do not normally compare. They have only an absolute meaning. These include words like *real, right, perfect, unique, elder* (statesman), *mere, utter* (idiot), *late* (president), *former, occasional,* etc.

Sequencing adjectives

If several adjectives are wanted to modify a noun, they tend to be placed in certain sequences or patterns. Look at the following, but remember too that English is very flexible, and that different emphases can permit all sorts of permutations:

    5   4   3   2   1
a brand-new green Japanese enamel birdcage

    5   4   3   2   1
an enormous nineteenth-century New York brownstone office building

    3   2   1
a small monthly cash payment

Working back from the noun:

1 Closest to the noun would go any other noun used adjectivally, almost as a compound noun, to indicate purpose (*office building*).
2 In second position from the noun would go any other noun used adjectivally, indicating materials (*brownstone, enamel*).
3 Third from the noun would go indications of nationality or origin (*Japanese, New York*).
4 Then comes colour, or vintage, or frequency (*brand-new, nineteenth-century, monthly*).
5 Last come adjectives indicating age, size, shape, temperature (*enormous, small*).

Multiple adjectives can also be found after the verb, as postmodifiers. They tend to be placed in more random order:

The house was *old, damp* and *smelly.*
We felt *cold, tired* and *hungry.*

Interrogative adjectives

Which? and *what*? are the **interrogative adjectives**. They ask for information about their nouns:

What plans do you have for the holidays?
Which book are you reading just now?
I saw a dog. *Which* dog did you see?

Interrogative adjectives often appear to be asking a speaker to 'fill in' the qualities of a noun. So they have sometimes been called 'blank cheque' adjectives:

Q: *Which* dress did you buy?
A: The *tie-dyed, blue and purple African cotton* one.

Demonstrative adjectives

This, that, these and *those* are called **demonstrative adjectives**. As their name indicates, they are used for pointing out or demonstrating the nouns which they modify:

That cottage was Wordsworth's.
These daffodils are most unusual.
This view of Windermere is my favourite.
Those hills in the distance are the Pennines.

Adjectives or nouns?

Sometimes adjectives can be used as nouns. This mostly happens when they appear with the definite article:

They have joined the ranks of *the unemployed* and *the homeless*.
We pray for *the sick* and *the poor* of all nations.
Give me *your tired, your poor,* your huddled masses . . . (Emma Lazarus)

Sometimes colour adjectives function as nouns:

She won't wear *green*.
Green is a restful colour.
A brighter shade of *green*

Conversely, nouns can function as adjectives:

the *city* hall, the *town* clock, the *ocean* liner

Nouns used adjectivally do not usually require to take a hyphen. (For more on **hyphenation**, see pp. 130–34.)

Adjectives or adverbs?

Several words function as both adjectives and adverbs. The context will indicate to which part of speech they belong:

Adjective	Adverb
It was **early** morning.	They left **early**.
It was a **wet** morning.	It looks **wet**.
They took a **late** bus.	They left **late**.

Adjectives or participles?

Again, there are some words which function as both adjectives and verb participles, and we have to examine the context before deciding to which part of speech they belong:

Adjective	Participle
We sat by the **roaring** fire.	The fire was **roaring** fiercely.
Her argument was **confusing**.	You are **confusing** two separate issues.
The news is **worrying**.	The dog was **worrying** the sheep.

Adjectives with prepositions

Some adjectives are used with a prepositional phrase in the following ways:

She is very *good at* languages.
I was *upset at* the decision.
He was *afraid of* his enemies.
He's terribly *fond of* you.
It was *rude of* them to walk out.
They were *rude to* her for no obvious reason.
She was pretty *angry about* the result.
You are *responsible for* this mess.

These are sometimes called postmodifying adjectives, because they come after the verb.

Common adjectival word endings

Certain word endings (or suffixes) commonly indicate an adjective. These include:

-**ish** redd*ish*, green*ish*, young*ish*, small*ish*, round*ish*, child*ish*, fever*ish*, styl*ish*, fool-*ish*, owl*ish*, devil*ish*, Brit*ish*, Span*ish*, Ir*ish*
-**ful** use*ful*, meaning*ful*, wonder*ful*, bash*ful*, sin*ful*, plenti*ful*, fear*ful*, skil*ful*, beauti*ful*, fright*ful*
-**ing** bor*ing*, charm*ing*, middl*ing*, shock*ing*
-**less** use*less*, meaning*less*, fear*less*, hat*less*, sun*less*
-**like** war*like*, glass-*like*
-**ly** king*ly*, saint*ly*, god*ly*, scholar*ly*, mother*ly*, hour*ly*, queen*ly*
-**y** sunn*y*, rain*y*, dust*y*, sand*y*, ston*y*, blood*y*, dirt*y*, tast*y*, hast*y*, nast*y*

-ous danger*ous*, glori*ous*, plente*ous*, courte*ous*, chivalr*ous*, tempestu*ous*, nutriti*ous*, delici*ous*, poison*ous*

-ic volcan*ic*, magnet*ic*, hero*ic*, microscop*ic*, systemat*ic*, (a)pathet*ic*, asthmat*ic*, atom*ic*, athlet*ic*, histor*ic*, dramat*ic*

-en flax*en*, wood*en*, molt*en*, braz*en*, wax*en*

-able/-ible charit*able*, hospit*able*, break*able*, indescrib*able*, defin*able*, eat*able*, incompar*able*, ed*ible*, vis*ible*, aud*ible*, tang*ible*, terr*ible*, access*ible*

-al herb*al*, region*al*, industri*al*, centr*al*, coloni*al*, music*al*, logic*al*, critic*al*, commerci*al*, provinci*al*, confidenti*al*, habitu*al*, vit*al*, norm*al*, dism*al*, abysm*al*

-ar circul*ar*, angul*ar*, molecul*ar*, muscul*ar*, sol*ar*, lun*ar*

-worthy blame*worthy*, news*worthy*, air*worthy*

-proof rain*proof*, bomb*proof*, water*proof*

There is more on adjective suffixes in Part 3, on **word formation**. For **suffix spelling rules**, see pp. 96–7.

Compound adjectives and hyphens

The main thing to note here is that adjectives are usually hyphenated when they precede a noun, to remind readers of their function. So:

Compound adjective	*Other use*
It was a first-class performance.	She is in the first class.
He broke his six-inch ruler.	His ruler was six inches long.
Ninth-grade students	Students in the ninth grade
He uses state-of-the-art equipment.	What is the current state of the art?

The adjective phrase

These are adjective-equivalents, and they operate just like adjectives in that they qualify or describe nouns. For example:

The shoes are not *the right size*.
The way *through the woods* is dark and long.
Her eyes were *the size of saucers*.
That car is *smaller than mine*.
***What part of speech* are these words?**

There is more on this under **phrases** (pp. 61–2).

Abuse of adjectives

Adjectives have been described as the enemy of the noun. That is to say, at the hands of wordy writers and speakers they often add nothing of substance to the nouns they modify. (A verbose writer might have written, 'nothing of *real* substance'.) We know how common it is to hear references to a subject being 'under *active* consideration at this *precise* point of time'. And how often do we hear that there is no cause for *undue* alarm (as if a modicum of alarm is appropriate), or that the outbreak of X poses no *serious* threat to our safety (perhaps just a teensy-weensy threat?). It is one thing to talk about a *diplomatic* crisis or a *naval* disaster; it is quite another to talk about a *serious* crisis or a *dreadful* disaster. Crises are serious and disasters are dreadful by definition. All these popular usages are examples of waffle; they are superfluous, and better avoided. (More on this under **tautology**, pp. 146–7.)

Determiners

Determiners, like adjectives, give information about nouns and pronouns. But they do not strictly speaking *describe* nouns and pronouns – which is one of the definitions of an adjective – and that is one reason why modern grammarians like to distinguish them from adjectives.

Determiners were so named because they *determine* the number and definiteness of the noun phrase to which they are attached. The commonest determiners are in the following categories:

> articles: *a, an, the*
> demonstratives: *this, that, these, those*
> possessives: *my, your, his/her/its, our, their; mine, yours, theirs*
> numbers: *one, two, three . . . first, second, third . . .*
> indefinite determiners: including *all, any, both, each, either, every, few, less, more, enough, neither, no, several, some, only*

Determiners are sometimes called 'function words', because they have very little meaning in themselves – they merely perform a function in the sentence. True adjectives, on the other hand, are called 'content words' – because they have some sort of finite content, or meaning, when they stand alone.

The article

There are two articles in English – the **definite article** (*the*), and the **indefinite article** (*a*, or, preceding a word beginning with a vowel, *an*).

The definite article

The definite article in English has the following functions:

> It refers back to a person or thing already identified:
You described a man with a beard. Is this *the* man?
Jason built a special ship for his voyage. *The* ship was called Argo.

This is called **anaphoric** reference. An author's use of something as apparently insignificant as the definite instead of the indefinite article can have a major impact on the resonance of a text. (See **Notes on 'the'**, pp. 26–7.)

> It defines or marks someone or something as the only one:

the Bible	*the* House of Commons
the Lord God	*the* Leader of *the* Opposition
the prophet Muhammad	*the* Prime Minister
the holy Koran	*the* Tsar of Russia

> It indicates a whole class or group or clan:

the Reptile family	*the* English
the working class	*the* Armstrongs and *the* Percys

> When stressed (and pronounced *thee)*, it indicates uniqueness:

Callas was *the* soprano of her generation.
It was *the* pub for live folk music and real ale.

The indefinite article

The indefinite article *a/an* has the following functions:

> It is a form of *one*:
A hundred years ago (not two hundred)
A mile wide
Wait *a* minute

If you wish to stress *one* – rather than a lot – you exaggerate the pronunciation, and say *ay*:

Take *a* biscuit, not a fistful!

> It singles out or introduces a particular and specific person or thing:
I'm going to tell you *a* story about *a* girl called Sally. She lived in *a* red sandstone
  terraced house . . .

> It has the indefinite meaning of *any;*
It was as big as *a* horse.
A peninsula is surrounded by water on three sides.

> It is distributive:
Fifty pence *a* kilo (= per kilo, each kilo)
Ten pence *a* slice

A is used before an initial consonant sound, *an* before an initial vowel sound, a rule which applies regardless of spelling:

A chair, *a* seat, *a* bed, *a* horse
An igloo, *an* egg, *an* ostrich, *an* heir, *an* SOS, *an* LP

There has been some disagreement in the past about words like *hotel, heredi-tary, habitual* and *historic* – should the 'h' sound be pronounced, thus requiring the words to be preceded by *a*? Or should it not be pronounced, leaving the words to be preceded by *an*? The consensus nowadays seems to favour *a hotel* over *an hotel, a historical event* over *an historical event*, though the latter are not wrong.

The zero article

The absence of an article is sometimes referred to as the **zero article**, and it helps us to refer to generic qualities. Thus:

Lions are dangerous animals.
(*Compare* **The lion is a dangerous animal.**)

The zero article is also used idiomatically:

They went by train/car/bus.
Have breakfast/dinner/lunch.
Go to bed/hospital/church.
At sea/work/home
In class/hospital

Demonstratives

The **demonstratives** are *this/that* (singular) and *these/those* (plural). *This/these* indicate nearness to the speaker, and *that/those* indicate distance from the speaker. The demonstratives are called determiners only if they precede a noun. If they stand alone, standing in place of a noun, then they are described as pro-nouns:

Determiners	*Pronouns*
Give me **that** gun.	Give **that** to me.
This girl is my best friend.	**This** is my best friend.

A special use of *this* is as a time marker:

Let's try and meet *this* week.
Can we fix a time? *This* Friday?

Possessives

Possessive markers may be either determiners (if they qualify a noun), or pronouns (if they are standing in for a noun). It all depends on their use in the sentence:

Possessives as determiners	Possessives as pronouns
This is my car.	The car is mine.
his	his.
her	hers.
your	yours.
our	ours.
their	theirs.

Numbers

One, two, three, etc. are called **cardinal numbers**, and they answer the question, *How many?* The **ordinal numbers** are *first, second, third,* etc., and they indicate an order. Numbers usually precede adjectives in a sentence:

ten green bottles
the **six** rowdy youngsters
my **third** and final shot

Indefinite determiners

These words function as determiners only when they modify a noun. The versions that stand alone are pronouns:

Determiners	Pronouns
All the good work is ruined.	**All** is not lost.
Both climbers are missing.	**Both** are safe and well.
Either bus goes into town.	**Either** is possible.
Neither answer is right.	**Neither** is right.
We see her **every** Tuesday.	
We have **no** bread.	(We have **none**.)
Each man had a gun.	**Each** had a gun.
Few people take holidays here.	**Few** come here on holiday.
Have you **enough** food?	I've had quite **enough**.

Notes on 'the'

Study this use of the definite article in the opening two paragraphs of Betsy Byars' novel for young people, *The Eighteenth Emergency* (1976):

The pigeons flew out of *the* alley in one long swoop and settled on *the*
    awning of *the* grocery store. A dog ran out of the alley with a torn Cracker
    Jack box in his mouth. Then came *the* boy.
The boy was running hard and fast. He stopped at *the* sidewalk, looked both
    ways, saw that *the* street was deserted and kept going. The dog caught
    the boy's fear, and he started running with him . . .

This use of *the* cannot be anaphoric reference – reference back to something which has gone before – since nothing has gone before these opening paragraphs of the novel. But does the reader sit back and wonder 'What pigeons?' or 'What alley?' or 'What boy?' No: the author's skilful use of *the* instead of the more obvious *a* has made the text especially gripping from the very start – which is part of the reason for the novel's appeal.

Always look at the context of the words you are analysing. *The* looks very simple, and of course usually it is. But what about this sentence:

There's not a single *the* in this sentence.

Here *the* functions as a noun.

Verbs

In many ways the **verb** is the most important of all the parts of speech. This was certainly the Romans' point of view: *verbum* in Latin meant '*the* word', so in this way its pre-eminence is still articulated in all the Romance languages as well as in English.

From school, we remember that verbs are 'doing' words or 'action' words, and for the vast majority of verbs this is a fair description. But we should remember that in addition to the main verbs of 'doing' (*run, jump, walk, stand, shake*), there are also auxiliary or 'helping' verbs (*be, have, will, can, may, shall, would, could, might, should, must;* see pp. 28–30). Indeed, **main verbs** and **auxiliary verbs** are the two key classes of verb.

The following sections look at the verb from a variety of grammatical perspectives.

Verb agreement or concord

The girl *speaks* good English.
The girls *speak* good English.

Concord, or agreement, is the rule that ensures the harmonisation of different grammatical units. **Number concord** is the most important type of concord in English, and ensures that a singular subject is always followed by a singular verb, a plural subject by a plural verb.

The following sentences are wrong because they break the rules of number concord:

The girl *speak* good English.
The girls *speaks* good English.

Apart from the rule of adding *-s* or *-es* in the third-person singular (he, she, it) of English verbs, there is not much left of verb concord in English. We used also to mark the second-person singular (you, or thou) for subject–verb concord:

The day *thou* gavest, Lord . . .
Where art *thou*, Sylvia?

This use has almost died out, and is now found only in poetry, in biblical writing and in certain dialects.

Auxiliary verbs

She *is* planning a visit to India.
I *haven't* seen her since last Tuesday.
Which bus *do* you plan to take?

The main **auxiliary**, or 'helping', verbs are *be, have* and *do*. They are used with main verbs to help them form specific tenses, as well as negatives and questions.

Be is used as an auxiliary with the *-ing* form of the main verb to form the continuous:

She *is living* in Poland.
We *were going* to the cinema.

Be is used with the past participle of the main verb to form the passive (see pp. 34–5):

The street *was covered* in mud.
These computers *are made* in America.

Have and *had* are used as auxiliaries along with the past participle to form the past tenses:

I *have changed* my mind.
She *has completed* her course.
I wish we *had visited* St Petersburg.

Be and *have* are also used as auxiliaries to form negative sentences, question forms and the passive:

She *isn't finished* yet.
***Haven't* you *finished* yet?**
***Was* the wallet *found* in the street?**

Do is used as an auxiliary to make negative and question forms:

I *don't smoke*. *Do* you?
***Do* you *like* my new shoes?**
He *didn't get* the job, *did* he?

See also **modal auxiliary verbs** (below).

Modal auxiliary verbs

Modal verbs are a category of the auxiliaries: they too are 'helping' verbs. They help the main verb to express a range of meanings: possibility, probability, certainty, permission, requests, instructions, suggestions, offers and invitations, wants and wishes, obligation and necessity. The modal verbs are:

can, could	**must, ought to**	**shall, should**	**need to**
will, would	**be able to**	**may, might**	**have (got) to**

Modals are very easy in one respect: they have only one form. Below are some examples of modals in use:

> Negatives and questions:
You *may not* walk on the grass.
He *couldn't* stop laughing.
Would you give me a lift into town?

> Possibility (*can, could, may, might*):
Can you unlock this door for me?
This *might* come in useful.
It *could* have been a disastrous accident.
When *may* she get up?

> Probability and certainty (*cannot/can't, must, ought to, should, will*):
You *must* be Dr Livingstone.
He *can't* have told me the whole story.
We *ought to* arrive home by noon.
That *must* be the postman now.

> Ability (*can, could, be able to*):
He *cannot* sing for toffee.
He *could* read and write from a very young age.
She *was able to* sign her name with difficulty.
She *couldn't* stop laughing.

> Permission (*can, could, may*):
You *can* use my car if you want.
You *may* speak now, John.
Can I ask a question?

> Instructions and requests (*can, could, will, would*):
Would you give John a message for me, please?
Would you do me a favour?
Could you explain that again for me?
I *would* like this work finished by Friday.

> Suggestions (*could, may, might, shall*):
You *could* try again later.
You *might* like to try this new shampoo.
You *may* as well start again.
Shall we change the subject?

> Offers and invitations (*can, could, shall, will, would*):
Will you have a cup of tea?
Would you like a biscuit?
I *could* give you a lift to the shops.
Shall we dance?

> Obligation and necessity (*must, mustn't, have to, have got to*):
I *have to* go now.
I *must* get to the interview in good time.

Finite and non-finite verbs

The dog *barks* when hungry.
It *is barking* now.
It *has been barking* for hours.

A **finite** verb is sometimes called a 'tensed' verb, because it varies for present and past tense. Auxiliaries and modals are finite, as are verb phrases which contain them: *eats, is eating, has eaten, has been eating, was eating, was being eaten* are all finite verb phrases.

Finite verbs have a subject with which they agree in person and number. Clauses with finite verbs are called **finite clauses**, while clauses with non-finite verbs are called **non-finite clauses**:

When I *was first looking* into the matter. . . (finite clause)
After Caesar *had crossed* the Rubicon . . . (finite clause)
On looking into the matter . . . (non-finite clause)
Having crossed the Rubicon . . . (non-finite clause)

There are three **non-finite** verb forms: the **infinitive** form, with or without *to*; the *-ing* form (or **present participle**, or **gerund**); and the *-ed* form (or **past participle**). Non-finite verbs do not have a subject, and they show no variation for tense.

All verbs have non-finite forms, except for **modal auxiliaries** (see pp. 28–30).

Infinitives, participles and gerunds

These are the **non-finite** parts of the verb (see above).

The infinitive

This is the part of the verb often prefixed by *to*:

I remembered *to lock* the door.
I wish *to see* him immediately.
To sleep, perchance *to dream* . . .
To err is human, *to forgive* [is] divine . . .
The infinitive, without the *to*, is often called the **base form** of the verb.

Split infinitives

There used to be a taboo dear to the hearts of grammatical purists which said that adverbs should never be inserted between *to* and the infinitive: as in *to boldly go*, *to fully understand*, etc. Sometimes, however, sense requires the splitting of infinitives. 'Completely failing to recognise' and 'Failing to completely recognise' are not quite the same thing, as Sir Ernest Gowers long ago pointed out.

Participles and gerunds

Verbs have **present participles**, formed with *-ing* (*running, jumping, standing*); and **past participles**, formed with *-ed* in regular verbs, or with *-en* or in other ways for irregular verbs (*finished, given, thought, forsaken*).

Participles are sometimes used adjectivally:

the *gusting* wind
the *forsaken* merman
A *rolling* stone gathers no moss.

To distinguish between participles and gerunds, look at the following:

A: He was *smoking* an enormous cigar.
B: *Smoking* is bad for your health.

In the A-type sentence, *smoking* is the participle in the verb phrase *was smoking*. In the B-type sentence, *smoking* functions as a noun, and this is the key characteristic of a gerund.

Linking verbs, or copular verbs

Linking verbs are so called because they link a subject with a complement. Unlike regular verbs, they do not denote an action so much as record a state. They are sometimes called **copula** or **copular verbs**, from Latin *copula*, 'a bond'. The main linking verb is *be* (see below, and also the section on **complements**, p. 72):

He *is* a Frenchman.
He *is* very ill.

The other main linking verbs are *appear, become, feel, get, grow, look, remain, seem*:

She *appears* distressed.
The room *became* quiet.
The condition *is getting* serious.
Andrew *grew* tall. (But not as in: Andrew grew radishes.)
She *looks* unconvinced.
She *seems* a very sincere person.

The verb 'to be'

Be is the most frequently used verb in the English language. It is also the most irregular. *Be* has three very important roles:

> It is a copula, or linking verb (see above). Instead of taking an object, it introduces a complement linked to the subject:

He *is* a bus driver.
She *was* very shy.
They *are* my next-door neighbours.
It *is* the River Nile.

> Sometimes this use is called **equative *be***, because the subject and the complement are the same thing:

He = bus driver
She = very shy
They = my next-door neighbours
It = the River Nile

> *Be* is an auxiliary and indicates the continuous or progressive aspect of a main verb:

They *are working* for charity.
He *was living* in France.
She *is being trained* to succeed the present director.

> *Be* is an auxiliary and indicates the passive voice:

The child *was named* Joseph.
I *am asked* for an explanation.

> A fourth use of *be* might be called the 'existential' use, because it conveys the meaning 'to exist'. This use is not now common:

When I have fears that I may cease *to be* . . . (Keats)
To be or not *to be*, that is the question. (Shakespeare)
A poem should not mean but *be*. (Archibald MacLeish)
I *am* – yet what I am, none cares or knows. (John Clare)
Whoever thinks a faultless piece to see,/Thinks what ne'er *was* nor *is* nor e'er *shall be*. (Pope)

Moods of the verb

These are verb categories which tell us about the degree of reality conveyed by the verb. There are three types of mood in English: showing whether a sentence is making a statement (the **indicative mood**), giving an order (the **imperative mood**), or expressing a wish or supposition or other non-factual utterance (the **subjunctive mood**).

Indicative or declarative mood

He *speaks* **German.**
She *was walking* **on the grass.**
He *is* **rather noisy.**

Imperative mood, or command

The verbs in these requests and commands all give an order; they are in the imperative mood:

Speak **to him in German, please.**
Keep **off the grass.**
Be **quiet.** *Sit* **in the corner.**

Note that imperatives need not necessarily be imperious:

Excuse **me.**
Have **a beer.**
Take **the first turning on the right.**

Subjunctive mood

The subjunctive mood is used in modern English only for certain hypothetical statements:

If I *were* **you . . .**
If this *be* **true . . .**
She wished she *were* **dead.**

Or for fixed forms:

So *be* **it!**
Be **that as it may. . .**
God *save* **the Queen.**
Good luck *be* **with you.**

Or as formal *that* subordinates:

I insist that Tom *pay* **his debt.**
I demand that he *write* **me an apology.**

The word **mood** comes from Latin *modus*, meaning 'way' or 'manner'. So in its original meaning it was said to indicate the verb's 'attitude' or manner of speaking.

    Subjunctive was also a Latin term, used to describe a mood confined to verbs in subordinate clauses. Latin grammarians described these clauses as dependants or subordinates of the main clause of the sentence, and marked the verbs accordingly. The main clause of a Latin sentence usually took the indicative mood and dealt in facts, while the *sub*ordinate clause took the *sub*junctive mood to express qualifications, conditions, suppositions, ideas and hypotheses dependent on those facts.

Transitive and intransitive

Subject	Verb	Object
He	**saw**	the crash.
She	**made**	a lovely meal.
They	**wrote**	an angry letter to their MP.

A **transitive verb** is one which takes a direct object. An **intransitive verb** does not:

Subject	Verb
Torrential rain	**fell**.
The volcano	**erupted**.

Many verbs can function transitively and intransitively:

John *played* the cello in the garden. (transitive)
John *played* in the garden. (intransitive)
The army *exploded* the bomb. (transitive)
The bomb *exploded*. (intransitive)

The word transitive is from Latin *transire*, 'to pass over', and in transitive verbs the action was thought to pass over to the object immediately following – like a spark jumping a break in an electrical circuit.

Active and passive

A: The Romans *invaded* Britain.
B: Britain *was invaded* by the Romans.

Transitive verbs occur in these two kinds of sentences. A-type sentences are called **active**, because the subject performs the action described by the verb. B-type sentences are called **passive**, because the subject is the recipient of the action.

The **passive auxiliary** is generally a form of the verb *to be*:

He *was* wounded in the leg.
They *were* told to take him to hospital.

Often, however, *get* performs a similar function (especially if the action received is disagreeable):

They *got* beaten up by some thugs.
She *got* run over at the pedestrian crossing.
He'll *get* knocked to smithereens.

Passive constructions are found much less frequently than active constructions. They are found in scientific writing, for instance, where we are not interested in who performs the action:

> A sample of soil *is placed* in a weighted evaporating basin which *is* then *reweighed*. The basin *is heated* over a water-bath for some hours or days according to the weight and nature of the sample, to drive off the soil water. The basin *is* then *allowed* to cool in a desiccator and *weighed* again. Heating and reweighing *are continued* until two weighings give identical results, showing that all the soil water has evaporated . . . (D G Mackean, *Introduction to Biology*, John Murray 1962)

Another common use of the passive is when the subject performing the action is unknown:

The woman was struck on the head.

A third frequent use of the passive requires a measure of vigilance on the part of the reader:

Thousands of civilians were tortured and executed. (By whom? The rebels? The government?)
A new tax called the poll tax was to be introduced.
You have been warned.

Verb tense

The word tense is from Latin *tempus*, 'time', and it is used to show the time when the action of a verb takes place. It is marked by inflection in English only for the **present tense** and the **past tense**:

Present tense

Here he *comes*.
She *likes* him very much.
The fighting in Afghanistan *continues* unabated.

The **present tense** marks an action now going on, or a state now existing. It also has one or two other uses:

He *gets up* at six o'clock every morning.
I don't *take* sugar in coffee.
She *teaches* chemistry.

The above shows the **habitual present**, marking habitual (repeated or recurring) events. An extension of this is the use of the present tense to denote what is true at all times – the **stative present**:

Lions *are* carnivorous animals.
Salt *dissolves* in water.

Sometimes the present is used with an **adverbial** (see p. 72) to indicate future time:

Term *begins* next Monday.
We *leave* tomorrow morning.

Past tense

Columbus *crossed* the Atlantic in 1492.
When they *woke*, the sun *was shining*.
We *arrived* yesterday.

The **past tense** describes an action or state which has taken place at a particular time before the present. It is formed by adding *-ed* or *-d* to the base form of regular verbs: *cross/crossed, arrive/arrived, talk/talked*. With irregular verbs, it is formed differently: *wake/woke, begin/began, leave/left*, etc. (See pp. 38–40 for more on irregular verbs.)

   Verb phrases can be made past by using the past tense of their finite verb:

When they woke, they *were rested* and the sun *was shining*.

The past tense is often used to mark reported speech:

I *am* ill.
He *said* that he *was* ill.
***Did* he *say* that he *was* ill?**

It also describes habitual actions in the past:

Last term, we *got up* at seven o'clock.
Long ago, everything *was run* by the monks.

Future tense

Tomorrow *will be* wet and windy.
We *shall arrive* on the midday flight.

The **future tense** describes actions or states which will take place at some future time, and it is marked by the use of *will* and *shall*. Traditionally, *will* was used with second- and third-person subjects, and *shall* with first-person subjects:

You/he/she/it/they *will go*
I/we *shall go*

These combinations were reversed to indicate emphasis, refusal, insistence, etc.:

I *will* not do it.
They *shall* not pass.

A verbal equivalent of stamping the feet, and certainly expressive of deep intransigence, would be a construction such as:

I *will* not and *shall* not do it.

Other future time markers are *to be about to* or *to be going to* + the base of the verb:

Hurry up – the train *is about to depart*.
I hope John Smith *is going to be* the next prime minister.

Other past tense forms

I *have visited* Paris several times.
I *had visited* New York when I was twelve years old.
By this time next week, I *shall have visited* Cairo.

These forms are called, respectively, the **perfect** (*have* + *-ed* form); the **past perfect**, or 'past in the past', sometimes called the **pluperfect** (*had* + *-ed* form); and the **future perfect** or 'past in the future' (*will/shall have* + *-ed* form).

Verb aspect

Aspect is a verb category indicating the point of time from which an action is seen to take place. Two contrasts of aspect are marked in English: **progressive aspect** and **perfect** (or **perfective**) **aspect**. The former states that the action is in progress, ongoing or continuous at that point of time; the latter states that the action is retrospective or has been completed.

Progressive/continuous aspect is marked by the use of *be* + present participle:

She *is driving* through the town.
She *was listening* to the car radio.

Perfect aspect is marked by the use of *have* + past participle:

He *has cooked* a splendid meal.
He *had fed* his guests by 10 o'clock.

Progressive and perfect aspect can be combined:

For years we *have been coming* here for our holiday.
We *had been looking* forward to a short break.

Verb suffixes and prefixes

Certain **prefixes** are associated with verbs. Here are some common verb prefixes:

a/ab- *ab*dicate, *ab*hor, *ab*ide, *ab*olish, *ab*ominate, *ab*ridge, *ab*rogate, *ab*sorb, *ab*stain

ac- *ac*celerate, *ac*cept, *ac*cede, *ac*company, *ac*count, *ac*cuse

ad-/af-/ap- *ad*here, *ad*mire, *ad*opt, *ad*ore, *ad*vance, *af*firm, *af*ford, *ap*peal, *ap*pal, *ap*pend

co- *co*exist, *co*habit, *co*produce, *co*operate

con- *con*cede, *con*cur, *con*cuss, *con*done, *con*fess, *con*fine, *con*firm, *con*form, *con*geal, *con*gratulate, *con*gregate, *con*nect, *con*sider, *con*struct, *con*sume, *con*tain, *con*tinue, *con*vene

com- *com*mit, *com*plain, *com*pile, *com*pose, *com*plete, *com*municate

de- de*cide*, de*ceive*, de*clare*, de*cline*, de*corate*, de*cree*, de*cry*, de*fy*, de*ject*, de*liver*, de*molish*, de*mur*, de*nounce*, de*pend*, de*plore*, de*plete*, de*prave*, de*spair*, de*tect*, de*velop*

dis- dis*able*, dis*cover*, dis*miss*, dis*qualify*, dis*tress*

en- en*gulf*, en*chant*, en*case*, en*velop*

in- in*fringe*, in*vade*, in*trude*, in*troduce*

inter- inter*cede*, inter*fere*, inter*pret*, inter*vene*

out- out*do*, out*fight*, out*jump*, out*play*, out*run*, out*swim*, out*produce*

over- over*come*, over*do*, over*flow*, over*ride*, over*see*, over*work*

sub- sub*ject*, sub*join*, sub*merge*, sub*mit*, sub*sist*, sub*vert*

tran-/trans- trans*act*, trans*cend*, trans*cribe*, trans*fer*, trans*fix*, trans*gress*, trans*late*, trans*pose*

un- un*bend*, un*do*, un*earth*, un*loose*, un*button*, un*zip*, un*tangle*, un*tie*, un*dress*, un*hitch*, un*veil*

with- with*draw*, with*hold*, with*stand*

Here are some common verb **suffixes**:

-ate chlorin*ate*, concentr*ate*, fascin*ate*, incapacit*ate*, orchestr*ate*, vener*ate*
-er batt*er*, clatt*er*, glitt*er*, mutt*er*, quav*er*, quiv*er*, sev*er*, shatt*er*, shiv*er*, stutt*er*
-ify beaut*ify*, de*ify*, glor*ify*, simpl*ify*
-ise/-ize advert*ise*, cauter*ise*, computer*ise*, final*ise*, hospital*ise*, modern*ise*, oxid*ise*, privat*ise*, real*ise*, sermon*ise*, verbal*ise*
-ish abol*ish*, establ*ish*, fam*ish*, fin*ish*, flour*ish*, nour*ish*, per*ish*, pol*ish*, pun*ish*
-mit ad*mit*, com*mit*, de*mit*, per*mit*, sub*mit*, trans*mit*

The *-ise/-ize* suffix is optional in some cases, and an occasional subject of debate. Some verbs are never spelt with *z* (*advertise, advise, arise, comprise, despise, exercise, revise, supervise, televise*, etc.), so for most British spellers *-ise* is the easier option. But American English prefers the *-ize* spelling for the remainder.

Regular and irregular verbs

The vast majority of English verbs are **regular** – that is, their forms can be established by rules. But there are about 300 **irregular** verbs, where some of the forms are unexpected. Instead of regular and irregular, we sometimes used to call them 'weak' and 'strong' verbs, because the weak ones toed the line and kept to the regular rules, while the strong ones were a law unto themselves!

All newly formed verbs are regular, or weak (e.g. *privatise, chlorinate*), and there has been a tendency over the years for certain strong verbs to become weak (e.g. *thrive* is listed below as following the same pattern as *drive*, but as well as *thrive/throve/thriven*, the weak *thrive/thrived/thrived* version is also used nowadays, especially by Americans).

There are four main forms of the **regular** verb, best indicated in the following table:

Infinitive or base form	-s form, or third-person singular	-ing participle	-ed past form and past participle
walk	walks	walking	walked
stop	stops	stopping	stopped
try	tries	trying	tried
love	loves	loving	loved
push	pushes	pushing	pushed
prefer	prefers	preferring	preferred

The **irregular** verb forms fall into three main types:

> Identical forms for the infinitive, past tense and past participle:

bet	hit	shut
bid	hurt	slit
burst	let	split
cast	put	spread
cost	quit	thrust
cut	set	

> Identical past tense and past participle:

Base form or infinitive	Past tense/participle	Other examples
burn	burned/burnt	learn, smell, spell, spill, spoil
bend	bent	build, lend, send, spend
bleed	bled	breed, feed, flee, hold, lead
sleep	slept	creep, keep, leap, sweep, weep
cling	clung	fling, sting, string, swing, wring
bring	brought	buy, catch, fight, seek, teach, think
bind	bound	find, grind, wind
get	got	
lose	lost	
shine	shone	
shoot	shot	
sell	sold	tell
(be)come	(be)came	
run	ran	
hear	heard	
light	lit	
make	made	
say	said	lay, pay
spit	spat	
stand	stood	

The two past tense forms of *burn* do not convey exactly the same meanings. The
-ed form is used to convey the duration of the action, while the *-t* form conveys a
completed action:

The fire burned for weeks.
Fetch me a bandage – I've burnt myself.

> Infinitive, past tense and past participle forms are all different:

Infinitive	Past tense	Past participle	Other examples
hew	hewed	hewn/hewed	mow, sew, saw, sow, show, swell
break	broke	broken	awake, choose, freeze, speak, steal, wake, weave
bear	bore	born/borne	
swear	swore	sworn	tear, wear
blow	blew	blown	grow, know, throw
bite	bit	bitten	
hide	hid	hidden	
take	took	taken	shake
drive	drove	driven	rise, ride, thrive, write
begin	began	begun	sing, sink, swim, shrink, drink, ring, spring
eat	ate	eaten	
fall	fell	fallen	
dive	dived/dove	dived	
do	did	done	
draw	drew	drawn	
fly	flew	flown	
forget	forgot	forgotten	
give	gave	given	
go	went	gone	
lie	lay	lain	
see	saw	seen	

Several irregular verbs are treated differently in the UK and USA. *Dove*, for example, as the past tense of *dive*, is an Americanism. The other common Americanism
is *gotten* (for UK *got*).

Phrasal verbs

Many English verbs are made up of a simple verb followed by a preposition or adverb such as *about, in, off*. Some of these verbs are called **phrasal verbs**, because the words in them combine to give a single meaning. Sometimes this meaning is obvious, i.e. it can be guessed from the meanings of the individual parts. But often the meaning of a phrasal verb is idiomatic and cannot be guessed from the meanings of the parts.

Look at these pairs:

A Tom *came off* the midnight train.
B I don't think his plan will *come off*.

A She *came round* to see us last night.
B She didn't *come round* till a week after the accident.

The B sentence in the first pair has *come off* with the idiomatic meaning of 'succeed'; the B sentence in the second pair has *come round* with the idiomatic meaning of 'regain consciousness'.

Warning: Not all verbs followed by a preposition or adverb are phrasal verbs. Look at these pairs:

1 He *looked/ up* the road. (verb *looked* + prepositional phrase)
2 He *looked up* the dictionary. (phrasal verb *looked up* = tried to find a meaning)

1 She *came/ by* bus. (verb *came* + prepositional phrase)
2 She *came by* a valuable painting. (phrasal verb *came by* = acquired)

Non-native English speakers need to work at these verbs, and are referred to specialist dictionaries. Examples are the *Collins COBUILD Dictionary of Phrasal Verbs* (2nd edn. 2002) and an accompanying workbook.

Phrasal verbs are especially common in spoken and colloquial English. People are more likely to say they have *climbed down* a ladder, rather than *descended* it; that they have *put up with* a noisy neighbour, rather than *tolerated* him or her, etc. Phrasal verbs are less pompous, less formal than verbs of classical origin. A list follows showing some of the commonest of the thousands of English phrasal verbs. Idiomatic meanings are also shown:

ask after seek information about *She phoned the hospital to ask after her father.*
back out (of) withdraw from *He backed out of the project when he realised what it would cost.*
back up support *Please back me up in this argument.*
bear up keep strong *He tried to bear up for the sake of his family.*
break down 1 stop functioning *The car broke down.*

2 cry, burst into tears *He broke down at the news of her death.*

3 reduce to its constituent parts *Try to break this data down a bit.*

break in(to) interrupt *The demonstrators kept breaking into the proceedings.*

break off sever *Negotiations were broken off this morning.*

bring about 1 cause *The accident was brought about by careless driving.*

2 turn a boat around *They managed to bring the ship about and head for port.*

bring in introduce *The government keeps bringing in new legislation.*

bring off complete successfully *The team brought off a famous victory.*

bring round revive *The lifeguard brought the child round after he'd been rescued from the water.*

bring up raise, educate *I was brought up by my grandmother.*

call for demand *The crisis calls for strong leadership.*

call in summon *They called in a doctor.*

call off abandon *The race was called off because of snow.*

care for 1 like *He didn't much care for her manner.*

2 look after *He cared for his invalid parent for many years.*

carry on 1 make a fuss *These children have been carrying on all morning.*

2 continue *Please carry on with your work.*

carry out undertake *The police will carry out a full investigation.*

check in register *She checked in at the Forest Lawn Hotel last night.*

check out 1 leave *We'll be checking out before noon.*

2 find out (about) *You'll have to check out his alibi.*

check (up) on investigate *We've checked on his story and it seems to be true.*

clear up 1 (of weather) get better *The weather is clearing up nicely.*

2 solve *The police are keen to clear the matter up quickly.*

come off prosper, succeed *His plans haven't come off very well.*

come round recover consciousness *Three hours after the operation, she still had not come round.*

count out exclude *Please count me out of your escapade.*

draw up stop (a vehicle) *The police drew up in front of the runaway car.*

get across communicate ideas *He got his message across to his audience with great force.*

get away with 1 steal *They got away with a million dollars.*

2 escape punishment *That man gets away with murder.*

get by cope, manage *She gets by on her widow's pension.*

get down depress *Don't let them get you down!*

give away betray confidences *She plays her cards close to her chest – never gives anything away.*

give up 1 stop, lose interest *Don't just give up because it's difficult.*

2 renounce, stop *He's been trying to give up smoking for years.*

go down with contract, become ill with *Half the class went down with flu.*

go in for 1 enter for *She went in for the Mastermind quiz.*

2 like *All my friends go in for football in a big way.*

go off 1 explode *The bomb went off without warning.*

2 go bad *Milk soon goes off in warm weather.*

3 begin to dislike *I used to like Mary, but I've gone right off her lately.*

go through 1 endure, suffer *She's gone through a lot lately.*

2 search, examine *The police went through the scene of the crime with a fine-tooth comb.*

hang about wait idly *He spent his days hanging about street corners.*

hang back hesitate *He always hangs back when he is in her company.*

hang on wait *Hang on a minute and I'll be right with you.*

hang on to retain *You should hang on to that Picasso painting – it's worth a lot of money.*

hang up end a phone conversation *We were in the middle of a chat when she just hung up on me.*

hold on wait *The telephone operator asked me to hold on.*

keep at persist with *You can learn anything if you keep at it.*

knock out stun, defeat *The boxer knocked out his challenger.*

let down disappoint *Don't cancel the game and let the teams down.*

let off 1 release *The plane let off a deafening blast of air.*

2 forgive, excuse *The culprit was let off with a warning from the magistrate.*

3 explode *They let off hundreds of fireworks on Guy Fawkes Night.*

look after take care of *The hospital looks after about 200 patients.*

look in call, visit *The doctor will look in on you on his way home.*

look into investigate *The police will look into any complaints.*

look up 1 improve, get brighter. *After the war, things started to look up a bit.*

2 consult *Look it up in the dictionary/telephone directory.*

look up to respect, admire *He had no role model to look up to.*

make for 1 go towards *When it started raining, we made for shelter.*

2 provide a basis for *Their management style doesn't make for good industrial relations.*

make out 1 understand *I can't make out his writing.*

2 write *She made out a cheque for £100.*

3 progress *How are you all making out with your map-reading skills?*

4 have sex *The room was full of disco noise and kids making out.*

make up 1 invent *He makes up the most amazing stories.*

2 renew friendship, return to good relations *They decided to kiss and make up.*

3 apply cosmetics *The actors were making up their faces before the performance.*

make up for compensate for *He tried to make up for his earlier outburst.*

pass away die *He passed away in his sleep.*

pass off 1 take place *The performance passed off very successfully.*

2 masquerade *He passed himself off as a Texan millionaire.*

pass out faint *He passed out in the crowded, airless compartment.*

press on continue to work hard *Regardless of all the interruptions, she pressed on with the job.*

pull up halt *The horses pulled up at the inn.*

put off postpone *The game was put off till Friday.*

put up accommodate *I can put you up for a couple of nights.*

put up with tolerate *She won't put up with any more nonsense.*

ring back telephone again *She'll ring you back in ten minutes.*

ring off end a phone conversation *She rang off when her boss came into the room.*

ring up 1 telephone *She rang up to tell me she'd arrived safely.*

   2 register cash in a till *The assistant rang up £29.95 for the garment.*

run down 1 knock down with a vehicle *He was run down by a speeding motorist.*

   2 disparage *She loves running people down behind their backs.*

   3 slowly bring to a halt *The Coal Board has been running that mine down for the last two years.*

run into 1 meet by chance *I ran into an old school friend yesterday.*

   2 add up to *His income runs into millions of pounds.*

run out of use up *The car's run out of petrol.*

see off say goodbye to *They saw me off from the station.*

see through 1 help through a difficult period *We'll see this problem through together.*

   2 assess to be untrue *We could see through most of their ploys and ruses.*

see to attend to *You'll need to see to that cut on your leg.*

set back delay, hinder *The fire has set back their plans for expansion.*

set off 1 start a journey *The bus set off at nine o'clock.*

   2 enhance *The large painting sets off the great hall very effectively.*

   3 ignite *The kids have been setting off fireworks all night.*

show off boast, display oneself *Small children love to show off to adults.*

show up 1 appear *Guess who showed up at the party?*

   2 shame *She enjoyed showing her boyfriend up in public.*

stand by support, help *We agreed to stand by the company and see it through its difficulties.*

stand for tolerate *He won't stand for any nonsense.*

stand up for defend, support *He always stands up for the underdog.*

take after resemble *Mary takes after her father.*

take in 1 dupe *He was very plausible and took us all in.*

   2 believe *It was such a surprise that we couldn't take it all in.*

   3 include *The tour took in all the main tourist spots.*

take off 1 leave the ground *The plane took off at 9 a.m.*

   2 imitate, mimic *He enjoys taking off Tony Blair.*

take on 1 undertake, accept *He has taken on a directorship of ICI.*

   2 challenge *We took on a strong team from America.*

take over absorb *Our company has been taken over by a multinational.*

think out reason, plan *We will have to think out our next move very carefully.*

turn down reject *The planning committee turned down his application.*

turn out end, transpire *His plan has turned out very well.*

turn up be found, appear *His baggage turned up a week late.*

wear off lose power *The power of the sedative began to wear off in the morning.*

work out solve *There was one clue I couldn't work out.*

When a phrasal verb is turned into a passive form, the preposition or adverb remains attached:

The result cannot be *wondered at*.
He was well and truly *done for*.
That practice has been *done away with* for years.
Try not to let yourself be *imposed upon* by your son.

When a phrasal verb is nominalised, or used as an adjective, a hyphen is normally used:

The *get-away* car was chased across town by the police.
Muhammad Ali scored another *knock-out* last night.
My sister has suffered a nervous *break-down*.
Please fasten your seat-belts for *take-off*.

Adverbs and adverbials

Adjectives qualify nouns and pronouns. **Adverbs** modify the other parts of speech – verbs, other adverbs, adjectives, prepositions and conjunctions. Thus they are a varied and heterogeneous word-class. But probably the most important and frequent function of an adverb is to modify the main verb in a sentence – hence its name.

So the two key functions of adverbs are:

> To modify the main verb of a sentence, so that the whole meaning of the sentence is affected. Thus:

Subject	Verb phrase with adverb
Aunt Agatha	arrived **yesterday**.
The bus	travelled **slowly**.

> To modify individual words and phrases (verbs, adverbs, adjectives, prepositions, conjunctions). Thus:
He managed to rest, even to sleep *fitfully*. (verb modification)
The weather changed *very* suddenly. (adverb modification)
She is *seriously* ill. (adjective modification)
The train left *just* before noon. (preposition modification)
Let me show you *exactly* how it works. (conjunction modification)

An adverb is a single word. But there are many multi-word constructions which have the same role and perform the same function. These are called **adverbials**; they are introduced in this chapter along with adverbs, but their role and function is described in more detail elsewhere. (See p. 72.)

Kinds of adverbs

Adverbs are commonly defined according to the kinds of questions they answer about the verbs they modify. They usually come after the verb, or after the object if there is one.

Adverbs and adverbials of time

Adverbs of time say *when* something happened, and they include words like *then, now, sometimes, afterwards,* etc.

They left the police station *later.*
Afterwards we all had dinner.

Many prepositional phrases may also be used as **time adverbials**:

I saw her *during the holidays.*
I saw her *for a brief five minutes.*
I talked to him *for a whole day.*
They stayed in London *over Christmas.*
They met us *before the match.*
She's been wearing glasses *since she was eleven.*

Some of the other commonest adverbial time constructions include *in the evening, last week, next year, in September, at 8 o'clock, for a fortnight, after three days, since 1945, a month ago,* etc.

Adverbs and adverbials of place

Adverbs of place say *where* something happened. They include words like *here, there, anywhere, nowhere, somewhere, hence, hither, thence, thither, upstairs, downstairs, away, abroad, indoors, outdoors, underground,* etc.:

John was *there* a moment ago.
Please go *downstairs* and answer the phone.

Adverbials of place include a range of notions of space, position, direction and distance:

She ran *to the house. (*direction to)
He came down *from the glen.* (direction from)
They drove *for 20 kilometres.* (distance)
He lives *in the end villa on the right.* (position)

Adverbs and adverbials of manner

They thanked us *fulsomely* for our hospitality.
The bad end *unhappily,* the good *unluckily.* That is what tragedy means. (Tom Stoppard)
The lava flowed *relentlessly* and *inexorably* downhill towards the village.

These adverbs tell us *how* something happened, and they are very often formed by adding *-ly* to an adjective:

Adjective	Adverb
absolute	absolute**ly**
bad	bad**ly**
beautiful	beautiful**ly**
careful	careful**ly**
exceptional	exceptional**ly**
quick	quick**ly**
quiet	quiet**ly**
soft	soft**ly**
sudden	sudden**ly**

Some adjectives require modification before the addition of *-ly*:

Adjective	Adverb
automatic	automatic**a**lly
easy	eas**i**ly
full	fully (full + y)
gentle	gently (no e)
true	truly (no e)

A few other suffixes indicate an **adverb of manner**:

-ways: **sideways**
-wise: **streetwise, clockwise**
-wards: **forwards, backwards, skywards, earthwards**
-fashion: **squirrel-fashion, Edwardian-fashion**
-style: **1960s-style, English-style**

Adverbials of manner also describe the way in which something happens or is done.

She listened *with great sadness* to his story.
The team did not play *well enough* to win the cup.
He looked at her *in the most furtive and nervous manner*.

Remember that not all words ending in *-ly* are adverbs of manner. Some adjectives also have this ending *(manly, elderly, friendly, lordly,* etc.).

Adverbs and adverbials of reason and purpose

These tell us something about the purpose behind an action, or *why* things have happened. They include adverbs like *purposely, deliberately, intentionally, accidentally,* etc. and adverbials like the following:

They went to France *for a holiday*.
He blares his stereo *to annoy*.

Adverbs and adverbials of frequency, degree and probability

These say *how often* something happens, *to what extent* something has happened, or *how sure* you are that something is going to happen. They include words like *always, ever, never, frequently, a lot, seldom, rarely, possibly, wholly, partially, thoroughly, probably, definitely, certainly, maybe, perhaps*. They usually come before the main verb (unless the main verb is *be*, when they come after):

I *definitely* saw him yesterday.
The taxi driver will *probably* know the quickest route.
I shall *never* forget that game.
Don't *ever* do that again!
I was only *partially* convinced by his story.

Adverbs of duration

These are words like *already, still, yet, any longer, any more, no longer*. You use them to say that an event is continuing, stopping, or not happening at the moment.

Is the sun out *yet*?
I can't stand this weather *any longer*.
Surely it can't *still* be raining?
Have they finished the job *already*?

Interrogative and conjunctive adverbs

Interrogative adverbs are words like *where, when, how, why, whence* and *whither*. They ask the questions that are answered by adverbs of place, time, manner, etc.:

When did they leave the hotel?
Why do you ask that question?
How was she keeping?

Conjunctive adverbs are the same words as interrogative adverbs, but they perform a slightly different function in the sentence. Instead of asking a question, they join two clauses together:

He asked the receptionist *when* they had left the hotel.
I wonder *why* you asked that question.

Other everyday adverbs

Words like *yes* and *no* are almost like sentences, in the sense that they are often used as stand-alone words, or sentence equivalents. But they were traditionally classed as adverbs, because they modified verbs – even if those verbs were as often as not unspoken ones. Look at an exchange like the following:

Question: Are you coming?
Answer: *Yes.*

Yes here actually means 'Yes, I am coming.' So traditional grammarians said *yes* was an adverb.

Other common adverbs are that range of words used mainly to qualify adjectives and other adverbs – *very, terribly, frightfully, excessively, too, quite, almost, so, more, most, scarcely, not* and *less.*

'Special' adverbs

A number of words function as both adjectives and adverbs, with only their context to tell you which they are. They include words like *cheap, clean* (as in completely, e.g. he clean forgot), *dead* (as in utterly, e.g. she was dead cool), *easy, fast, fine, free, hard, high, just, late, loud, low, pretty, quick, real, sharp, slow, straight, sure, well, wide, wrong.*

Comparison of adverbs

Adverb comparison is very similar to adjective comparison (see pp. 18–19); you use *-er/-est* or add *more/most* to the adverb to convey comparative and superlative forms.

The job was completed *more promptly* than last time.
John was affected *more seriously* by the accident than I was.
I object *most strongly* to these insinuations.
He drove the car *faster and faster.*
His cough sounded *worse and worse.*

Position of adverbs

Adverbs are extremely mobile in their deployment, and in many cases they can go at the beginning or in the middle or at the end of a sentence:

***Suddenly* I heard a noise upstairs.**
I was *suddenly* aware of a noise.
He left the party quite *suddenly.*

A word like *originally* can be inserted at any of the points marked / in the following sentence:

/The dress/must/have/been/purchased/in Marks and Spencer's/.

Generally speaking, adverbs should be so positioned as to make quite clear which particular words they are intended to modify. Compare, for example:

She smiled at him *foolishly.* (i.e. she gave him a foolish smile)
***Foolishly,* she smiled at him. (i.e. it was unwise of her to do so)**

The split infinitive

For a reason which was once perhaps more persuasive than it now is, many people professed an objection to the use of an adverb between *to* and the verb's infinitive form. They insisted that the 'unity' of the infinitive must be respected, and they objected to split infinitive constructions like the following:

He tended *to frequently interrupt* the conversation.
She intends *to really work* this semester.

Nowadays, it is perhaps enough to avoid split infinitives in formal writing, although most people would not object to the following even in writing:

He wants *to so organise* his agenda that . . .
He forgot *to fully extend* the aerial.

See also p. 31.

Prepositions

It was *on* the table.
He is *at* school.
We drove *to* the shops.
We had to be there *before* 5 o'clock.

Prepositions are words like *on, at, to* and *before*. They show the relation of a noun or noun equivalent to the rest of a sentence. As the name suggests ('pre[ced-ing] position'), they usually come before the words they complement. Most often, they show how two parts of a sentence are related in time or space.

Simple and complex prepositions

Simple prepositions consist of a single word. **Complex prepositions** consist of two or three words. Here are some of the commonest:

Simple prepositions

about	down	over
above	during	round
across	for	since
after	from	through
against	in	to
along	inside	towards
among	into	under
around	of	up
at	off	with

Simple prepositions (cont.)

before	on	within
behind	onto	without
beneath	opposite	
by	out	

Complex prepositions – two words

ahead of	due to
apart from	except for
because of	instead of
close to	near to

Complex prepositions – three words

as far as	in spite of
by means of	in terms of
in accordance with	on account of
in addition to	on behalf of
in front of	with reference to

Preposition or adverb or conjunction?

Many of the simple prepositions listed above have several other possible functions. Before we can be sure they are indeed prepositions, we need to check the context in which the words are used:

> If the words are followed by nouns or noun equivalents, they are **prepositions**: 'I gave you that information *before* tea.'
> If they are used to link clauses, they are **conjunctions**: 'I gave you that information *before* you asked for it.'
> If they are not followed by nouns and don't link clauses, they are **adverbs**: 'I gave you that information *before*. Don't ask for it again.'

Prepositional meanings

Prepositions cover a wide range of meanings. First, they express **spatial meanings**. Many of these spatial meanings can be best illustrated diagrammatically (see pp. 52–3).

Prepositions are also used to convey a sense of:

> time ('*at* 5 o'clock', '*for* six weeks', '*by* next Tuesday')
> cause ('He was sacked *for/on account of* his laziness', 'She did it *out of* kindness')
> manner ('I paid *by* travellers' cheque', 'He worked *like* a demon')
> accompaniment ('You must go *with* them')
> support or opposition ('I was *against* the plan', 'They are *with* you all the way')

> concession ('She came *despite* her illness')
> possession ('a musician *of* rare talent', 'a bag *with* a purple handle')
> addition and exception ('The car was a bargain *apart from* its rusty bonnet',
  'We had a great time *except for* the weather')

Prepositional phrases

The combination of the preposition and its noun phrase complement is called a
prepositional phrase. These can come after, or **post-modify**, a noun:

The villain was the man *in the blue suit*.

Or they can be adverbials:

At 5 o'clock *in the afternoon*, the rain came on.

Or they can complement verbs or adjectives:

He fell *off the table*.
We were very sorry *for him*.

Or they indicate possession:

Two Gentlemen *of Verona*

Space prepositions

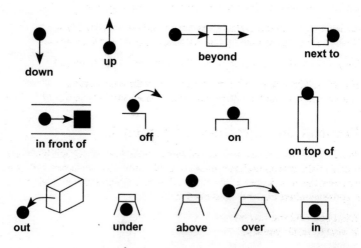

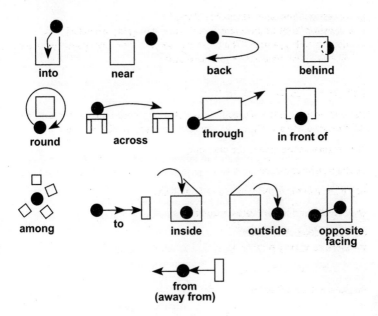

into   near   back   behind

round   across   through   in front of

among   to   inside   outside   opposite facing

from (away from)

Prepositions governing two elements

A preposition need not be repeated if it has two complements:

An operetta *by* Gilbert and Sullivan, NOT *by* Gilbert and *by* Sullivan
He spoke *with* passion and humour, NOT *with* passion and *with* humour.

But you do need to repeat the preposition if there is a risk of ambiguity:

She was talking *about* health education and smoking cigarettes.
She was talking *about* health education and *about* smoking cigarettes.

Prepositions at the end of sentences

Because a Latin sentence could not end with a preposition, some English scholars used to claim that an English sentence shouldn't end with one either. If it ever was one, this is no longer a rule of English usage. A better rule is to place the preposition where it sounds most natural:

What hotel did you stay *in*?
***In* what hotel did you stay?**

Either of these alternatives is acceptable, though the latter is more formal and sounds stiffer. In some examples, there is no alternative:

What was she looking *for*?
NOT: *For* what was she looking?

Winston Churchill (a master of plain, punchy and memorable English – the right word in the right place) poked fun at the former reluctance to put a preposition at the end of a sentence with his well-chosen example of contorted English:

This is the sort of behaviour *up* with which I shall not put.

Prepositional idioms

Many prepositions are embedded in **idioms** (see pp. 156–7). There are no easy rules for deciding which preposition to use in such phrases. They just have to be learned. A person who is overcharged is said to pay *through* the nose; one who is made to do as we wish is led *by* the nose; and when we do something without a person noticing we say that we have done something *under* his very nose.

Other examples include:

off colour   an ear *for* music
against the grain   *with* the stream/flow
stick *at* nothing   beating *about* the bush
straight *from* the shoulder   *above* board
beyond your means   *into* the bargain
soldiers *under* arms   *on* call

Conjunctions

Conjunctions are link words or 'joining together' words. There are two types: coordinators and subordinators.

Coordinating conjunctions

The **coordinators** are so called because they join units of equal status. The units may be words ('fish *and* chips', 'tired *but* happy', 'tea *or* coffee'); or they may be sentences ('John is working in the garden *and* Mary is working in the house', 'His name is Steven *and* he lives in Leeds').

The coordinating conjunctions are:

and   both . . . and
but   either . . . or
or   neither. . . nor
then
so
yet

Look at these:

The weather will be (*both***) dry *and* windy tomorrow.**
The weather will be dry *but* windy tomorrow.
The weather will be dry *or* windy tomorrow.
The weather will be *neither* dry *nor* windy tomorrow.
She was born in Zagreb *and* raised in Philadelphia.
She didn't complain *or* even protest.
When she saw John she blushed, *then* walked away.

These sentences show some of the range of meanings afforded by coordinating conjunctions. Note that in the last three examples, the clauses have the same subject (*she*); when you use a coordinating conjunction you do not always need to repeat the subject in the second clause.

These are all examples of **linked coordination**. When there is no conjunction, the coordination is said to be **unlinked**:

The weather was wet *and* windy *and* cold. (linked coordination)
The weather was wet, windy, cold. (unlinked coordination)

Subordinating conjunctions

The **subordinating conjunctions** join subordinate or dependent clauses to the main clause of a sentence. (For more on this, see under **sentence** structure, p. 74.) The main subordinators are:

after He laughed *after* she cracked a joke.
(al)though *Although* it is sunny now, the forecast is for rain.
as The car braked hard *as* the dog ran across the road.
as . . . as They left the scene *as* quickly *as* they could.
as if He talked *as if* money were no problem.
because He climbed the hill *because* it was there.
before Tell me one thing *before* you go.
even if I don't want to go *even if* you give me a free ticket.
except I'd go *except* I've no time.
if *If* you drop litter you'll get a £10 fine.
in case We left some supper *in case* John dropped by.
in order to She left early *in order to* get her train.
more . . . than I've grown far *more* potatoes *than* I can use.
rather than I'd starve *rather than* eat snails.
since The business has flourished *since* it was taken over.
so that The management worked hard *so that* it would succeed.
that The reason *that* I am here today . . .
till/until They drew no salaries *till* the company's prospects were secure.
when They relaxed a bit *when* they got their first big contract.
whenever They still work flat out *whenever* they have to.

where They go *where* the good orders are.

whereas They are real professionals *whereas* their competitors are a lot of amateurs.

wherever You'll find them *wherever* there's business to be had.

whether Now they have to decide *whether* they will consolidate or expand the business.

while Nero fiddles *while* Rome burns.

Some subordinating conjunctions also function as prepositions:

Subordinator	Preposition
He arrived **before** I did.	He arrived **before** me.
He left **after** I did.	He left **after** me.

Most subordinating conjunctions can also be used to link sentences, rather than just to link a subordinate clause with a main clause in the same sentence:

'When can I have it?' – '*When* John's finished with it.'
'Can I take the car?' – '*So long as* it's back by tea time.'
'That goes by e-mail.' – '*Then* the client gets it right away.'

And as an idiom

Sometimes *and* has a special idiomatic use, and isn't really a conjunction at all:

> In expressions like 'You're looking fine *and* comfortable/dandy' or 'This towel is nice *and* soft', *and* is used almost as an adverb equivalent.

> In 'Try *and* remember where you put it' or 'Let's try *and* find it', *and* really equals *to* as part of an infinitive verb phrase.

> In 'He ran *and* ran *and* ran', the repeated *and* functions as a sort of emphatic, or **intensifier**.

> In 'There are universities *and* universities', the idiomatic *and* carries the intensifier sense that there are various kinds of universities and only some of them are worthy of the name.

Interjections

Oh!	Ah!	Ooh!	Alas!
Help!	Ow!	Eh?	Sh!
Pooh!	Whew!	Tut-tut!	Look out!
Cheers!	Nice one!	Damn!	Gosh!
Hem!	Oh dear!	Look here!	Bless my soul!

These are exclamations, or emotional noises. As a part of speech, they are termed **interjections**. Sometimes they are formed by actual words, sometimes not.

We use them to express sudden feelings of joy, pain, surprise, disgust, anger, etc. They are generally marked by an exclamation mark or a question mark. They stand alone, as above, or they may be loosely added on to a sentence.

Oh no – I can't bear to watch any longer!
Dear me – what has happened to your clothes!
There now – don't cry!

Many interjections or exclamatory statements are elliptical – that is, they refer to previous parts of a conversation or text, with words left out or implied:

What an ass/night/experience!
Poor fool/kid/lamb/lad!

Being colloquial, interjections are being generated all the time, different social groups favouring different expressions:

Gordon Bennett! Blimey! (Southern English)
Crivvens! Help-ma-boab! Jings! (Glasgow)
Cool! Gee! (US)

Taboo versions are currently popular in speech, but not appropriate for formal writing (Shit! Fuck! etc.).

Phrases

So far in this book, we have looked at the traditional eight parts of speech, although by adding determiners we have made it nine. Part 2 of the book will examine larger chunks of meaning – sentences and clauses. But if words are the smallest building blocks of language, the next category in the hierarchy is **phrases** (about which a little has already been said). We will look now at phrases, before going on to consider sentences and clauses.

Basically, a phrase is a small group of words that function as a grammatical unit. If you look at a sentence you can usually break it up into phrases:

The cat / sat / on the mat / waiting / for its tea.

This sentence has been broken into five phrases. (In grammar, it is important to remember that a phrase may consist of one word or more than one word.)

What about this?

The / cat sat on the / mat waiting / for its / tea.

This version of the same sentence is made up of rather unnatural breaks. It has been broken into groups of words which do not function as grammatical units. Thus we see that not all groups of words make phrases. A certain internal structure is required.

In grammar, we distinguish five kinds of phrase. Each is named after the word class which plays the key part in its structure:

> noun phrase:
a great big balloon (main word: noun *balloon*)
the most ghastly accident (main word: noun *accident*)

> verb phrase:
may have been sleeping (main word: verb *sleeping*)
will have surrendered (main word: verb *surrendered*)

> adjective phrase:
frightfully smart (main word: adjective *smart*)
very very old (main word: adjective *old*)

> adverb phrase:
quite inadvertently (main word: adverb *inadvertently*)
very stupidly (main word: adverb *stupidly*)

> preposition phrase:
in the river (main word: preposition *in*)
for your private information (main word: preposition *for*)

Structurally, a phrase is analysed in terms of a main word and its modifiers. In grammar, as we have noted, a phrase may contain one word or several. The subject of each of the following sentences, for example, may be described as a noun phrase. This is true even of the first sentence, where the noun phrase is in fact a single noun:

Balloons were bobbing about in the sky.
The balloons were bobbing about in the sky.
A great big blue and yellow balloon was bobbing about in the sky.

It is not uncommon for one phrase to embed another, or several other, phrases. So:

on the edge of a busy street (prepositional phrase: main word *on*)
the edge of a busy street (noun phrase: main word *edge*)
of a busy street (prepositional phrase: main word *of*)
a busy street (noun phrase: main word *street*)

A phrase may also embed a clause. So:

the house that Jack built (noun phrase: main word *house)*
that Jack built (relative clause, introduced by *that*)

Noun phrases

The main word – sometimes, as we have seen, the only word – of a **noun phrase** is usually a noun or pronoun:

buds

Often there is a **determiner**:

a bud   *the* buds

Then there are the **modifiers**:

green buds   *darling* buds *of May*

If the modifiers come before the main word, they are called **pre-modifiers**; if they come after it, they are **post-modifiers**.
    The modifiers may themselves be modified:

a *distinctly* ramshackle bus
the red bus standing at platform 16 *with its engine running*

Apposition is not uncommon in noun phrases. The noun phrase is followed by a second, explanatory, noun phrase, which is said to be 'in apposition' to the first:

Zagreb, *the capital of Croatia,* is once again a peaceful place.
A well-known media personality, *namely Terry Wogan,* is present.

Certain types of clauses feature commonly as modifiers in a noun phrase:

She has an Alsatian which barks constantly.
The man who spoke to me is an Egyptian.

The first sentence contains the noun phrase 'an Alsatian which barks constantly', in which is embedded the **relative clause** 'which barks constantly'. The second sentence contains the noun phrase 'the man who spoke to me', in which is embedded the relative clause 'who spoke to me'. (See p. 76 for more on relative clauses.)
    Appositive clauses (clauses in apposition) are also commonly embedded in a noun phrase. They are introduced by *that*, functioning as a conjunction:

The fact that he insulted her . . .
The reason that he is here today . . .

Compound nouns (see pp. 9-10), especially multi-word technical terms, are best treated as noun phrases:

automatic speech output device
lexical stress assignment process
airport flight information systems

Sometimes a noun phrase is made up of adjectives: *the poor, the famous.*
The poor are always with us; the famous too, alas.

Verb phrases

The main word of a **verb phrase** is a main verb, which may be preceded by up to four auxiliaries. Some of the verb phrases are:

see
have **seen**
shouldn't have been **seeing**
must have been being **seen**

The main verb of the verb phrase will be in one of these forms:

> the base form: *see, speak, run, jump*
> the -*s* form: *sees, speaks, runs, jumps*
> the -*ing* participle form: *seeing, speaking, running, jumping*
> the -*ed* past or participle form (regular or irregular): *saw, spoke, ran, jumped*

The verb phrase may be active or passive. Here are some active and corresponding passive verb phrases:

Active	Passive
sees	is seen
ate	was eaten
is cooking	is being cooked
has built	has been built
will elect	will be elected
may have affected	may have been affected
should be delivering	should be being delivered

The auxiliaries precede the main verb in a specified order or sequence:

> modals, such as *can, may, will, must*
> perfect auxiliary *have*
> progressive auxiliary *be*
> passive auxiliary *be*

These auxiliaries in turn specify the form to be taken by the main verb which follows:

> can *read*, may *speak*, must *work* . . .
> have *read*, have *spoken*, have *worked* . . .
> was *reading*, was *speaking*, was *working* . . .
> was *read*, was *spoken*, was *worked* . . .

Verb phrases which contain a phrasal verb or a multi-word verb may occasionally be interrupted:

He *has handed in* his resignation.
He *has handed* his resignation *in*.

You *should put off* your decision.
You *should put* your decision *off*.

A verb phrase is the essential and pivotal element of a **clause** (see p. 69).

Adjective phrases

The main word in an **adjective phrase** is an adjective. The other words are modifiers, which may precede the adjective (pre-modifiers) or follow it (post-modifiers):

happy	*sad*
ecstatically and deliriously *happy*	very obviously *sad*
happy to see you all	*sad* to the point of despair

Some adjectives need to have post-modifiers:

John is very *keen* (+) *on cricket*.
She is fully *aware* (+) *of your criticism*.
I'm very *fond* (+) *of golf*.

Adjective phrases function mainly in the following ways.

> they are pre-modifiers in a noun phrase:
It was a *very eloquent and witty* speech.

> they are post-modifiers in a noun phrase:
She has done something *rather silly*.

> they are subject complements:
The job was *extremely difficult*.

> they are object complements:
He made her *very happy*.

> they complete the meaning of certain adjectives:
She is *afraid of the big bad wolf*.

Sometimes adjectives are used as the main word in what then effectively becomes a noun phrase. Adjectives of nationality do this:
the Americans
the Welsh
the Germans

So do classes of society:
the poor
the sick
the old

And so do certain superlatives:
the latest
the worst

Examples of these usages:
The wounded have now been evacuated from the war zone.
The French have pioneered this approach.
What's *the latest* from Downing Street?

Adverb phrases

The main word in an **adverb phrase** is an adverb. The other words are called modifiers, which may precede the adverb (pre-modifiers) or follow it (post-modifiers):
amazingly
so *amazingly*
amazingly for him
very *amazingly* indeed

There are two main functions for adverb phrases:

> they modify an adjective:
Her advice was *extremely and surprisingly* constructive.

> they modify an adverb:
She spoke *somewhat* inappropriately about the economy.

Prepositional phrases

The components of a **prepositional phrase** are the preposition and its complement. The prepositional complement is most commonly a noun phrase.

across *the barricades*
into *the abyss*

But it can also be certain types of clause:

He'll drive you to *wherever you want to go.*

Prepositional phrases function mainly in the following ways:

> they are post-modifiers in a noun phrase:
a man *in a brown suit*
the boys *in blue*

> they are adverbials:
He drove *to the city* (1) *in the early evening* (2).

> they are verb or adjective complements:
Tom was *in a great hurry.*
She was sitting *on the floor.*
I was very sorry *for them.*

Remember that prepositional phrases often occur in clusters:

He lives *in a bungalow* (1) *near a nice beach* (2) *in Cornwall* (3).

Remember too how prepositional phrases may be embedded in one another:

It was a disaster in the annals of international diplomacy.
> *in the annals of international diplomacy* (prepositional phrase)
> *the annals of international diplomacy* (noun phrase)
> *of international diplomacy* (prepositional phrase)
> *international diplomacy* (noun phrase)

Two

Sentences and clauses

How to do things with words.

> J L Austin, William James Lectures at Harvard University, 1955

Backward ran sentences until reeled the mind.

> Wolcott Gibbs, satirising the style of *Time* magazine in the *New Yorker*, 1936

I will not go down to posterity talking bad grammar.

> Benjamin Disraeli, correcting proofs of his last parliamentary speech, 1881

I don't want to talk grammar, I want to talk like a lady.

> George Bernard Shaw, *Pygmalion*, 1916

He lays sentences like eggs, but forgets to incubate them.

> Elias Canetti, *The Human Province*, 1973

the sentence

major and minor sentences
simple and multiple sentences and clauses
sentence types
positive and negative sentences
active and passive sentences
when is a sentence not a sentence: the comma splice

sentences and clauses

clause elements
subject
predicate
verb
object
complement
adverbial
compound and complex sentences
independent and dependent clauses
coordination
subordination
subordinate clauses
nominal or noun clauses
adverbial clauses
relative clauses
comparative clauses
finite and non-finite clauses
restrictive and non-restrictive clauses
dangling modifiers
reading difficulty

The sentence

It is helpful to think of the **sentence** as the largest unit of grammar. In the hierarchy of the nuts and bolts of language, we can say that:

A **sentence** consists of one or more clauses.
A **clause** consists of one or more phrases.
A **phrase** consists of one or more words.
A **word** consists of one or more **morphemes**.

We have looked at words and phrases in Part 1 of this book, and we will look at word formation in Part 3.

Grammar deals with the rules for combining words and phrases into sentences. We all think we know what we mean by a sentence in English, even if it is rather hard to define.

Some people say that a sentence is a group of words which begins with a capital letter and ends with a full stop (or one of the equivalents of a full stop, i.e. a question mark or an exclamation mark). This has been called the 'formal' definition of a sentence, because it defines the term by describing its form or shape. It is obviously a better definition of the written than of the spoken language!

Others tell us that a sentence is a 'complete expression of a single thought'. This is called the 'notional' definition, because it defines the term by the notion or idea it conveys. But it begs the rather large question of exactly what is a single thought.

According to these definitions, the following are all sentences:

Good morning!
No parking.
Come in.
For her last holiday, Jane took a trip to Tunisia, where she visited lots of interesting places, swam in a warm sea, ate some splendid meals, and contrived in the course of a hectic courtship to get herself married to the wealthy proprietor of a large ceramic-tile factory near Carthage.

They all comply with the 'formal' definition, although the last example seems rather to test the 'notional' definition.

Perhaps a simpler way to define a sentence in English is to apply three criteria to it:

> It is a construction that can stand alone, without people feeling it to be incomplete.
> It is constructed according to agreed rules of grammar; that is, it has a certain structure.
> It is the largest structure to which the rules of grammar apply. The unit beyond the sentence is the **paragraph** (see pp. 134–7), which is more accurately a part of the specialised topic of punctuation than grammar.

Following these rules, most people will probably be able to pick out the sentences from the non-sentences in the following list:

Time for bed, said Zebedee.
The car won't start.
Where are my football boots?
Go away.
Even for adults.
In the street.
Here I you wish were.
Them stop coming from.
Yesterday was my birthday, I got lots of presents.

The fifth and sixth items are incomplete, while the seventh and eighth are unstructured jumbles of words; they are not grammatical, so they are not sentences. The last item in the list would be better converted into two sentences; its comma might be better changed to a full stop or a semicolon.

Major and minor sentences

Sentences come in all shapes and sizes, as the merest glance across the range of printed media will confirm. Students of grammar often divide them into 'major' and 'minor' types. **Major sentences** are often described as 'regular', and **minor sentences** as 'irregular'.

Major sentences are said to break down into certain structural patterns, like these:

John Brown	has scored	a winning goal	for Chelsea.
I	lost	the car keys.	
Tom and Yvette	went back	to Canada	yesterday.

(We will look at the patterns of the major sentence later.)

Minor sentences are the ones that cannot be broken down in this way. They include:

> Interjections (see pp. 56–7): *Shhhh! Oh dear! Ahem! Whew!*
> Proverbs (see p. 165): *Once bitten, twice shy. Easy come, easy go.*
> Phrases used as questions: *Milk and sugar? Feeling better?*
> Short forms: *Road closed. No smoking. Weather dreadful.*
> Formula expressions: *Well done! How do you do? Hello! Good evening. Nice to see you!*

Simple and multiple sentences and clauses

Consider this sentence:

It was a lovely day.

This is called a **simple sentence**. It cannot be broken into smaller sentences.

Now look at this sentence:

It was a lovely day and I golfed in the afternoon.

This second sentence can be broken into two sentences:

It was a lovely day. (+) I golfed in the afternoon.

This is said to be a **multiple sentence**, made up of *two clauses* joined by *and*. Thus simple sentences contain only one verb or verb phrase, and can be analysed into only one clause. Multiple sentences contain more than one verb or verb phrase, and can be analysed into more than one clause:

It *was* a lovely day, I *was* up to date with most of my work, my good friend John Brown *called* at the door unexpectedly with his golf clubs after lunch, and thus we *ended up* playing a pleasant afternoon game of golf.

This is a multiple sentence with four verb phrases (italicised) and four clauses. It would be easy enough to change it into four sentences: substitute full stops for the commas and add capital letters.

Sentence types: declarative, interrogative, imperative, and exclamative

These are the four main types of sentence.

> Declarative sentence (conveying information):
She lives in Jamaica.
The capital city of the new republic, normally picturesque and prosperous, is at present a dispirited and shell-shocked shadow of its former self.

> Interrogative sentence (requesting information):
Where is the bus station?
Have you had a nice holiday?

> Imperative sentence (requesting action):
Take a letter, please
Let's have a cup of tea.

> Exclamative sentence (expressing feelings):
Get you!
How wonderful!

Most of this chapter is about declarative sentences.

Positive and negative sentences

Sentences are either **positive** or **negative**. They are made negative by the use of *n't* or *not* after the auxiliary. If there is no auxiliary, a 'dummy auxiliary' *do/does* is incorporated:

Positive: Elizabeth speaks good French.
Negative: Elizabeth *doesn't speak* good French.
Positive: I'll send you the bill tomorrow.
Negative: I *won't send* you the bill tomorrow.
Positive: John is running a profitable business.
Negative: John *is not running* a profitable business.

Certain other words convey a negative meaning to a sentence:

He has *never* met her.
She saw *nothing*.
I can *by no means* condone this behaviour.

Active and passive sentences

Sentences are either **active**, with an agent doing something, or **passive**, with something being done to an agent:

Active: The man addressed the crowd.
Passive: The crowd was addressed by the man.

The first sentence is made passive by moving *the man* and *the crowd* to the opposite ends of the sentence, by adding *by* before *the man,* and by changing the active verb *addressed* to the passive form *was addressed.*
    Other examples of active and passive sentences:

Active: Tiger Woods yesterday won the PGA Golf Championship at
    Pinehurst, North Carolina.
Passive: The PGA Golf Championship was won yesterday at Pinehurst, North
    Carolina, by Tiger Woods.
Active: The Labour whips have warned backbenchers that the PM will be
    finished if they do not tonight support the Government motion in the
    House of Commons.
Passive: Backbenchers have been warned by the Labour whips that . . .

Most of the examples in this chapter are of active sentences, which are very much commoner than passive ones.

When is a sentence not a sentence: the comma splice

We've described a sentence as a 'construction that can stand alone, without people feeling it to be incomplete', or as a 'complete expression of a single thought'. We've described how two **simple sentences** may be joined (by *and, but, yet, so, while,* etc.) to make a **multiple sentence**. So what are the following:

Titanic was a big box-office success, I'd really like to see it.
It's almost 5.30 already, we'll not get the job finished tonight.

These are examples of the **comma splice**, a punctuation error in which a comma with no connecting joining word tries to splice two independent clauses into a single sentence. The resulting sentences don't really work; they'd be better left as two sentences.

The other misuse of the comma splice is to use it with the conjunctions *however* or *nevertheless*. These two words carry a certain force, as the examples show:

They cooked me a delightful lunch, however I wasn't hungry.
A spell-checker is a useful aid, nevertheless there are lots of misspellings it
cannot be programmed to correct.

Again, both of these examples would work better as two sentences; so they should be separated by full stops or semicolons, not commas.

Sentences and clauses

As we have seen, a **simple sentence** has a single verb phrase (in italics below), and is made up of a single clause:

John *is digging* his garden.

A **multiple sentence** is one which has more than one clause:

John *is digging* his garden and *whistling* a tune.

The second sentence has two verb phrases; so it has two clauses, joined by the linking word *and*.

Clause elements

Simple clauses are made up of certain elements, or components, each of which conveys a particular kind of meaning. The five elements of a clause are:

subject S

---

verb V
object O   } predicate
complement C
adverbial A

Clauses need not contain more than some of these elements, although some will contain all of them. All clauses contain a verb element:

He (S) is drinking (V).
He (S) is drinking (V) a mug of coffee (O).
Christopher Robin (S) is saying (V) his prayers (O).
The tax office (S) has sent (V) me (O) two reminders (O) this month (A).

US voters (S) in 2004 (A) re-elected (V) George W Bush (O) the 42nd president (C).
Give (V) me (O) that book (O).

Unless the clause has an imperative function (as in the last example) or an inter-rogative one, the subject is usually the first element in the clause, and gives it its theme or topic. Then, usually, comes the verb element, the key to the clause in the sense that this is the one component that every major clause has. The object and complement elements usually follow the S + V in a clause. The adverbial element usually adds information about details like the time or the location of the action. It is highly mobile, and is placed closest to the element it modifies.

Subject (S)

Subjects of a declarative sentence are usually any of the following:

> noun phrases:
The people **voted for a change of government.**

> pronouns:
They **have become disillusioned with the current regime.**

> proper nouns:
Rome **is the capital of Italy.**

> *-ing* forms:
Smoking **is bad for you.**

> *to* forms:
To work **hard is all you are asked.**

> inverted finite clauses:
That the PM should resign **is clear for all to see.**

The subject of a clause is important. Often therefore, in the absence of a mean-ingful subject, a 'dummy subject' is introduced:

There **is a slight problem. (Where?)**
It **is wet and windy. (What is *it*?)**

Predicate

This is a traditional grammatical term covering the part of the clause that makes a statement about the subject of the clause. As the table below shows, the **predi-cate** includes all the parts of the clause that are not contained in the subject:

Subject	Predicate
Elizabeth	slept.
Elizabeth	was ever so tired and sleepy.
Elizabeth	slept deeply if fitfully for upwards of fifteen hours.

Verb (V)

In English clause analysis, it is important to remember the two types of verb – the '**doing' words**, like *sing, jump, dance*; and the **copular verbs**, which are *be, appear, become, get, grow, look* and *seem*. Ordinary 'doing word' verbs – the vast majority of verbs – take an object:

S	V	O
John	has bought	a house in London.
Mary	gave	me a kiss.

Copular verbs take an object equivalent called a **complement**:

S	V	C
He	is	a fisherman.
She	seems	in a great hurry.

As already stated, the verb element is the most important and pivotal element of the clause. A few of the commonest verb patterns are listed below, with the verb in italics:

SVO	The post office *has opened* a new branch.
SV	Andrew's pet rabbit *has died*.
SVC	The dinner *was* a great success.
SVA	She *departed* secretly.
SVOO	Alison *cooked* him his favourite meal.
SVOC	Alison's cooking *is driving* him mad.

There is more on verbs on pp. 27–45 and 60–61.

Object (O)

The **object** of a declarative clause normally follows a verb. Sometimes two objects follow the verb:

James ate *his lunch*.
John passed *James* (1) *the salt* (2).

The verbs here are **transitive verbs**, or verbs which take an object. Some verbs can take both a **direct** and an **indirect object**:

S	V	O (indirect)	O (direct)
Paul	brought	Vicky	a bunch of flowers.
Vicky	gave	him	a kiss.

An indirect object is one which can be preceded by *to* or *for*.

Paul brought [*for*] Vicky a bunch of flowers.
Vicky gave [*to*] him a kiss.

The direct object of a declarative clause is usually either a noun, a noun phrase, or an object pronoun:

He plays *soccer*.
He has attended *two hundred league matches*.
The police followed *him* to a deserted house.

Occasionally a finite or non-finite clause functions as the object:

I explained *what I had done*.   **He denied *that he was involved*.**
He denied *being involved*.   **He proposes *to build a house*.**

Complement (C)

This is the name given to the object equivalent in a clause taking a copula or linking verb:

S	V	C
Mary	is	a vet. (noun phrase complement)
She	appears	very competent. (adjective phrase complement)
She	seems	in a great hurry. (prepositional phrase complement)
She	is	downstairs. (adverbial complement)

Adverbial (A)

Adverbials, as we have seen, are clause elements and function like adverbs and adverb phrases. They can be found more or less anywhere in the clause. They are often optional, and peripheral to the drift of the clause:

After ten days I began to suspect an accident.
We got the good news *last Friday*.

There may be several adverbials in one clause.

He left the house *very angrily* (1) *at 12.15* (2) *to meet his creditors* (3).

In spite of their name, adverbials do not necessarily contain adverbs. In the above case, they comprise an adverb phrase (1), a prepositional phrase (2), and a non-finite verb phrase (3). But they all answer adverbial questions:

***How* did he leave? – Very angrily.**
***When* did he leave? – At 12.15.**
***Why* did he leave? – To meet his creditors.**

Compound and complex sentences

So far, most of the example sentences in this chapter have been patterned on simple sentences, containing only one clause. Sentences with more than one clause can be analysed into **compound** and **complex sentences**.

In compound sentences, the clauses are linked by coordinating conjunctions – usually *and, or, but* – and each clause can potentially stand on its own.

Main clause 1	Coordinator	Main clause 2
I travelled by bus	and	John went by taxi.
I liked Florence	but	I didn't like Rome.

These sentences are made up of two main clauses linked by coordinating *and* and *but*.

In complex sentences, there is a main clause and one or more subordinate clauses. Subordinate clauses lack the potential to stand on their own, and require a main clause before they can make much sense:

Main clause	Subordinate clause
I phoned the police	when I heard the shooting.

Subordinate clause	Main clause
After she'd completed the report	she went to a meeting.

Subordinate clauses may be **finite**, like the two examples above; that is, they have a finite verb. Or they may be **non-finite**:

I phoned the police *after hearing the shots.*
***After completing the report,* she went out.**

In none of these versions can the subordinate clauses stand on their own.

Independent and dependent clauses

A main clause is sometimes called an **independent clause**. As the name indicates, this is a clause which can stand alone and is not dependent on another clause:

[The noise got louder] and [the children screamed].

The above sentence has two independent – or main – clauses joined by *and*. If we change it to read:

[When the noise got louder], [the children screamed].

we still have two clauses, but the first clause has now become **dependent** on the second, or subordinate to it. In this next example:

[She thought [that I was serious] [when I spoke to her]], [but she was wrong].

there are two independent clauses (*She thought* and *but she was wrong*) and two dependent clauses (*that I was serious* and *when I spoke to her*).

The terms independent and dependent are more or less synonymous with main and subordinate.

Coordination

In sentence grammar, **coordination** tells us that the elements that are joined have the same status. The joined elements may be words, phrases or clauses. Coordination is signalled by the use of the coordinating conjunctions – usually *and, but, or*:

She can speak to you *in German* or *in English* or *in French*.
He has lost *his cheque card* and *his driving licence*.
John worked all morning and Alison worked all afternoon.

Here phrases and clauses are coordinated. Sometimes the coordinating conjunctions are left out; the coordination is then said to be unlinked:

She speaks German, English, French.

Sometimes more than the coordinating conjunction is left out, and there is an ellipsis:

John worked all morning, Alison all afternoon.

Subordination

In **subordination**, we see that the joined elements do not have the same status. Subordination may be between clauses or phrases, and is usually marked by one of the subordinating conjunctions. When introducing an adverbial clause, these include *although, since, when, if, until*:

She'll help you *if you ask nicely*.
She talked on and on *until I nearly screamed*.

When introducing noun clauses, they include *that* and *what*:

It was clear *that he was badly hurt*.
He always gets *what he wants*.

When introducing 'adjective' or relative clauses, they include *that, which, who* and *whom*:

The present *that I received yesterday* is delightful.

There are also multi-word subordinators which introduce subordinate clauses, such as *in order that, as long as, insofar as, so that, assuming that*, etc.:

He drives very competently, *given that* he has only one arm.
I'll see you next week, *as long as* you don't forget.

In all these clauses, the subordinate clauses depend for their meaning on the main clauses. That is why they are often also called dependent clauses.

Subordinate clauses

As we have seen, a **subordinate clause** is dependent on another clause, the main clause. There are four types of subordinate clause, depending on their position or function in relation to the main clause:

> **nominal** or **noun clauses**
> **adverbial clauses**
> **relative clauses**
> **comparative clauses**

Nominal or noun clauses

These are subordinate clauses with a function in the sentence similar to that of the noun phrase. They can act as the subject, object, or complement of the main clause:

[What you think] is of no interest to me. (subject)
I'm not asking [what you think]. (object)
The plan is [that we will fly to New York]. (complement)

There are finite and non-finite nominal clauses:

She tells me [that her father is in prison]. (finite *that* clause)
[What you need now] is a spot of good luck. (finite nominal relative clause)
[Giving him a bottle of whisky] is the same thing as [giving him a loaded pistol]. (non-finite nominal -*ing* clause)

Sometimes nominal clauses come after a preposition:

It depends on [what you think].

Adverbial clauses

These are subordinate clauses with a function in the sentence similar to adverbials. Thus they modify the main clause by adding information about time, location, concession, cause, etc. They are usually linked to the main clause by a conjunction. They can occur in most parts of a sentence:

She must phone the police [if she is bullied].
[If she is bullied], she must phone the police.

Adverbial clauses cover a wide range of structures and meanings:

He pulled the cord [to set off the alarm].
[Gasping audibly], he completed his speech.
She retired [heartily detested by the electorate].

These non-finite adverbial clauses all answer basic adverbial questions:

Why did he pull the cord?
How did he complete his speech?
How did she retire?

Relative clauses

These are subordinate clauses with an 'adjectival' function in the sentence, as modifiers of a noun phrase:

The car [*which* I bought] was a mini.
I talked to the people [*who* were selling it].

In these sentences, the relative clauses are joined to the main clauses by the relative pronouns *which* and *who*. They refer back to the noun phrases *the car* and *the people*, which are called the **antecedents** of the relative clauses.

Often, especially in speech, the relative pronoun is missed out:

The man [he works for] is American. (= *whom* he works for)
I won't reply to the letter [you wrote]. (= *which* you wrote)

Comparative clauses

These are subordinate clauses which modify comparative adverbs and adjectives. The main comparative adjectives are the ones with regular -*er* endings – *older, fatter, harder, simpler,* etc. Other comparative words are *more, less, better, worse,* etc.:

It's less difficult [than I thought].
This melon seems a bit riper [than the last one was].
She tried [as hard as she could].
Things are even worse [than you might have imagined].

Finite and non-finite clauses

Finite clauses are those with a finite verb:

When he's working, he chews gum.

Both clauses in the above sentence are finite, because their verbs are finite (*is working; chews*).

A **non-finite clause** has a non-finite verb:

He chews gum to help his concentration.

The second clause in the above sentence is non-finite, because its verb is the non-finite *to* form (an infinitive).

Restrictive and non-restrictive clauses

This is a subdivision of relative clauses in which punctuation (or, for spoken language, intonation) plays a crucial part. Look at these sentences:

My sister *who lives in Canada* is coming to stay.
My sister, *who lives in Canada,* is coming to stay.

In the first sentence, the relative clause *who lives in Canada* is **restrictive**, specifying which sister. The informant thus perceives a certain emphasis in the first sentence:

My sister who lives in *Canada* . . . Not the one who lives in *London* . . .

In the second sentence, the relative clause has been marked off in commas, and is **non-restrictive**. The information between the commas is not restricted, so the sentence has two things to say: (1) the informant has a sister who is coming to stay; (2) that sister happens to live in Canada.

Punctuation – or intonation – thus conveys the information that the informant in the first sentence has more than one sister, while the informant in the second sentence has only one sister, and that sister is resident in Canada.

Dangling modifiers

We know that a modifier is a word, phrase or clause which is added to another word to specify more exactly what that word refers to. We talk about a **dangling**, or 'hanging', **modifier** when it has been misplaced in the sentence, often with ridiculous results. For example:

The explosive was found by a security man in a plastic bag.
The boy picked the flowers that his mother had been growing for a friend.
I have a canary in a cage that can talk.
Visitors with dogs who wish to enter the garden must keep them on a lead.
Children with parents who are under ten are admitted free.
You see few signposts driving across Dartmoor.
Although big enough, she did not take the apartment.

These sentences all need to be rethought. They all point out the moral that modifiers need to be carefully 'tucked in' to the sentence. Can you rewrite them to make better sense?

Reading difficulty

Academic studies of **readability** point to a number of specific and obvious constructions causing difficulty to the reader. Among these are areas such as the following:

> a high number of clauses per sentence
> use of the passive

> nominalisations deriving from verbs, e.g. *reduction* from *reduce*
> ellipsis, as in 'The car [. . .] I bought was red.'

It is of course impossible and inadvisable completely to avoid such constructions in writing. But it is sometimes useful to remember that certain constructions are known to give difficulty to the reader, and to double-check one's writing if such constructions have been used.

A few specific examples of 'difficult' constructions follow. Usually the difficulty is fairly obvious, and not always easy to avoid. This merely means that certain kinds of text – e.g. scientific or legal documents – have to be read more slowly and carefully than others:

> Extended noun phrase as subject:

The conversion of the products obtained from the crackers of the oil refineries into the basic raw materials of the plastics industry **occupies a large part of the world chemical industry.**

> Embedded relative clauses (or 'interrupting constructions'):

Meanwhile the Normans, *who earlier in the Confessor's reign had failed to gain a commanding position in the kingdom,* **were now preparing a landing somewhere along the coast.**

> Non-subject noun phrases in first position in the sentence (inversion):
The clothes and personal effects **we disposed of.**

> Nominalisations:

The *exploration* **and** *subjugation* **of this coast were the work of Portuguese seamen.**

> Use of multiple subordinate clauses in subject position:

The fact *that the monomers and similar chemicals that are the starting materials for the manufacture of plastics can now be made cheaply in large quantities* **is a result of extensive research and development.**

> Adverbials in first position:

Returning from its feeding grounds in the Antarctic Ocean, **the emperor penguin leaps to a height twice its own length.**

> Subordinators in first position:

Had the journey been undertaken in the eighteenth century, **they would have found the countryside far more open.**

> Concealed or double negatives:

These experts *seldom* **made** *any* **effort actually to improve the quality of people's everyday lives.**

> Ellipsis:

The internationally renowned physicist forgot [*that***] his college tutor had suggested the key experiment in the first place.**

Three

Word formation

acronyms
analogy
back formation
blending
borrowing
clipping
coining
compounding
reduplication

prefixes and suffixes

Philologists who chase
A panting syllable through time and
*   space,*
Start it at home, and hunt it in the
*   dark,*
To Gaul, to Greece, and into Noah's Ark.

William Cowper, 'Retirement', 1782

Some word that teems with hidden
meaning – like Basingstoke.

W S Gilbert, *Ruddigore*, 1887

You see it's like a portmanteau – there
are two meanings packed up into one
word.

Lewis Carroll, *Through the Looking*
Glass, 1872

Word formation is the study of how words are formed, particularly of how longer and more complex words are formed from shorter and simpler ones.

Many words comprise only a **base form** (or 'root' or 'stem'). The base form of a noun is the singular form (e.g. *cat* not *cats*); for an adjective it is the positive (e.g. *old* not *older* or *oldest*); and for a verb it is the infinitive or imperative (e.g. *speak* and not *speaks, spoke, spoken* or *speaking*; *walk* and not *walks, walked* or *walking*). So words like *apple, house, sad, big, learn, jump* and *go* comprise only the base form; words like *applejack, housekeeper, sadly, splendiferous, unlearn, jumping jack* and *go-between* are **complex forms**, with something added to the root.

The two key ways in which base words are changed are:

> Inflection, e.g.:
apple/apples
house/houses
sad/sadder/saddest
big/bigger/biggest
learn/learns/learned/learning
jump/jumps/jumped/jumping
go/goes/going

> Word formation, e.g.:
indigestible: in + digest + ible (affixation)
hyperinflationary: hyper + inflate + ion + ary (affixation)
scuba diver: *s*elf-*c*ontained *u*nderwater *b*reathing *a*pparatus (acronym) + diver
glitzy: *gl*amour + *ritzy* (blending)
birthday: birth + day (compounding)
eyeball: eye + ball (compounding)
street cred: street credibility (clipping)
café, restaurant: (borrowing, from French)
automate: automation (back formation)
enthuse: enthusiasm (back formation)

This chapter concentrates on word formation, the second of these aspects, the main inflections of English having been covered in Part 1. The biggest part of the present chapter is given over to lists of key prefixes and suffixes, the use of which has been and remains one of the main and most productive methods through which the stock of English words has grown and developed.

Affixation is a very long-standing process. Prefixes such as *an-* and *apo-, mis-* and *be-*, have been in full production for many centuries. *De-* is in a similar mould, with an interesting flurry of contemporary creativity with coinages like *deskill, deregulate, decommission* and *destabilise*, etc. Even *mega-* has had a burst of glory from the 1980s. Other affixes, such as *ab-, exo-, -et* and *-id*, may look pretty dormant, but it is tempting fate to write off even the most classical and Latinate of affixes: their days of productivity may well come again.

It is important to remember that words are not invariably formed by tight adherence to formal rules. Language is much more dynamic and fluid than that. As Dwight Bolinger expressed it in his *Aspects of Language* (1968):

> Practically all words that are not imported bodily from some other language . . . are made up of old words and their parts. Sometimes those parts are pretty well standardized, like the suffix *-ness* and the prefix *un-*. Other times they are only broken pieces that some inventive speaker manages to refit. . . *Hamburger* yields *-burger*, which is reattached in *nutburger, Gainesburger,* and *cheeseburger. Cafeteria* yields *-teria*, which is reattached in *valeteria, groceteria,* and *washeteria.* Trade names make easy use of almost any fragment, like the *-roni* of *macaroni* that is reattached in *Rice-a-Roni* and *Noodle-Roni.* The fabrication may re-use elements that have been re-used many times, or it may be a one-shot affair such as the punning reference to being a member of the *lowerarchy*, with *-archy* extracted from *hierarchy.* The principle is the same. Scientists and scholars may give themselves airs with high-bred affixes borrowed from classical languages, but they are linguistically no more sophisticated than the common speakers who are satisfied with leftovers from the vernacular.

The list of prefixes and suffixes is given on pp. 89–107. Some of the other main forms of word formation are listed below.

Acronyms

Acronyms are abbreviations pronounced as if they were words, and they are a fairly recent method of word formation. They proliferated throughout the twentieth century alongside the many abbreviations of our time. Here are a few:

AIDS	*Acquired Immuno-deficiency Syndrome* (1982)
AWOL	*Absent Without Leave* (US military, 1919)
BUPA	*British United Provident Association*
CD-ROM	*Compact Disk–Read Only Memory*
IATA	*International Air Transport Association*
NAAFI	*Navy Army and Air Force Institutes*
NATO	*North Atlantic Treaty Organisation*
OPEC	*Organisation of Petroleum Exporting Countries*
SALT	*Strategic Arms Limitation Talks*
SAM	*Surface-to-Air Missile*
TEFL	*Teaching English as a Foreign Language*
TIF	*Tag Image Format* (file, 1990s)
UFO	*Unidentified Flying Object*
UNESCO	*United Nations Educational Scientific and Cultural Organisation*
dinky	*double income no kids* (1980s)

laser	*Light Amplification by Stimulated Emission of Radiation* (1957)
nimby	*not in my back yard* (1980s)
quango	*quasi-autonomous non-governmental organisation* (1970s)
radar	*Radio Detecting and Ranging* (1941)
scuba	*self-contained underwater breathing apparatus* (1952)
snafu	*situation normal all fowled up* (UK military, 1940s)
spam	*stop pornography and abusive mail* (junk mail, 1990s)
spin	*significant progress in* (the) *news* (1990s)
yuppie	*young urban* [or *upwardly mobile*] *professional* (1980s)

Note that the first set of examples are spelled out as capital letters, while the second set are written as ordinary words. One of the earliest acronyms is found in both forms: OK, or okay (USA, 1830s, meaning 'ol korrect').

Analogy

Another, and a much more seminal and multifarious, method of word formation is **analogy**. Many words and expressions are formed in this way, whether one describes an unmemorable person as *underwhelming* (by analogy with *overwhelming*), or says that a person has *hidden shallows* (by analogy with *hidden depths*), or coins words like *motorcade* by analogy with *cavalcade*, *telethon* by analogy with *marathon*, or *technobabble* by contrast with *nukespeak*.

Back formation

This is the process whereby a new word is formed by removing an element from – rather than adding one to – an imagined root or base. A change of word class usually occurs. For example, the verbs *edit* and *psych* are back formations from the nouns *editor* and *psychology*. Or again, the noun *permutation(s)* has recently been observed attempting to back-form a verb, *permutate*, when the verb has in fact existed for many centuries, albeit little-used nowadays, as *permute*. More frivolously, *gruntled* (whatever that may mean) is a back formation from *disgruntled*. It is worth noting in passing that the verb *back-form* is itself a back formation. Here are a few common back formations:

automate	*from*	automation
burgle	*from*	burglar
craze	*from*	crazy
donate	*from*	donation
eavesdrop	*from*	eavesdropper
enthuse	*from*	enthusiasm
greed	*from*	greedy
henpeck	*from*	henpecked

intuit	*from*	intuition
televise	*from*	television
vivisect	*from*	vivisection

Blending

Blending is a form of word compounding where new words are formed from the overlap and amalgamation of two existing words. Lewis Carroll, himself rather fond of creating such words, called these creations 'portmanteau words'. Examples are:

beresk	*from*	bereaved / berserk
biodegradable	*from*	biologically / degradable
blog	*from*	web / log (internet)
blooper	*from*	bloomer / pooper
Bollywood	*from*	Bombay / Hollywood
breathalyser	*from*	breath / analyser
brunch	*from*	breakfast / lunch
camcorder	*from*	camera / recorder
chocaholic	*from*	chocolate / -aholic (analogy alcoholic)
chortle	*from*	chuckle / snort
electrocute	*from*	electro- / execute
Eurocrat	*from*	European / bureaucrat
Eurovision	*from*	European / television
fanzine	*from*	fan / magazine
ginormous	*from*	gigantic / enormous
glitzy	*from*	gleaming and glamour / ritzy
moped	*from*	motor / pedal bike
motel	*from*	motor / hotel
motorcade	*from*	motor / cavalcade
netiquette	*from*	internet / etiquette
Oxbridge	*from*	Oxford / Cambridge
Oxfam	*from*	Oxford / famine relief
pixel	*from*	picture / element
raunchy	*from*	rancid / paunchy
sitcom	*from*	situation / comedy
slithy	*from*	slimy / lithe
smog	*from*	smoke / fog
telecast	*from*	television / broadcast
televangelism	*from*	television / evangelism
Wikipedia	*from*	wiki-wiki (Hawaiian 'quick') / encyclopedia

Blending is popular with advertisers, with words like 'Schwepper-vescence' and 'Ricicles' (which we all know are 'twicicles' as 'nicicles').

Borrowing

This is one of the simplest kinds of word formation: a term is quite simply lifted from a foreign language. The new word may be needed in English because it describes something not previously known to English speakers. Hence nouns for much flora and fauna: *lemon, orange, lilac, yam, jute, tea, shamrock, paprika, yak, kangaroo, wombat.* Many borrowed words are from foreign diets and *cuisine* (itself a borrowed word from French): *frankfurter, pretzel, cinnamon, ginger, yogurt, chop suey, fricassee, patisserie, lasagna, pasta, vodka.* Walter Scott popularised in his novel *Ivanhoe* the realisation that while the names of many animals in their lifetime are English (*ox, cow, calf, sheep, swine, boar, deer*) they reach the table with French names (*beef, veal, mutton, pork, bacon, brawn, venison*). This is a relic from the time when Norman masters left the care of the living animals to the Anglo-Saxon lower classes, while the superior French *cuisine* was kept in the hands of Norman cooks and *chefs.* Many other borrowings testify to this superiority: *sauce, boil, fry, roast, toast, pastry, soup, sausage, jelly, dainty.* And while the humbler *breakfast* is English, the more sumptuous meals, *dinner* and *supper,* as well as *feasts* generally, are French.

Most of the borrowings that date from the Norman Conquest are no longer perceived to be foreign words. We tend to be more aware of certain recent borrowings, such as *pogrom, blitzkreig, glasnost* and *perestroika.* But how many of us are actually aware that when we say *nix* with a negative shake of the head, we are actually using the German negative word *nicht*? Or that a *shanty town* is a direct borrowing of French *chantier,* the name Quebec lumbermen gave to their log cabins in the forest, and more generally in standard French the name for a building site? Or that if we tell an unruly child to *vamoose,* or go away, we are using the Spanish verb *vamos* or *vamonos,* meaning 'let's go'? These are more recent borrowings, and contribute to the ongoing patchwork called English.

A notorious old borrowing, dating to the Norman Conquest of England in the eleventh and twelfth centuries, is the expression *apple-pie order.* We all know this means 'neat and tidy', but what have apple pies to do with neatness and tidiness? The answer is: nothing at all. This borrowing too goes back to the French-speaking Norman lords and ladies at the dinner table and their lower-class English servants. The French-speaking lady of the house would have asked the English-speaking servant girl to put smart-looking clean white folded linen at each place at the high table – folded napkins, in other words, for important guests. The French for folded napkins is *nappes pliées,* and the English-speaking servant girl called that smart and tidy-looking table *apple pie,* because that's what the words sounded like to her. A thousand years later, we continue to use the expression for the most part without the slightest knowledge of its original meaning.

There follows a list of selected borrowings under the headings of the source languages. Latin, Greek, and French are not listed, since borrowings from these sources are wholesale:

Celtic languages ambassador, bijou, blarney, bog, breeches, brogue, bug, cairn, car, carriage, clan, corgi, crag, dolmen, flannel, galore, glen, hooligan, leprechaun, loch/lough, minion, peat, piece, shamrock, slogan, sporran, Tory, trousers, whisky

Dutch/Afrikaans apartheid, bluff, boss, brandy, bully, bumpkin, clamp, coleslaw, commando, cookie, cruise, dapper, dope, drill, drum, frolic, golf, grime, hunk, kink, landscape, loiter, poppycock, rant, skipper, sledge, slim, smack, smuggle, snap, snoop, spook, spoor, stoop, trek, yacht

German blitz, dachshund, Fahrenheit, flak, frankfurter, glockenspiel, hamburger, hamster, kindergarten, kitsch, leitmotif, nix, pretzel, quartz, schnitzel, strafe, waltz, yodel

Norse and the Scandinavian languages anger, auk, balderdash, bleak, blether, blink, bloom, blunder, blur, clamber, creek, crook, die, dirt, doze, dregs, egg, eider, fellow, flat, fleck, gasp, gaze, geyser, girth, glint, glitter, gloat, happen, harsh, inkling, kettle, kick, law, leg, meek, muck, nasty, nudge, oaf, odd, raise, roof, saga, scalp, scant, scold, scowl, seat, skewer, ski, skid, skill, skin, skull, sky, slalom, sniff, squall, squeal, take, they, thrift, thrust, tungsten, ugly, want, weak, window

North American languages anorak, caucus, chipmunk, igloo, kayak, moccasin, moose, papoose, persimmon, pow-wow, raccoon, skunk, squaw, toboggan

South American languages alpaca, avocado, barbecue, buccaneer, cashew, chilli, chocolate, condor, coypu, hammock, iguana, jaguar, petunia, poncho, potato, quinine, tobacco, tomato, toucan

Caribbean languages cannibal, canoe, hurricane, maize, papaya, vicuna, yucca

African languages chimpanzee, gnu, harmattan, impala, mumbo-jumbo, okra, quagga, raffia, tsetse fly, voodoo, yam, zombie

Arabic admiral, alchemy, alcove, algebra, alkali, almanac, apricot, assassin, aubergine, azimuth, bedouin, cypher, gazelle, ghoul, giraffe, hazard, henna, jasmine, jihad, Koran, lemon, magazine, minaret, mohair, monsoon, Muslim, safari, saffron, salaam, scarlet, sherbet, sofa, syrup, talisman, tariff, zero

Hebrew alphabet, cabal, camel, cinnamon, hallelujah, hosanna, Jehovah, leviathan, manna, maudlin, messiah, rabbi, sabbath, shibboleth

Indian languages anaconda, bungalow, carmine, cheetah, chintz, chutney, crimson, curry, dinghy, dungarees, gymkhana, juggernaut, jungle, jute, lacquer, mango, mantra, mongoose, mulligatawny, nirvana, pakora, pariah, pundit, sapphire, shampoo, sugar, sutra, swastika, tomtom, yoga

Chinese and Japanese bonsai, chopsticks, geisha, ginseng, kaolin, ketchup, kimono, kung-fu, sampan, samurai, shogun, tea, tycoon, yen, zen

Clipping

Clipping is a type of word formation which occurs when a word or group of words is abbreviated. The resulting terms are often colloquial, and found more often in spoken than in written English. Examples are:

ad	advertisement
amp	ampere

artic	articulated lorry
bus	omnibus
cello	violoncello
chimp	chimpanzee
demo	demonstration
disco	discotheque
exam	examination
fan	fanatic
fax	facsimile
flu	influenza
fridge	refrigerator
gent	gentleman
goalie	goalkeeper
hippo	hippopotamus
lab	laboratory
mob	*mobile vulgus* (Latin: 'the masses')
phone	telephone
photo	photograph
piano	pianoforte
pram	perambulator
pro	professional
revs	revolutions
spec	specification
telly	television

Personal names are often subject to clipping:

Alexander	Alex, Sandy, Lex
Katherine	Kath, Kate
Elizabeth	Liz, Beth
Vivienne	Viv
William	Will, Bill

Coining

Given the enormous range of opportunities in English for creating new words from old, it is perhaps unsurprising that the actual **coining** of new words is comparatively rare. Inventive writers like Lewis Carroll and Roald Dahl give us polysyllabic *jabberwocky* or *frobscottle* or *snozzcumbers* from time to time, by a combination of known and novel elements. Others, like J M Barrie or William Sharp, 'create' new personal names like *Wendy* (1904, from reduplicative 'friendly-wendy') or *Fiona* (1880s, with careful attention to the rules of Gaelic). Advertisers and creators of brand names are prolific coiners, but few of their creations enter the language – *Hoover*, *Kodak* and *Kleenex* are rare exceptions. Probably the best-known coinages are *fun* and *pun*, both dating from around 1700.

Neologism (from Greek *néos* new, *logos* word) is another term used to describe a new word or a new connotation of a word. Many neologisms drop out of the language as quickly as they drop in: so the term is perhaps slightly pejorative, and best confined to words that are still awaiting the verdict of history. If they pass the green light, as it were, they move up the hierarchy and become coinages. If they fail the test they drop back into faddish obscurity.

Compounding

Compounding occurs with the joining up of two or more smaller words to form a bigger one. It is important because it has always provided many new words, from well-established items like *housewife, nostril (nose + thirl,* or 'hole'), *eyeball, birthday, cupboard, armchair, bookcase, butterfly, blackbird, sheepdog, breakwater, steamboat, limestone, headmaster, gentleman, clergyman, playboy, teapot,* etc., to more recent creations like *astronaut, biorhythm, skinhead, thermonuclear,* not to mention the torrent of computer-speak: *laptop, website, desktop, touchpad, firewall, broadband,* etc. Compounds may be written as single, fused words, like the foregoing, or they may take hyphens: *men-at-arms, commander-in-chief.* Or they may be written as two words: *fairy tale, honey bee, time warp.* Some compounds, especially of abstract or technical English, form large clusters: *first-degree murder, photoelastic stress analysis, X-ray spectrometer, liquid-crystal display hand, short-range nuclear warhead.*

Some complete words affix particularly easily and yield numerous compounds. A selection of these (*news-, out-, -down, -head,* etc.) is listed under prefixes and suffixes below.

Reduplication

This is the name given to the process whereby words are created by partial or complete repetition. Some of the resulting words are commonest among children: *abracadabra, puff-puff* (for train, in the days of steam), *wee-wee, teeny-weeny, bye-bye.* Some of the creations are echoic: *tomtom, tut-tut, tick-tock.* Many involve contrasting sounds: *hanky-panky, helter-skelter, hocus-pocus, hugger-mugger, knick-knack, mish-mash, ping-pong, mumbo-jumbo.* The resulting words are often spelled with a hyphen.

Many of these reduplicative words involve an element of rhyme, which is what makes them memorable and ensures the contemporary colloquial popularity of this aspect of word formation. Nowadays we all seem to love a rhyme.

Other reduplications:

Rhyming	**Nonrhyming**
Ally Pally (for Alexandra Palace)	dilly-dally
argy-bargy	ding-dong
arty-farty	flimflam
backpack	shillyshally
Delhi belly	singsong

easy-peasy
fat cat
heebie-jeebies
hi-fi
hoity-toity
namby-pamby
pub grub
razzle-dazzle
razzmatazz
silly-billy
sin-bin
toy-boy
willy-nilly

Repetitive
chin-chin
chop-chop
gaga
go-go
goody-goody
no-no
so-so

Prefixes and suffixes

Affixation is the general name for the fixing of something in front of a word or base (when it is called a **prefix**), or after a word or base (when it is called a **suffix**). Affixation is by far the most prolific and enduring form of English word formation. English prefixes and suffixes are formed from a variety of source languages, including Old English, Old French, Latin and Greek. When a prefix contributes obviously to the meaning of the word (as *un-* does in *unkind* or *unclean* or *unfair*), it is sometimes called **productive**. Where it does not make an obvious contribution to the meaning of the word (as *ana-* does not in *anagram, anatomy* or *analysis* – unless one is a classical Greek scholar), it is sometimes called **unproductive**. Nowadays many affixes which were once productive have become unproductive, especially to users of the English language with scanty knowledge of Latin or Greek. The notorious example of *history/herstory* illustrates the point. Some members of the anti-sexist lobby took the view that world history as a subject was male-dominated, and that the very construction of the word illustrated this point nicely. They may have been entirely right about the subject, but they were wrong about the word, since it was taken into English from the Greek word *historia*, meaning 'knowing' or 'inquiry', and demonstrably not made up of 'story' as a base plus 'his' as a prefix or compound.

Other etymologically daft, if 'politically correct', constructions are nonwords like *efemcipate* and *femstruate* (for *emancipate* and *menstruate*). These terms may eliminate the (by some people) hated elements *man* and *men*, but they do no more than represent crude and rather ridiculous attempts at thought-policing by people who seem to have little feeling for how language evolves and works. They are the farther reaches of the movement that has tended to replace *mankind* with *humankind*, *spokesmen* with *spokespersons*, and *chairmen* with *chairs*, etc.

That is one thing, of course; but even to threaten *Herman* with his *Walkman* is perhaps not far away!

There follows a selective list of some of the more common prefixes and suffixes in modern English, with brief notes on their etymologies, and examples of some of the words formed. Some of the more common compounds are also listed:

Prefixes

a-, an- from Greek 'without' or 'not' or 'opposite to'. For example, an '*a*political' person is without views about politics. Other words formed from this prefix: *a*moral, *a*phasic, *a*tonal, *a*typical, *a*sexual, *a*gnostic, *a*narchy, *a*theist, *anon*ymous

a- from Old English 'on', as in *a*stern, *a*bed, *a*board, *a*foot, *a*live, *a*shore

ab- (a-, abs-) from Latin 'from' or 'away', as in *a*version, *a*vert, *ab*dicate, *ab*stract, *ab*stain, *ab*ound, *ab*use, *ab*duction

ad from Latin 'to' or 'towards', as in *ad*ore, *ad*vise. This prefix generally assimilates before *b, c, f, g, l, n, p, r, s, t*, and converts into *ab*breviate, *ac*cident, *ac*cord, *ac*cuse, *ac*cede, *af*firm, *af*fix, *ag*grieve, *al*lude, *an*nounce, *an*nexe, *ap*pear, *ar*rive, *as*similate, *as*cribe, *as*sent, *as*sure, *as*sault, *at*tend, *at*tain, *a*vow

aero- from Greek 'air', as in *aero*dynamics, *aero*plane, *aero*naut, *aero*space, *aer*ial, *aero*bic, *aero*batics, *aero*foil

after- from the Old English preposition, giving compound nouns like *after*noon, *after*birth, *after*life, *after*thought, *after*math, *after*-effects. A wide range of adjectives is also derived: *after*-school, *after*-dinner, *after*-hours, etc. The adjectives usually take a hyphen, the nouns not.

agro-, agri- from Greek 'field', giving *agri*culture, *agri*business, *agro*nomy, *agro*chemical

am-, ambi- (1) from Latin 'around' or 'about', akin to **amphi-**, as in *am*bassador, *amb*ient, *am*putate, *amb*ition, *ambi*guous, (2) from Latin for 'both', as in *ambi*dextrous, *ambi*valent

amphi- from Greek 'on both sides' or 'round', as in *amphi*bious, *amphi*theatre

ana- from Greek 'on', 'up', 'throughout', or 'backwards', as in *ana*tomy, *ana*lysis, *ana*chronism, *ana*gram, *ana*logy

ante-, anti- from Latin 'before', as in *ante*date, *ante*cedent, *ante*natal, *ante*diluvian, *ante*-room, *anti*cipate

anti-, ant- from Greek 'against', usually forming words indicating opposition or prevention, as in *anti*thesis, *anti*dote, *anti*pathy, *anti*-biotic, *anti*freeze, *anti*nuclear, *anti*-inflationary. Not to be confused with **ante-**, and vice versa.

apo- from Greek 'from' or 'off from', as in *apo*crypha ('things hidden from'), *apo*logy, *apo*stle, *apo*gee, *apo*strophe, *apo*rism (*apo* + *horizein*, 'within a limit', meaning a pithy definition)

arch- from Greek for a 'ruler' or 'chief', giving words like *arch*angel, *arch*bishop, *arch*duke, *arch*itect. The prefix also functions as a sort of intensifier, as with *arch*-enemy, *arch*-rebel, *arch*-competitor, etc. (See also the suffix **-arch**, below.)

astro-, astron- from Greek 'star', giving *astron*omy, *astro*dome, *astro*-physics, *astro*logy, *astro*naut, *astr*al

at- from Old English, giving *at*one ('bring together into one'), *a*do ('at do'), *t*wit (verb, 'at wit')

audio-, aud- from Latin 'hear', as in *audio*cassette, *audio*-tape, *audio*-lingual, *audio*-visual, *audi*tion, *audi*tory

auto- from Greek 'of or by itself', as with (1) things that work 'automatically', such as *auto*mobile, *auto*mation, *auto*cue, *auto*-reverse; (2) things to do with 'oneself', such as *auto*biography, *auto*nomy, *auto*graph, *auto*crat; (3) words to do with cars, or 'autos', such as *auto*sport, *auto*-industry

be- from Old English intensifier, giving (1) words suggesting a 'covering' or item of dress, such as *be*wigged, *be*spattered, *be*jewelled, *be*spectacled; (2) words suggesting a certain state, such as *be*calmed, *be*fuddled, *be*sotted, *be*trothed, *be*witched, *be*mused; and (3) various transitive verbs, such as *be*friend, *be*moan, *be*queath, *be*siege, *be*set, *be*hold. Also *be*head, *be*come, *be*have, *be*lieve, *be*ware

bi- from Latin 'two', as in *bi*cycle, *bi*focal, *bi*ped, *bi*sect, *bi*annual, *bi*furcation, *bi*lingual, *bi*noculars, *bi*centenary, *bi*gamy, *bi*carbonate. There is some potential for confusion with this prefix, because it can sometimes mean 'half' and sometimes 'twice', with the result that words like *bi*weekly or *bi*monthly can mean 'twice a week/month', or 'once every two weeks/months'. These terms should therefore be used with care

bio- from Greek for 'life', as in *bio*chemistry, *bio*graphy, *bio*logy, *bio*degradable, *bio*psy, *bio*fuel; and recent coinages like *bio*nic, *bio*rhythms. Note that **bio-** also appears within certain words: anti*bio*tics, sym*bio*tic

by- from Old English 'by', giving compounds like *by*stander, *by*pass

cardi-, cardio- from Greek 'heart', as in *cardi*ac, *cardi*ology, electro-*cardio*gram

cata- from Greek '(broken) down', as in *cata*logue, *cata*strophe, *cate*chism, *cat*hartic, *cat*hedral (from Greek *kata*, 'down', and *hed*, 'sit', giving Latin *cathedra*, 'seat' or bishop's 'throne')

cent-, centi- from Latin 'hundred', as in *cent*enary, *centi*grade, *centi*metre, *centi*pede, *cent*ury, per*cent*(age)

chron-, chrono- from Greek 'time', as in *chron*ology, *chron*ometer, *chron*icle, ana*chron*ism, syn*chron*ise

cine- from Greek 'movement', which gave *cinema* (moving pictures) and hence *cine*-camera, *cine*-film, *cine*matography

circum-, circu- from Latin 'round', as in *circum*stance, *circum*navigate, *circum*ference, *circum*vent, *circu*late, *circu*it, *circum*cise

con-, com- from Latin *com-*, 'together with', as in *com*pound, *com*pact, *com*pare, *con*sonant, *con*tend, *con*duct, *con*nect. This prefix often combines with other consonants, as in *col*lide, *col*lect, *cor*rect, *cor*rupt, *co*erce. Compounds such as *co*operate, *co*-star, *co*-publish, etc. are also formed from this prefix.

contra-, contro-, counter- from Latin *counter*, 'opposite' or 'against', as in *contra*ry, *contra*dict, *contra*vene, *contra*ceptive, *contra*flow, *contra*distinction, *contro*versy, *contra*band, *counter*attack, *counter*balance, *counter*weight, *counter*feit

cyber- from Greek 'steer' or 'govern', giving *cyber*netics, *cyber*space, *cyber*phobia, *cyber*punk and many other IT-related terms

de- from Latin 'down' or 'from', yielding (1) verbs indicating an opposite or reverse action, as in *de*activate, *de*classify, *de*congestion, *de*militarise, *de*mystify; (2) verbs indicating the removal of something, as in *de*-ice, *de*coke, *de*capitate, *de*frost, *de*scale, *de*skill; and (3) a reduction, as in *de*grade, *de*value, *de*fuse. There is also by analogy a wide range of other verbs: *de*press, *de*scend, *de*part, *de*pend, *de*note, *de*scribe, *de*vise, *de*mure, *de*legate, including recent creations like *de*criminalise, *de*segregate, *de*-escalate.

deca- from Greek 'ten', as in *deca*thlon, *deca*de, *deca*hedron

deci- from Latin 'tenth', as in *deci*bel, *deci*mal, *deci*mate

demi- from Old French 'half', as in *demi*john, *demi*god. See also **half-** and **semi-**, below.

demo-, dema- from Greek for 'town', as in *demo*crat, *dema*gogue, *demo*tic, *demo*graphy

derm- from Greek 'skin' or 'hide', giving *derm*al, *derm*atology, (suffix) epi*derm*is

di-, dis- from Greek 'two', as in *di*phthong, *di*lemma, *dis*aster (from Latin, 'two stars' in conflict), *di*syllable

dia- from Greek 'through' or 'apart', as in *dia*logue, *dia*meter, *dia*phanous, *dia*phragm, *dia*lectic

dis-, dif-, di- from Latin 'apart' or 'asunder'. This prefix can elide or combine with other consonants, giving words like *dif*fuse, *di*vide, *dif*fer. More importantly, it also combines with many existing verbs to give their opposites: *dis*agree, *dis*appear, *dis*approve, *dis*sociate (*dis*associate), *dis*connect, *dis*embark, *dis*infect, *dis*inherit, *dis*integrate, *dis*like, *dis*lodge, *dis*obey, *dis*organise, *dis*qualify, etc.

double- from Old French meaning 'two', as with *double*-glazing, *double*-locked, *double*-sided, *double*-jointed, *double* Dutch, etc. There is also a connotation of deception with compounds such as *double*-talk, *double*-dealing, *double*-cross.

down- from Old English, giving compounds such as *down*fall, *down*cast, *down*beat, *down*grade, *down*trodden, *down*turn, as well as terms like *down*side, *down*sizing

dys- from Greek 'bad', usually with the sense 'abnormal', as in *dys*function, *dys*lexic, *dys*pepsia, *dys*entery, *dys*trophy

eco-, ec- from Greek 'house', now with the sense of 'habitat' or 'environment', giving words like *eco*logy, *eco*species, *eco*sphere, *eco*system, *eco*science, *eco*-freak, *eco*-nut, *eco*-disaster

en-, em-, el- from Greek 'in', as in *en*ergy, *en*thusiasm, *en*demic, *em*phasis, *em*porium, *em*blem, *el*lipse. The prefix also functions as a sort of intensifier in words like *en*rich, *en*able, *en*close, *en*courage, *en*danger, *en*dear, *en*force, *en*rage, *en*rapture, *en*slave, *en*tangle, *en*trance, *en*twine.

endo- from Greek 'within', as in *endo*gamy ('inbreeding'), *endo*crine, *endo*thelium

epi- from Greek 'on', 'upon', 'for', as in *epi*gram, *epi*logue, *epi*stle, *epi*phany, *epi*taph

equi- from Latin 'equal', giving *equi*valent, *equi*vocal, *equi*lateral, *equi*distant, *equi*librium

Euro- a prefix now synonymous with the European Union (EU) and related activities, spawning items such as *Euro*sceptic, *Euro*bond, *Euro*vision, *Euro*crat, *Euro*currency, *Euro*bank, *Euro*market

ex-, ef-, e- from Latin 'out of', as in *ex*hale, *ex*tol, *ex*ceed, *ex*haust, *ex*hume, *ex*patriate, *ex*pire, *ex*onerate. The prefix forms **ef-** and **e-** before certain consonants, as in *ef*fusive, *e*merge, *e*lapse, *e*rase, *e*vade, *e*scape, *e*duce, *e*ducate. Words such as *ex*-husband, *ex*-boxer, *ex*-king, *ex*-president, indicating people who 'used to be' something, are also from this prefix.

exo- from Greek for 'outside', as in *exo*tic, *exo*gamy, *exo*dus, *exo*rcise

extra- from Latin for 'beyond', as in *extra*ordinary ('beyond the ordinary'), *extra*-special, *extra*-marital, *extra*-curricular, *extra*vagant, *extra*neous. In many of its hyphenated constructions popular with advertising scriptwriters, the prefix means 'very' and functions as an intensifier: *extra*-large, *extra*-bright.

for- from an Old English preposition usually indicating prohibition (*for*bid, *for*fend), abstention (*for*bear, *for*go, *for*swear), or neglect (*for*sake, *for*get, *for*lorn)

fore- from Old English 'before' or 'in front', giving compounds such as *fore*tell, *fore*cast, *fore*father, *fore*warn, *fore*going, *fore*noon, *fore*stall, *fore*legs, *fore*head. Not to be confused with **for-**.

gain- from the same source as Old English 'again' and 'against', giving *gain*say

hand- from Old English, giving compounds with the meaning 'made or operated by the hands' or 'for the use of the hands', such as *hand*-made, *hand*-stitched, *hand*writing, *hand*bag, *hand*kerchief, *hand*cuff, *hand*shake, *hand*stand

hetero- from Greek 'other' or 'different', giving words like *hetero*sexual (sexual relationship between people of different sexes), *hetero*geneous, *hetero*dox

hom-, homo- from Greek 'same', giving *homo*geneous, *home*opathy, *homo*phobe, *homo*sexual, *homo*nym, *homo*phone

hyper- from Greek for 'over' or 'above', in the sense of 'excessively', as in *hyper*active, *hyper*critical, *hyper*inflation, *hyper*market, *hyper*sensitive, *hyper*bole. A prefix functioning as an intensifier, **hyper-** also functions nowadays as an independent noun, meaning 'agitated' or 'keyed up', and appears in the words *hype* and *hyped*-up.

hyph-, hypo- from Greek for 'under' (therefore the opposite of **hyper-**), as in *hypo*crite, *hypo*dermic, *hypo*tenuse, *hypo*thermia, *hypo*thesis, *hyph*en (two words 'under one', or 'into one')

in- from Latin for 'into', as in *in*born, *in*come, *in*side, *in*vade, *in*cite, *in*duce, *in*nate, *in*trude. The prefix also forms **im-, en-, em-, il-, ir-** before certain consonants, as with *il*lusion, *im*mense, *im*prove, *im*pulse, *im*pel, *em*brace, *em*broil, *en*courage, *en*dure, *ir*radiate.

in- from Latin for 'not', as with *in*advertent, *in*capable, *in*curable, *in*convenient, *in*nocent. The prefix also forms **ig-, il-, im-, ir-** with certain consonants, as with *ig*noble, *il*logical, *il*legitimate, *il*literate, *im*mortal, *im*proper, *ir*regular, *ir*rational.

in- from an Old English preposition, giving compound items such as *in*sight, *in*-bred, *in*let, *in*come, *in*hale, as well as *en*dear, *en*thral, *en*grave, *em*bed/*im*bed

infra- from Latin 'beneath' or 'lower', giving *infra*structure, *infra*sonic, *infra*-red, *infra* dig ('beneath one's dignity')

inter- from Latin for 'between', as in *inter*act, *inter*continental, *inter*marriage, *inter*view, *inter*rupt, *inter*course, *inter*com, *inter*-city. The prefix also forms **intel-** and **enter-**, giving *intel*ligent, *enter*prise, *enter*tain.

intra- from Latin 'within', now used as an opposite of **extra-**, as in *intra*-European, *intra*venous, *intra*muscular, *intra*-uterine. Not to be confused with **inter-**, or vice versa.

intro- from Latin 'to or towards' or 'within', giving *intro*duce, *intro*vert, *intro*spection

low- productive contemporary compound, giving *low*-key (restrained), *low*-profile (unsensational), *low*-budget (cheap), *low*-grade (inferior)

macro- from Greek 'large' or 'long', the opposite of **micro-**. Most words formed with this prefix are technical: *macro*economics, *macro*biotic, *macro*structure, *macro*cosm.

mal- from Old French 'bad', used in words describing imperfection, such as *mal*formation, *mal*nutrition, *mal*adjusted, *mal*practice, *mal*function

mega- from Greek 'large', a buzz prefix of the 1980s giving *mega*buck, *mega*star, *mega*rock, *mega*bid, *mega*thon, *mega*trend, as well as the independent adjective *mega* (equivalent to the 'cool' of an earlier generation). This prefix suited the spirit of an age ever in search of the new superlative. Earlier constructions were *mega*phone, *mega*lithic, *mega*lomania, *mega*lopolis. The prefix also has the technical meaning of a unit of measurement one million times bigger than the unit referred to: *mega*hertz, *mega*watt, *mega*ton, *mega*cycle, *mega*byte.

meta- from Greek 'change' or 'transformation', as with *meta*morphosis, *meta*phor, *meta*physics, *met*onymy, *met*hod

micro- from Greek 'small', as in *micro*scope, *micro*cosm, *micro*biology, *micro*film, *micro*processor, *micro*computer, *micro*electronics, *micro*wave

mid- from Old English 'middle', giving *mid*most, *mid*night, *mid*day, *mid*summer, *mid*-term

milli- from Latin 'thousand', as in *milli*metre, *milli*bar, *milli*micron, *milli*pede

mini- from Latin 'lesser' and 'least', as in *mini*mum, *mini*m, *mini*bus, *mini*cab, *mini*skirt

mis- partly from Old English for 'wrongly' or 'badly', and partly from Latin *minus* via Old French *mes*, which came to have a similar meaning, giving *mis*behave, *mis*judge, *mis*apply, *mis*construe, *mis*manage, *mis*place, *mis*truth, *mis*deed, *mis*hap, *mis*chief

mono- from Greek 'one alone', giving *mono*logue, *mono*chrome, *mono*tonous, *mono*xide, *mono*gamy, *mono*cle

multi- from Latin 'many', as in *multi*tude, *multi*farious, *multi*form, *multi*ply, *multi*plicity, *multi*dimensional, *multi*purpose

nano- from Greek 'dwarf' meaning tiny or minuscule, as with *nano*technology, *nano*second, *nano*gram

neo- from Greek 'new' or 'recent', akin to Latin *novus*, giving *neo*logism ('new wordism'), *neo*lithic, *neo*-natal (recently born, i.e. less than a month old). The prefix also means a follower of a person or school of thought: *neo*-classical, *neo*-Marxist, *neo*-Nazi, *neo*-Freudian.

neur-, neuro- from Greek for 'nerve', giving *neuro*logy, *neur*asthenia, *neuro*-surgery, *neuro*n, *neur*algia

news- an example of an English noun which readily combines with others to form new compounds: *news*agent, *news*cast, *news*desk, *news*paper, *news*worthy, *news*print, *news*flash, *news*letter

non- from Old French 'not', giving *non*sense, *non*entity, *non*committal, *non*conformist, *non*flowering, *non*involvement, *non*resistant, *non*smoking. There is a contemporary tendency to overuse this prefix, creating words (*non*words?) like *non*presence (for absence), *non*permanent (for temporary), *non*success (for failure), *non*obligatory (for optional).

ob- from Latin 'towards' or 'facing against', as in *ob*ject, *ob*verse, *ob*fuscate, *ob*durate. The prefix assimilates before certain consonants as **oc-, of-, op-, os-,** giving also *op*pose, *oc*cur, *of*fer, *oc*cult, *os*tentation.

off- from Old English, giving compounds such as *off*set, *off*cut, *off*spring, *off*shoot, *off*hand, *off*al ('off-fall')

omni- from Latin 'all', as in *omni*potent, *omni*present, *omni*vorous

out- from Old English, giving compounds with the meaning 'do better than', where the root is stressed, such as *out*strip, *out*wit, *out*do, *out*run, *out*smart, *out*manoeuvre; and others such as *out*fall, *out*rage, *out*law, where the prefix is stressed; and Americanisms such as *out*asight, *out*front

over- from Old English, giving compounds such as *over*come, *over*take, *over*do, *over*see, *over*eat, *over*reach, *over*react

para-, par- from Greek for (1) 'beside', as in *para*military ('beside the military'), *para*medic, *para*normal, *para*typhoid; (2) '(defence) against', giving *para*pet, *para*sol; (3) other meanings such as *para*graph, *para*phrase, *para*noia, *para*digm, *para*dise, *para*plegic, *para*dox; and (4) actions involving *para*chutes, such as *para*gliding, *para*scending, *para*trooper

pene- from Latin 'almost', as in *pen*insula, *pene*plain

per-, pel- from Latin 'through', as in *per*ambulate, *per*secute, *per*turb, *per*vert, *per*mit, *per*form, *per*tain, *pel*lucid, *pil*grim (from *per + ager*, a person travelling 'through the country')

peri- from Greek 'round', as with *peri*meter, *peri*scope, *peri*phery, *peri*od

poly- from Greek 'many', denoting plurality and diversity, as in *poly*andry, *poly*anthus, *poly*chromatic, *poly*gamy, *poly*glot, *poly*gon, *poly*syllabic, *poly*technic

post- from Latin 'after', as in *post*pone, *post*humous, *post*script, *post*date, *post*-war, *post*-Saddam

pre-, prae- from Latin 'before', as in *pre*face, *pre*cede, *pre*decease, *pre*judge, *pre*vent, *pre*mature, *pre*dict, *pre*destination, *pre*text, *pre*-Christian, *pre*-war, *pre*monition

pro- from Greek 'before', as in *pro*boscis, *pro*scenium, *pro*logue, *pro*phet, *pro*gramme, *pro*blem

pro-, por-, pur-, pol- from Latin 'on', 'forth' or 'before', and akin to the Greek prefix, giving *pro*ceed, *pro*gress, *pro*ject, *pro*noun, *por*tend, *por*tray, *pur*loin, *pur*chase, *pol*lute. Also in the sense of an agent 'holding the line', in titles such as *pro*consul, *pro*-vice-chancellor, *pro*curator. Finally, and very productively, in the sense of 'in favour of' or 'on behalf of', there is the wide range of compounds like *pro*-British, *pro*-communist, *pro*-feminist, *pro*-life, etc.

pros- from Greek 'towards' or 'in addition to', as in *pros*ody, *pros*elytize

proto- from Greek 'first' or 'earliest', as in *proto*type, *proto*col, *proto*-hacker

pseud- from Greek 'false' or 'spurious', used pejoratively to suggest bogus or sham or pretentious qualities, as in *pseudo*-friend, *pseudo*-literary, and yielding in the 1960s the independent noun *pseud*, 'a bogus intellectual'; *Pseuds' Corner* in the magazine *Private Eye* popularised this use. Earlier terms from this prefix were *pseudo*nym ('fictitious name') and *pseudo*pregnancy ('false pregnancy').

psych-, psyche-, psycho-, from Greek 'soul' or 'mind', giving *psyche*, *psych*ology, *psych*iatry, *psycho*dynamic, *psycho*somatic, and more recent flowerings of the Beat generation such as *psyche*delic, and phrasal verbs *psych* up and *psych* out

re-, red- (1) from Latin 'back', as in *re*turn, *re*tract, *re*cant, *re*fute, *re*deem, *re*duce, *re*nounce, *re*sound, *re*sign, *re*veal; (2) the prefix can also be used for 'again', and requires a hyphen where the meaning might otherwise be ambiguous, as in *re*-sign, *re*-bound, *re*-cover

retro- from Latin 'backwards', as in *retro*grade, *retro*spect, *retro*rocket

se-, sed- from Latin 'aside' or 'apart', as in *se*cede, *se*lect, *se*clude, *sed*ition, *se*duce, *se*crete

semi- from Latin 'half', as in *semi*circle, *semi*-acid, *semi*-detached, *semi*-liquid, etc. By extension, the prefix can be used as a more general qualifier meaning 'partly', as in *semi*-dark, *semi*-literate, *semi*-invalid, *semi*-official, *semi*-permanent, *semi*-skilled, *semi*-skimmed.

sub-, suc-, suf-, sug-, sup-, sur-, sus-, su- from Latin 'under' or 'up from below', as in *sub*marine, *sub*terranean, *sub*merge, *sub*due, *sub*ject, *sub*vert, *sub*conscious. **Sub** also assimilates variously before consonants, as with *sus*pect, *suc*ceed, *suf*fer, *sug*gest, *sup*pose, *sus*pend, *sus*pect, *suc*cinct, *sup*press, *sur*rogate, *sus*ceptible, *suf*fuse, *sup*plant.

subter- from Latin 'beneath', as in *subter*fuge

super-, sur- from Latin 'over', as in *super*intend, *super*structure, *super*natural, *super*cilious, *super*fluous, *super*lative, *super*stition, *super*vene, *sur*plus, *sur*vive, *sur*feit, *sur*charge, *sur*name, *sur*face

syn-, sy-, syl-, sym- from Greek 'together with', as in *syn*thesis, *syn*tax, *syn*onym, *syn*agogue, *syl*lable, *sy*stem, *sym*ptom, *sym*pathy

techn- from Greek 'craft' or 'skill', giving *techn*ical, *techn*ology, *techn*ocrat, *techn*ique, pyro*techn*ic ('skill with fire'), hi-*tech*, as well as pejoratives like *techn*ofreak, *techn*obabble

tele- from Greek 'distance', giving *tele*vision (and *telly*), *tele*graph, *tele*printer, *tele*pathy, *tele*scope, *tele*phone

thorough-, through- from the Old English preposition with variant spellings, giving *thorough*going, *thorough*fare, *thorough*bred, *through*out

to- from the Old English intensive meaning 'this', giving *to*day, *to*morrow, *to*night

trans-, tran-, tra-, tres- from Latin 'across', suggesting 'movement' or 'change', giving *trans*atlantic, *trans*action, *trans*late, *tran*scend, *tran*scribe, *trans*fusion, *trans*port, *trans*plant. Prefix assimilations give *tra*dition, *tres*pass, *tra*duce, *tra*jectory, *tra*verse.

ultra- from Latin 'beyond', giving *ultra*marine, *ultra*montane, *ultra*modern, *ultra*-violet

un- from Old English meaning (1) 'not', as in *un*clean, *un*wise, *un*true, *un*fair, *un*tidy; or (2) 'back', with the connotation of reversal, as in *un*tie, *un*fold, *un*bend, *un*do

under- from Old English, giving compounds such as *under*stand, *under*growth, *under*wear, *under*hand, *under*cover

uni- from Latin 'one', giving *uni*form, *uni*fy, *uni*ty, *uni*te, *uni*on, *uni*lateral, *uni*sex, *uni*cycle, *uni*verse

up- from Old English, yielding compounds such as *up*roar, *up*land, *up*set, *up*right, *up*river, *up*stage, *up*stream, *up*thrust, *up*tight, *up*wind, *up*front, *up*chuck

vice- from Latin for 'in place of', as in *vice*-chancellor, *vice*-president, *vice* versa

wel-, **well-** from the Old English adverb, giving *wel*come, *wel*fare, *well*-bred, *well*-trained, *well*-tried, *well*-to-do

with- from the Old English preposition, giving *with*stand, *with*hold, *with*draw (*with*drawing room = drawing room)

Suffixes

Before listing the suffixes alphabetically, it is perhaps appropriate to draw attention to certain rules of spelling. If the suffix begins with a vowel, it is necessary to double the final single consonant for:

> monosyllables, as in drop/dropping, pat/patting, sit/sitting
> stressed last syllables, as in admit/admittance, repel/repellent, regret/regrettable
> a consonant following a single stressed vowel, as in grit/gritter, refer/referral, infer/inferring (but refer/reference, infer/inference, because here the second syllable is not stressed)

These are called the **gemination** ('twinning') **rules**, because they govern the doubling of consonants before a suffix.

Another simple rule governs words ending with -*e*. If they add a suffix beginning with a vowel, the -*e* is usually dropped. If they add a suffix beginning with a consonant, the -*e* is usually retained. Thus:

Drop the -e	Retain the -e
sense + ory = sensory	shame + ful = shameful
creative + ity = creativity	care + free = carefree
cube + oid = cuboid	gentle + ness = gentleness

Exceptions include: mile*age*, acre*age*, aw*ful*.

Note that the –able/-ible dilemma is one of the commonest causes of spelling error. Some of the -ible spellings that worry people are:

accessible	audible	collapsible
combustible	compatible	comprehensible
convertible	corruptible	credible
deductible	defensible	destructible
digestible	discernible	divisible
edible	eligible	fallible
feasible	flexible	forcible
horrible	incorrigible	indelible
intangible	intelligible	legible
negligible	perceptible	permissible
plausible	possible	resistible
responsible	reversible	sensible
terrible	visible	

Some of the -able spellings that worry people are:

advisable	adaptable	adorable
amiable	approachable	available
believable	calculable	capable
changeable	conceivable	curable
definable	demonstrable	dependable
desirable	despicable	dissolvable
durable	excitable	excusable
expendable	foreseeable	forgettable
forgivable	immovable	impassable
impeccable	implacable	impressionable
indescribable	inimitable	insufferable
manageable	measurable	pleasurable
preferable	readable	recognisable
reconcilable	regrettable	removable
reputable	transferable	understandable
unmistakable	usable	washable

(Several of these words are also listed in the list of **commonly misspelled words**, on pp. 196–205.)

-able, -ible, -ble Latin adjective suffixes, as in admirable, amiable, capable, culpable, edible, drinkable, flexible, horrible, indigestible, permissible, predictable, probable, soluble, washable

-acious Latin adjective suffix, denoting a tendency, sometimes excessive, as in loquacious, voracious, vivacious, veracious, tenacious, fallacious, sagacious

-age Latin abstract noun suffix, as in breakage, bondage, courage, drainage, heritage, homage, leakage, marriage, measurage, personage, savage, shrinkage, tillage, verbiage, voyage, umbrage. The suffix also gives a place, as anchorage, cott*age*, orphan*age*, hermit*age*, vicar*age*; and a reference of measure, as in acre*age*, foot*age*, mile*age*, tonn*age*, volt*age*.

-aholic suffix of the 1970s blended from the latter part of *alcoholic* (NB NOT alc*a*holic), with the meaning 'addicted to', and forming adjectives by analogy, as work*aholic*, choc*aholic*, shop*aholic*, writ*aholic*, golf*aholic*

-al, -ar Latin suffix giving (1) adjectives, as in comic*al*, equ*al*, gener*al*, leg*al*, loy*al*, norm*al*, or*al*, politic*al*, regul*ar*, secul*ar*, singul*ar*; (2) nouns denoting action, as in buri*al*, betray*al*, dismiss*al*, renew*al*, rent*al*, withdraw*al*

-an, -ian, -ane, -ain, -on Latin suffixes giving (1) nouns denoting a person, as in artis*an*, grammari*an*, vill*ain*, surge*on*, sext*on*; (2) adjectives such as pag*an*, urb*an*, urb*ane*, hum*an*, hum*ane*, mund*ane*, cert*ain*, sylv*an*; (3) adjectives from places, as in Americ*an*, Australi*an*, Brazili*an*, Ethiopi*an*, Nigeri*an*

-ance, -ancy, -ence, -ency Latin abstract noun suffixes, as in dist*ance*, resist*ance*, cad*ence*, const*ancy*, dec*ency*, inf*ancy*, persist*ence*. Many of these nouns are formed from a corresponding verb, as in admitt*ance*, observ*ance*, accept*ance*, disturb*ance*, disappear*ance*, entr*ance*, guid*ance*, insur*ance*, mainten*ance*, perform*ance*, resist*ance*; or from an adjective, as in arrog*ance*, brilli*ance*, fragr*ance*, ignor*ance*, irrelev*ance*, reluct*ance*, repugn*ance*, vigil*ance*.

-ant, -ent Latin suffixes giving (1) nouns denoting a person, as in assist*ant*, attend*ant*, claim*ant*, combat*ant*, depend*ant*, ten*ant*, ag*ent*, assail*ant*, serv*ant*, stud*ent*; (2) adjectives such as arrog*ant*, const*ant*, depend*ent*, ignor*ant*, pleas*ant*, pregn*ant*, pat*ent*, innoc*ent*, flu*ent*

-arch, -archy from Greek 'chief', giving mon*archy*, hier*archy*, matri*archy*, patri*archy*, olig*archy*, squire*archy*

-ary, -arian, -arious Latin suffixes giving (1) adjectives as in contr*ary*, exempl*ary*, mercen*ary*, milit*ary*, necess*ary*, sedent*ary*, station*ary*, antiqu*arian*, agr*arian*, veget*arian*, sect*arian*, parliament*arian*, utilit*arian*, octogen*arian*, greg*arious* – with several forms becoming independent nouns, words like libr*arian*, gramm*arian*, formed by analogy in this category; (2) nouns with the connotation 'belonging to', as in libr*ary*, infirm*ary*, penitenti*ary*, gran*ary*, avi*ary*; or agent nouns, as in actu*ary*, mission*ary*, advers*ary*, secret*ary*, lumin*ary*, emiss*ary*; or nouns with other meanings, as annivers*ary*, bound*ary*, diction*ary*, gloss*ary*, obitu*ary*, sal*ary*, summ*ary*, vocabul*ary*

-ate, -ee, -ey, -y Latin suffixes denoting (1) nouns indicating a person or agent, as in advoc*ate*, cur*ate*, episcop*ate*, magistr*ate*, nitr*ate*, legat*ee*, nomin*ee*, trust*ee*, committ*ee*, attorn*ey*, cov*ey*, all*y*, deput*y*, jur*y*; (2) verbs, as advoc*ate*, antici-p*ate*, complic*ate*, concentr*ate*, eradic*ate*, fascin*ate*, incapacit*ate*, supplic*ate*, vener*ate*

-ate, -ete, -eet, -ite, -ute, -te Latin adjective suffixes, as in deliber*ate*, desol*ate*, emascul*ate*, fortun*ate*, concr*ete*, eff*ete*, discr*eet*, erud*ite*, min*ute*

-ation see **-ion**

-bound English adjective suffix, as in house*bound*, duty-*bound*, earth-*bound*, snow*bound*, out*bound*, hide*bound*, spell*bound*

-centric Greek adjective suffix, relating to 'a centre', as in con*centric*, ego*centric*, ec*centric*, anthropo*centric*

-cide Latin noun suffix from 'kill', as in infanti*cide*, geno*cide*, parri*cide*, pesti*cide*, sui*cide*, fungi*cide*, insecti*cide*, herbi*cide*, spermi*cide*

-craft English noun suffix, giving (1) words to do with transport, formed by analogy with air*craft*, as in hover*craft*, space*craft*, landing*craft*; and (2) words to do with particular skills, as in handi*craft*(s), needle*craft*, wood*craft*, bush*craft*, stage*craft*, film*craft*, witch*craft*

-cred a recent suffix meaning 'acceptability among young people' and formed from an abbreviation of *street credibility*, giving compound terms like street *cred*, and by analogy star *cred*, stage *cred*, work *cred*

-cy Old French noun suffix indicating (1) a state or quality, as in accura*cy*, buoyan*cy*, decen*cy*, deficien*cy*, diploma*cy*, discrepan*cy*, infan*cy*, litera*cy*, pregnan*cy*, transparen*cy*; (2) a trade or rank, as in accountan*cy*, baronet*cy*, captain*cy*, pira*cy*, consultan*cy*, presiden*cy*; and (3) a wider range of words formed by analogy – agen*cy*, constituen*cy*, falla*cy*, lega*cy*, pharma*cy*, prophe*cy*, tenden*cy*

-dom English abstract noun suffix, indicating (1) a state or condition, as in bore*dom*, free*dom*, hippie*dom*, official*dom*, martyr*dom*, star*dom*; and (2) a territory, as in king*dom*, earl*dom*, Christen*dom*, heathen*dom*

-down English suffix giving (1) compound adjectives, as in head-*down*, face-*down*, top-*down*, nose-*down*; and (2) a range of nouns as in break*down*, crack*down*, melt-*down*, shut*down*, splash*down*, show*down*, touch*down*, tumble*down*, sun*down*

-ed, -t English suffixes forming (1) the regular past tense and past participles of verbs, as in start*ed*, stopp*ed*, talk*ed*, wait*ed*. With some of these verbs, both the *-ed* or the *-t* ending are possible, as burn*t*/burn*ed*, knel*t*/kneel*ed*, lean*t*/lean*ed*, leap*ed*/leap*t*, learn*ed*/learn*t*, smell*ed*/smel*t*, spell*ed*/spel*t*, spill*ed*/spil*t*, spoil*ed*/spoil*t*; (2) past participles used as adjectives, as in cook*ed* meat, excit*ed* children, escap*ed* convicts; (3) compound adjectives, as in magenta-colour*ed*, brown-ey*ed*, three-legg*ed*

-ee from the French ending, giving nouns describing persons affected by an action, as in amput*ee*, deport*ee*, employ*ee*, franchis*ee*, interview*ee*, licens*ee*, train*ee*, trust*ee*; or performers of an action, as in absent*ee*, divorc*ee*, refer*ee*. Also gives matin*ee*, soir*ee*, neglig*ee*, toup*ee* by analogy.

-eer Latin suffix giving verbs and nouns, as in car*eer*, domin*eer*, volunt*eer*, gazett*eer*, mulet*eer*, privat*eer*, pion*eer*

-el, -le English suffix producing (1) nouns that denote an object or instrument, as in shov*el*, shutt*le*. There is also a diminutive connotation, as in thimb*le* (from 'thumb'), sett*le* (a small seat, from 'sit', from which also comes sadd*le*), ridd*le* (a small reading problem, from 'read'); (2) adjective suffix, as in britt*le*, fick*le*, id*le*, litt*le*; (3) verb suffix, giving a **frequentative** meaning (expressive of the repetition of an action), as in dazz*le* (from 'daze'), wadd*le* (from 'wade'), dribb*le* (from 'drip'), kne*el* (from 'knee'), swadd*le* (from 'swathe'), spark*le*, start*le*, strugg*le*, crumb*le*, gobb*le*, ming*le*, hurt*le*.

-el, -le Latin diminutive suffix, as in citad*el*, chap*el*, dams*el*, mongr*el*

-en English suffix giving (1) diminutive nouns, as in chick*en*, kitt*en*, maid*en*; (2) verbs denoting making or doing, as in broad*en*, deep*en*, fatt*en*, soft*en*, op*en* (from 'up'), fright*en*, gladd*en*, light*en*, length*en*, sweet*en*; (3) adjectives to indicate what something is made of, as in wood*en*, wooll*en*, silk*en*, wax*en*, earth*en*, gold*en*, lead*en*

-ence Latin suffix that combines with verbs to give abstract nouns, as in coher*ence*, correspond*ence*, depend*ence*, insist*ence*, pret*ence*, refer*ence*, reminisc*ence*, resid*ence*, rever*ence*, subsist*ence*. See also **-ance**.

-ent Latin suffix, which combines with verbs to form nouns and adjectives, as in correspond*ent*, insist*ent*, persist*ent*, stud*ent*, differ*ent*, depend*ent*

-er highly productive English suffix giving (1) the standard form of the comparative adjective, as in old*er*, young*er*, bigg*er*, small*er*, fatt*er*, thinn*er*; (2) nouns denoting a person or doer of an action, often indicating a job or a pastime, as in sing*er*, bak*er*, employ*er*, lawy*er*, sail*or*, speak*er*, mill*er*, manag*er*, photograph*er*, report*er*, farm*er*, teach*er*; sometimes spelt **-ar**, as in begg*ar*, li*ar*; see also **-or**; (3) nouns denoting equipment or machinery, as in blend*er*, cook*er*, mix*er*, comput*er*, record*er*, print*er*, slic*er*, strain*er*, wip*er*, cutt*er*, mow*er*; (4) frequentative verbs, as in batt*er*, flutt*er*, glimm*er*, spatt*er*, stagg*er*, stutt*er*, wand*er*

-ery Latin noun suffix, giving (1) words suggesting actions or behaviour, as in discov*ery*, deliv*ery*, cook*ery*, forg*ery*, mock*ery*, recov*ery*, flatt*ery*, buffoon*ery*, snobb*ery*; (2) places, as in bak*ery*, brew*ery*, cream*ery*, distill*ery*, nurs*ery*, refin*ery*, shrubb*ery*, tann*ery*; (3) collections of items, as in crock*ery*, drap*ery*, artill*ery*, machin*ery*, pott*ery*, ironmong*ery*, scen*ery*

-esce Latin verb suffix, suggesting the start of an action, as in coal*esce*, efferv*esce*, acqui*esce*

-ese Latin suffix 'belonging to', giving place of origin/language, as in Japan*ese*, Chin*ese*, Portugu*ese*, Vietnam*ese*; by extension, it has given words indicating various sorts of jargon and dialect, as in journal*ese*, comput*erese*, official*ese*, American*ese*, Pentagon*ese*

-esque adjective suffix adopted from Old French, giving pictur*esque*, statu*esque*; added to certain proper names, it means 'derivative' or 'after the fashion of', as in Pinter*esque*, Swinburn*esque*, Runyon*esque*

-ess Latin noun suffix denoting a female agent, as in actr*ess*, empr*ess*, duch*ess*, govern*ess*, heir*ess*, host*ess*, steward*ess*, mistr*ess*. There is a tendency now to avoid some of these nouns entirely, female writers favouring the neutral term author rather than author*ess*, for example. Other redundant nouns in this category are poet*ess*, sculptr*ess*, manager*ess*.

-est English suffix giving the standard form of the superlative adjective, as in bigg*est*, small*est*, old*est*, young*est*, dark*est*, fair*est*

-et, -ete, -ate Greek noun suffix denoting an agent, as in po*et*, proph*et*, athl*ete*, com*et*, plan*et*, apost*ate*

-ette, -et Latin diminutive noun suffix via Old French, as in cigar*ette*, coqu*ette*, etiqu*ette*, nymph*ette*, ros*ette*, servi*ette*, flor*et*, isl*et*, pock*et*

-fold English adjective suffix meaning 'multiplied by', as in two*fold*, three*fold*, hundred*fold*, mani*fold*

-folk English noun suffix, as in towns*folk*, country*folk*, kins*folk*, men*folk*, women-*folk*. These words were old-fashioned until the 1980s, when they were thrown a lifeline by writers keen to avoid sexist language and words like townsmen, countrymen, kinsmen, etc.

-free English adjective combining with nouns to form new adjectives, as in care*free*, duty-*free*, interest-*free*, rent-*free*, stress-*free*, tax-*free*, trouble*free*, additive-*free*, pollution-*free*

-friendly contemporary compound adjective, on the model of user-*friendly*, now giving customer-*friendly*, ozone-*friendly*, environment-*friendly*, child-*friendly*

-ful English adjective suffix, showing (1) quantity, as in bag*ful*, hand*ful*, pocket*ful*, spoon*ful*; (2) characteristics, as in aw*ful*, beauti*ful*, dread*ful*, scorn*ful*, shame-*ful*, tear*ful*, truth*ful*, wil*ful*, youth*ful*. There is some debate about pluralising (1), and bags*ful*/bag*fuls*, hands*ful*/hand*fuls*, etc. are both found; the latter form is commoner.

-gate suffix coinage of the 1970s and 1980s denoting some sort of political or financial scandal, formed by analogy from the Water*gate* affair (which brought down the Nixon presidency in the USA in 1972), as in Iran*gate*/Contra*gate*, Mulder*gate*, Westland*gate*, Maxwell*gate*, sleaze*gate*

-gon Greek 'angle', giving poly*gon*, octo*gon*, penta*gon*

-gram Greek 'writing' or 'drawing', as in tele*gram*, ana*gram*, dia*gram*, holo*gram*, picto*gram*

-graph Greek 'written', as in mono*graph*, tele*graph*, auto*graph*, photo*graph*

-hand English noun affixed to other nouns giving (1) a job, as deck*hand*, farm-*hand*, field*hand*, cow*hand*; (2) position, as right-*hand*, left-*hand*

-head English noun affixed to other nouns giving (1) a range of mainly pejorative nouns, as egg*head*, hot*head*, muddle*head*, fat*head*, sleepy*head*, thick*head*, dick*head*; (2) the top or front of something, as in mast*head*, pin*head*, spear-*head*, letter*head*, pit*head*, stair*head*, beach*head*, figure*head*

-headed adjective formed from **-head**, suggesting characteristics or appearance, as in cool-*headed*, hard-*headed*, muddle-*headed*, bare*headed*, bald-*headed*, shock-*headed*, curly-*headed*

-hood English abstract noun suffix, often suggesting a state or condition, as in boy*hood*, child*hood*, man*hood*, widow*hood*, neighbour*hood*, brother*hood*, priest*hood*

-ian, -an, -ean Latin suffix which gives (1) nouns indicating a job or pastime, as in come*dian*, electri*cian*, histor*ian*, magi*cian*, musi*cian*, opti*cian*, physi*cian*, politi-*cian*, techni*cian*; (2) nouns and adjectives based on proper names of famous people, as in Elizabeth*an*, Shakespear*ean*, Dicken*sian*, Victor*ian*, Wagner*ian*

-iana Latin noun suffix, which combines with famous names to describe memorabilia or collections of items relating to these people, as in Victor*iana*, Churchill*iana*, Wordsworth*iana*

-ible, -ibility Latin adjective and noun suffixes, giving digest*ible*/digesti*bility*, corrupt*ible*/corrupt*ibility*, resist*ible*/resist*ibility*. See also **-able**, which is more frequent and is the currently productive suffix.

-ic, -ical Latin adjective suffixes meaning 'like', as in (1) angel*ic*, barbar*ic*, bucol*ic*, class*ic*, enthusiast*ic*, histor*ic* (or histor*ical*), moron*ic*, meteor*ic*, rhythm*ic*, vitriol*ic*, volcan*ic*, unique, Byron*ic*, Milton*ic*; (2) philosoph*ical*, geograph*ical*, scept*ical*, metr*ical*, satir*ical*

-ice, -ise Latin abstract noun suffix, as in avar*ice*, just*ice*, serv*ice*, exerc*ice*, merchand*ise*

-ics Greek suffix, originally a marker for the study of a scientific subject, as econom*ics*, acoust*ics*, electron*ics*, linguist*ics*, obstetr*ics*, genet*ics*, athlet*ics*, polit*ics* (all singular nouns); and tact*ics*, statist*ics*, eth*ics*, hero*ics*, hyster*ics* (all plural nouns)

-id Latin adjective suffix, as in ac*id*, cand*id*, ferv*id*, morb*id*, plac*id*, rab*id*, sol*id*, splend*id*, turb*id*, tep*id*, vap*id*

-ide suffix from Old French, for scientific compounds, as in ox*ide*, sulph*ide*, cyan*ide*, fluor*ide*, brom*ide*

-ie, -y English diminutive noun suffix, as in Ann*ie*, Charl*ie*, Jimm*y*, Bobb*y*, lass*ie*, bab*y*, dogg*y*

-ify Latin verb suffix descriptive of processes, as in ampl*ify*, beaut*ify*, clar*ify*, dign*ify*, ident*ify*, not*ify*, pur*ify*, satis*fy*, simpl*ify*

-ile, -il, -eel, -le Latin adjective suffixes, as in frag*ile*, mob*ile*, serv*ile*, sen*ile*, civ*il*, fra*il*, gent*eel*, gent*le*, humb*le*, ab*le*

-ine Latin adjective suffix, denoting 'belonging to', as in can*ine*, div*ine*, equ*ine*, fel*ine*, femin*ine*, sal*ine*, lacustr*ine*

-ing standard suffix of the English verb when forming the present participle or gerund, as in runn*ing*, jump*ing*, stand*ing*, used also as nouns and adjectives

-ion, -tion, -ition, -sion, -som, -son Latin abstract noun suffixes which originally denoted the action of the verb from which they were formed, as in act*ion*, decis*ion*, direct*ion*, exhibit*ion*, ignit*ion*, operat*ion*, react*ion*, reduct*ion*, situat*ion*; as well as pot*ion*, opin*ion*, ran*som*, rea*son*, sea*son*, posit*ion*, nat*ion*, occas*ion*, tens*ion*, fus*ion*

-ise, -ize Greek verb suffix signifying action, as bapt*ise*, critic*ise*, eulog*ise*, final*ise*, hospital*ise*, paraly*se*. **-ize** is an alternative spelling favoured by Americans (and also by many British dictionaries with an eye for sales into US markets). But note that some verbs must be spelled **-ise**; these include advert*ise*, adv*ise*, ar*ise*, compr*ise*, comprom*ise*, desp*ise*, dev*ise*, disgu*ise*, exerc*ise*, improv*ise*, pract*ise*, prom*ise*, rev*ise*, superv*ise*, surm*ise*, surpr*ise*, telev*ise*.

-ish English adjective suffix, indicating (1) characteristics diluted in quantity from those indicated by the original adjective, as in bigg*ish*, small*ish*, old*ish*, young*ish*, boy*ish*, brut*ish*, child*ish*, fool*ish*, girl*ish*, good*ish*, green*ish*, slav*ish*, swin*ish*, wasp*ish*; (2) nationality, as in Brit*ish*, Ir*ish*, Scott*ish*, Pol*ish*, Turk*ish*, Kurd*ish*, Span*ish*; (3) age or time, as in thirty*ish*, eight-*ish*

-ish Latin verb suffix, as in abol*ish*, ban*ish*, cher*ish*, establ*ish*, fin*ish*, flour*ish*, nour-*ish*, per*ish*, pol*ish*, pun*ish*. English fam*ish* is formed by analogy.

-isk Greek noun suffix signifying a diminutive, as in aster*isk* (originally a 'little star'), obel*isk*, basil*isk*, tamar*isk*

-ism Greek noun suffix denoting (1) the result of an action, as in barbar*ism*, critic*ism*, de*ism*, despot*ism*, ego(t)*ism*, fatal*ism*, hero*ism*, alcohol*ism*, plagiar*ism*; (2) a following or a school of thought, as in Gaull*ism*, Marx*ism*, Hitler*ism*, Thatcher*ism*, Catholic*ism*, Presbyterian*ism*, sex*ism*, age*ism*

-ist Greek noun suffix denoting (1) a person with certain beliefs or behaviour, as in athe*ist*, fasc*ist*, femin*ist*, pessim*ist*, ideal*ist*, Method*ist*, terror*ist*; (2) certain occupations, as in botan*ist*, cartoon*ist*, dent*ist*, physic*ist*, psychiatr*ist*, guitar*ist*, trombon*ist*, cell*ist*

-ite, -ete Latin suffix forming (1) verbs, as in exped*ite*, un*ite*, del*ete*; (2) nouns indicating a committed follower of someone/something, sometimes carrying a derogatory inference, as in Trotsky*ite*, Thatcher*ite*, aesth*ete*

-ition see **-ion**

-itis Latin suffix indicating an illness, as in arthr*itis*, appendic*itis*, hepat*itis*, mening-*itis*; or – informally – any general obsession, as in election*itis*, consumer*itis*

-ity Latin suffix combining with adjectives to form abstract nouns, as in absurd*ity*, complex*ity*, creativ*ity*, curios*ity*, familiar*ity*, hostil*ity*, popular*ity*, productiv*ity*, simplic*ity*; also nouns like local*ity*, minor*ity*, personal*ity*, public*ity*, univers*ity*

-ive, -iff Latin suffixes forming (1) nouns denoting persons and things, as in capt*ive*, fugit*ive*, plaint*iff*, detect*ive*, representat*ive*, addit*ive*, contracept*ive*, locomot*ive*, sedat*ive*; (2) adjectives originally denoting inclination, as in act*ive*, pass*ive*, rest*ive*, plaint*ive*, mass*ive*, capt*ive*, fugit*ive*, nat*ive*, conclus*ive*

-ize see **-ise**

-k English frequentative verb suffix, as in har*k* (from 'hear'), stal*k* (from 'steal')

-kin English diminutive noun suffix, as in cat*kin*, lamb*kin*, mani*kin*

-less English adjective suffix, indicating (1) a lack or absence of something, as in fear*less*, heed*less*, hope*less*, god*less*, law*less*, tooth*less*, worth*less*; (2) an infinity of something, as in count*less*, age*less*, number*less*, price*less*, time*less*

-let Old French diminutive noun ending, as in drop*let*, pig*let*, stream*let*, star*let*, book*let*, flat*let*, cut*let*; also items of jewellery, as in arm*let*, wrist*let*, brace*let*, ank*let*, circ*let*

-like, -ly English adjective suffix, as in bird*like*, child*like*, dream*like*, war*like*, life*like*, business*like*, heaven*ly*, man*ly*, ghast*ly*, like*ly*, father*ly*, love*ly*, order*ly*, saint*ly*

-ling English diminutive noun suffix, as in duck*ling*, gos*ling*, nest*ling*, suck*ling*, dar-*ling* (from 'dear'), year*ling*

-ly (1) the standard and most productive English adverbial suffix, denoting manner, as in clean*ly*, sad*ly*, sweet*ly*, cheap*ly*, frequent*ly*, quick*ly*, and very many more; (2) a suffix indicating frequency, as in week*ly*, dai*ly*, night*ly*, hour*ly*, year*ly*, quarter*ly*

-ma Greek ending connoting 'the product or result of' the relevant verb, giving aro*ma*, asth*ma*, diplo*ma*, dog*ma*, dra*ma*, ene*ma*, enig*ma*, panora*ma*, stig*ma*

-man English noun combining with others to form new nouns indicating (1) a man's job, as in bar*man*, business*man*, camera*man*, clergy*man*, fire*man*, fisher*man*, frog*man*, milk*man*, ombuds*man*, post*man*, states*man*, tax*man*, trades*man*; (2) a man's origins, as in Cornish*man*, English*man*, French*man*, Scots*man*, Ulster*man*. In the past, the term applied to both men and women. Nowadays, words like chair*man*, spokes*man*, lay*man*, sales*man*, yes-*man* are often substituted by chair*person* (or chair), spokes*person*, lay*person*, sales*person*, yes-*person*.

-mate from Old English noun for 'a person who shared your meat', now giving compounds like bed*mate*, class*mate*, in*mate*, mess*mate*, play*mate*, ship*mate*, work*mate*

-ment Latin suffix which combines with verbs to form nouns, as in abandon*ment*, achieve*ment*, arrange*ment*, commit*ment*, develop*ment*, entertain*ment*, ex- cite*ment*, manage*ment*, punish*ment*, retire*ment*

-meter from Greek 'measure', giving an instrument for measuring things, as in gaso- *meter*, baro*meter*, speed*ometer*, therm*ometer*. Often confused with **-metre**.

-metre from Greek 'measure', giving units of length, as in kilo*metre*, milli*metre*, centi*metre*. Often confused with **-meter**.

-monger from Old English word for a 'dealer', gives compound nouns for (1) occu- pations, as in fish*monger*, iron*monger*; (2) certain petty or discreditable people, as in gossip*monger*, scare*monger*, rumour*monger*, war*monger*

-most English adjective suffix, used as an intensifier, as in inner*most*, hind*most*, top*most*, upper*most*, fore*most*, ut*most*

-n, -en English adjective suffix (1) from the participle ending, as in drunk*en*, shak*en*, molt*en*, tor*n*; (2) denoting the material or coloration of an object, as in gold*en*, lin*en*, wood*en*, flax*en*, hemp*en*, leather*n*

-naut from Greek 'sailor', giving various kinds of navigator, as in cosmo*naut*, astro*naut*, aero*naut*, argo*naut*. (Note that jugger*naut*, a heavy lorry, is from a Hindu word for a massive object.)

-ness English abstract noun suffix, as in sad*ness*, happi*ness*, good*ness*, bad*ness*, gentle*ness*, weak*ness*, wilder*ness*, dark*ness*, wit*ness* (= one who wits)

-nik Russian or Yiddish suffix first used in the 1950s to describe a person connected with the word that precedes it, as in beat*nik*, refuse*nik*, peace*nik*, kibbutz*nik*

-ock English diminutive noun suffix, as in bull*ock*, hill*ock*, padd*ock*

-ocracy Greek suffix for 'form of government', as in dem*ocracy*, the*ocracy*, aut- *ocracy*, arist*ocracy*, bureau*cracy*, techno*cracy*, plut*ocracy*. Supporters of these forms take the suffix **-ocrat**.

-oholic see **-aholic**

-oid Greek noun or adjective suffix, indicating 'something resembling', as in spher- *oid*, glob*oid*, petal*oid*, cub*oid*, tabl*oid*, ster*oid*

-ology Greek noun suffix for 'word' meaning 'study of', as in tech*nology*, ge*ology*, archae*ology*, meteor*ology*, gynaec*ology*. The adjective is **-ological**.

-or Latin agent noun suffix, as in act*or*, collect*or*, competit*or*, conduct*or*, direct*or*, govern*or*, inspect*or*, narrat*or*, prosecut*or*, spectat*or*, visit*or*; also forms certain objects, as calculat*or*, refrigerat*or*, escalat*or*, react*or*. See also **-er** (2, 3).

-ory Latin adjective suffix, as in audit*ory*, sens*ory*, amat*ory*, admonit*ory*, illus*ory*

-osis Greek suffix used to indicate (1) illness or disease, as in cirrh*osis*, psych*osis*, thromb*osis*, tubercul*osis*; (2) a state or process, as hypn*osis*, diagn*osis*, progn*osis*, metamorph*osis*, osm*osis*

our, -or Latin abstract noun suffix, as in lab*our*, hon*our*, clam*our*, ard*our*, sav*our*. Americans have reverted to the **-or** of the original Latin spelling of these words.

-ous, -ose Latin adjective suffix denoting a particular quality, often 'full of', as in fam*ous*, glori*ous*, graci*ous*, copi*ous*, assidu*ous*, querul*ous*, anxi*ous*, grandi*ose*, joc*ose*, ingenu*ous*, danger*ous*

-person English agent word preferred nowadays by many writers to **-man** as a general suffix, as chair*person*, spokes*person*, ombuds*person*, news*person*

-phile from Greek 'love', giving a person who likes a particular place or thing very much, as in franco*phile*, Euro*phile*, Germano*phile*, biblio*phile*. Compare **-phobe**.

-phobe, -phobic from Greek 'fear', giving a person who dislikes or fears a particular place or thing very much, as in Anglo*phobe*, Russo*phobe*, agora*phobe*, claustro*phobe*, arachno*phobe*. The condition itself is conveyed by the suffix **-phobia**.

-phone from Greek 'sound' or 'voice', giving (1) names of instruments which produce or transmit sound, as in dicta*phone*, mega*phone*, tele*phone*, saxo*phone*, xylo*phone*; (2) names for people who understand or use a particular language, as anglo*phone*, franco*phone*, germano*phone*

-piece English noun which combines with others, as in mouth*piece*, centre*piece*, frontis*piece*, master*piece*, show*piece*, mantel*piece*

-proof English noun which combines with others to produce adjectives describing certain qualities, as in heat*proof*, weather*proof*, water*proof*, sound*proof*, bullet-*proof*

-red English abstract noun suffix, as in hat*red*, kind*red*

-ridden from the English verb, past participle of *ride*, which combines with nouns to form an adjective suggesting harassment and oppression, as in guilt-*ridden*, bullet-*ridden*, class-*ridden*, disease-*ridden*, maggot-*ridden*, priest-*ridden*, scandal-*ridden*, debt-*ridden*. A similar construction is **-stricken**.

-scape suffix thought to be from Dutch 'to shape (a picture)', giving land*scape*, and by analogy sea*scape*, sky*scape*, moon*scape*, city*scape*

-ship English abstract noun suffix, suggesting (1) personal qualities and skills, as in friend*ship*, hard*ship*, wor*ship* (from worth*ship*), fellow*ship*, leader*ship*; (2) craft qualities, as in craftsman*ship*, oarsman*ship*, musician*ship*, seaman*ship*, workman*ship*; (3) various types of ship, as in air*ship*, battle*ship*, flag*ship*, war*ship*

-side English noun combining with others to suggest the edge of something, as in bed*side*, grave*side*, ring*side*, river*side*, track*side*; or more generally, a part of something, as in hill*side*, country*side*, under*side*, top*side*, back*side*, in*side*, off*side*

-sis Greek noun suffix denoting 'state', as in analy*sis*, cataly*sis*, empha*sis*, gene*sis*, paraly*sis*

-some English adjective suffix denoting a quality, as in quarrel*some*, tire*some*, win*some*, whole*some*, liss*om* (from lithe), bux*om*, hand*some*

-speak English verb which combines with nouns to form new nouns referring to the particular language or jargon of a group, derived from George Orwell's 'new*speak*' in the novel *Nineteen Eighty-Four* (1949), and now by analogy in nuke*speak*, legal*speak*, media*speak*, computer*speak*, double*speak*, army*speak*, Euro*speak*

-ster English noun suffix to denote a person, originally a feminine ending, as in spin*ster* (= an unmarried woman, whose occupation was to spin), song*ster*, young*ster*, bax*ter* (or baker, from bake*ster*), fo*ster* (from food*ster*)

-stricken from the past participle of English verb *strike*, which combines with nouns to form adjectives that refer to unpleasant emotions, as in grief-*stricken*, terror-*stricken*, guilt-*stricken*, horror-*stricken*, poverty-*stricken*. See also **-ridden,** which is a similar construction.

-style English noun which combines with others to form new words, as in life*style*, free*style*, hair*style*, Indian-*style*, old-*style*, 1980s-*style*

-ther English adverbial suffix, indicating direction towards, as in hi*ther*, thi*ther*, -whi*ther*

-tor, -sor, -or, -our, -er, -eer, -ier, -ar Latin noun suffixes denoting persons, as in act*or*, audit*or*, auth*or*, doct*or*, chancell*or*, emper*or*, jur*or*, monit*or*, spons*or*, success*or*, vict*or*, savi*our*, arch*er*, found*er*, enchant*er*, preach*er*, ush*er*, auction*eer*, engin*eer*, brigad*ier*, grenad*ier*, vic*ar*, registr*ar*, premi*er*, farri*er*

-trix Latin noun suffix denoting a female agent, as in execu*trix*, proprie*trix* (now old-fashioned), domina*trix*

-tude Latin abstract noun suffix, as in alti*tude*, forti*tude*, lati*tude*, magni*tude*, servi*tude*

-ular Latin adjective suffix, giving qualities, as in mus*cular*, gran*ular*, mod*ular*; and shapes, as in ang*ular*, circ*ular*, rectang*ular*, tub*ular*

-und Latin adjective suffix, as in joc*und*, rot*und*, morib*und*, orot*und*

-ure Latin abstract noun suffix formed from verbs, as in clos*ure*, depart*ure*, expos*ure*, expendit*ure*, fail*ure*, mixt*ure*, pleas*ure*, sculpt*ure*, seiz*ure*; as well as a wider range of words, as cens*ure*, cult*ure*, gest*ure*, junct*ure*, meas*ure*, pict*ure*, literat*ure*, legislat*ure*

-ward(s) English suffix originally denoting adjectives and adverbs of direction, as in home*ward*, sea*ward*, north*ward*, to*ward*, awk*ward* (from awk, 'turned the wrong way'). The adverbs favour a final **-s,** as in home*wards*, heaven*wards*, in-*wards*.

-ware English word for 'manufactured articles', which combines with others to form more specific nouns, as tin*ware*, brass*ware*, earthen*ware*, glass*ware*, stone*ware*, silver*ware*, Denbigh*ware*, Wemyss*ware*

-wise, -ways (1) English adverbial suffix, denoting manner or fashion, as in clock-*wise*, any*wise*, no*wise*, other*wise*, al*ways*, side*ways*, length*ways*, straight*way*; (2) the English noun meaning 'clever' also functions as a compound, as in street*wise*, worldly-*wise*, penny-*wise*

-woman English noun which combines with others to indicate a particular job or nationality, as in horse*woman*, needle*woman*, spokes*woman*, yachts*woman*, English*woman*, Dutch*woman*

-work English word which combines with nouns to indicate (1) the material from which objects are made, as in brass*work*, iron*work*, wood*work*, scroll*work*, pastry*work*; (2) particular types of job or activity, as in brain*work*, needle*work*, case*work*, house*work*, farm*work*, shift*work*

-worthy English word which combines with nouns to form adjectives, as in news*worthy*, note*worthy*, credit*worthy*, trust*worthy*, sea*worthy*

-wright English noun for a person who has 'worked' or 'wrought', as in ship*wright*, wheel*wright*, play*wright*

-y adjective suffix (1) with English derivatives suggesting a quality, as in health*y*, hair*y*, might*y*, mood*y*, greed*y*, bush*y*, stick*y*, sorr*y* (from sore), guilt*y*, blood*y*; (2) with more general Latin derivatives, as in famil*y*, fanc*y*, cop*y*, memor*y*, miser*y*, stor*y*, victor*y*, aristocrac*y*; (3) used as an ending in familiar names, as in Jimm*y*, Ronn*y*, Bett*y*, Lizz*y*

Four
Punctuation

'?': The entire content of a telegram sent by Victor Hugo to his publishers, asking how well Les Miserables *was selling. The publishers replied in similar vein : '!'*

In R Hendrickson, *The Literary Life*

Mr Speaker, I said the honourable member was a liar it is true and I am sorry for it. The honourable member may place the punctuation where he pleases.

R B Sheridan, 1751–1816, on being asked to apologise for calling a fellow MP a liar

Intellectually, stops matter a great deal. If you are getting your commas, semi-colons and full stops wrong, it means that you are not getting your thoughts right, and your mind is muddled.

William Temple, Archbishop of York, in the *Observer*, 23 October 1938

I cannot take seriously the criticism of someone who doesn't know how to use a semicolon.

Shirley Conran, in the *Observer*, 29 March 1992

[Punctuation] is a large subject. Taste and common sense are more important than any rules; you put in stops to help your reader to understand you, not to please grammarians. And you should try so to write that he will understand you with a minimum of help of that sort.

Sir Ernest Gowers, *The Complete Plain Words*, 1954

Punctuation

Punctuation is used to mark off units of grammar and clarify a writer's meaning. In speech, emphasis and pauses are used to help get the spoken message across. In written English, punctuation has to serve the same purpose. Here the conventions are – for example – to mark off **sentences** by a combination of full stop + space; **words** are marked off by the insertion of spaces between them; **paragraphs** are marked off by indenting text on a new line, etc. Punctuation also indicates specific points of grammar. For example, an apostrophe indicates the possessive or the omission of a letter.

Punctuation and good writing

Punctuation is essential to good writing. Without it, we are unable to say where a sentence ends or a paragraph begins, or how the nuances of a text are to be understood. Yet since the 1970s and despite many recent mantras about trying harder, the trend of British education has been firmly away from the formal teaching of this basic subject, with the predictable result that generations of students and teachers (and teachers of teachers) are unsure of their ground. This chapter has three ambitions: firstly to offer simple guidelines for writers of text; secondly to show that punctuation is easy; and thirdly to suggest that it remains important. But such a short chapter cannot pretend to be the authoritative work on the subject of punctuation: that would take a much longer book. Here we mainly try to cover all the basic aspects, not only in those areas where agreement is general, but also on matters of stylistic preference.

Generally speaking, the times favour a minimalist approach to punctuation. Nowadays when we read a text from the 1950s or earlier, we are often struck by the amount of punctuation in use; and indeed it may seem excessive to our latter-day eye. This book goes along with the minimalist philosophy, seldom recommending the intervention of punctuation if none is strictly necessary. However, as stated above, it also takes the view that punctuation is important; so it takes issue strongly with those time-and-motion 'experts' who may advise the Civil Service and other hapless bodies that secretaries can pound out more letters per hour if they do away with the commas. This may be true, but it is worthless advice; and if followed, it helps to explain much bureaucratic gobbledygook.

There are few absolutes in good punctuation. Like so many other aspects of language, it is a moving target. The advent of the typewriter, of the popular press and, most recently, of the word processor and the internet (to say nothing of text-messaging), have all had a huge impact on our approach to punctuation; and the commonly heard current recommendation regarding a text to 'Bung it up on the web', symptomatic as that is of our rush-rush-rush business lifestyles, is unconducive either to clear thinking or writing. In speech, emphases, pauses, gesticulation and eye contact are all called into service in order to help get the spoken message across. In written English, we rely on punctuation to serve this purpose. It also indicates points of grammar: for example, an apostrophe indicates the possessive or the omission of a letter. So, lack of punctuation or incorrect punctuation often causes ambiguity or misunderstanding. There is a world of a difference, for example, between 'ten year-old children' and 'ten-year-old children'; ask any teacher. And as Lynne Truss has famously pointed out, 'extra marital sex' is not the same kettle of fish as 'extra-marital sex'.

One of the last bastions for the stickler for decent punctuation is consistency. If you are embarking on the writing of an extended text – whether a novel, a dissertation or a textbook – it is important to try and ensure that your use of quotation marks and other features is consistent from start to finish of your text. This aspect of text creation is frequently covered by 'house style'. Most of the serious or academic publishers supply their new or would-be authors with a set of house-style guidelines. These guidelines cover not only punctuation preferences such as quotation marks, but also such matters as whether to use the *-ise* or *-ize* spelling, or whether to leave single or double spaces between sentences. Needless to say, house-style guidelines vary from publisher to publisher, from the most cursory checklist to the most exhaustive not to say pernickety manuals.

If punctuality is the politeness of princes, it might also be said that punctuation is the politeness of publishers. Unfortunately, politeness (or at least presenting your text in a user-friendly way) is not a notable feature of writing today, particularly if it's writing that has been 'bunged up on the web'.

Apostrophe [']

The **apostrophe** has two main functions in punctuation. It marks the possessive or genitive case, and it indicates contractions or the omission of letters in the spelling of certain words.

Diminutive as it may be, the apostrophe must be the most abused punctuation mark in English today. From children who insist on apostrophising every plural in sight; to the leader pages of our 'quality' press; via the highly visible manifestations of signwriters' and advertisers' uncertainty on every high street in the land: the confusion seems universal. Yet the rules governing the use of the apostrophe are very simple.

Possession

In the broadest sense, the apostrophe mark is the sign of ownership or possession. In English singular nouns it is shown by the addition of *s* preceded by the apostrophe mark. Thus: *John's car*. In plurals that already have an *s* the apostrophe alone is used. Thus: *the girls' night out*. In irregular plurals without *s*, the rule is the same as for the singular. Look at these:

Singular nouns: the lion's mane, Mary's hat, the ship's captain, the knight's
   shining armour, the busman's holiday, Monday's child, Dick Turpin's horse,
   etc.
Regular plural nouns: two horses' mouths, two boys' bikes, two ships' crews,
   the ladies' golf club, the Mothers' Union, the Strangers' Gallery, ten years'
   imprisonment, etc.
Irregular plural nouns: the children's toys, the Women's Institute, etc.

Unlike possessive nouns such as the above, possessive pronouns (apart from *one's*)
do not require an apostrophe:

She took hers, we took ours, and they took theirs.

A problem associated with possessive nouns sometimes arises in words that already
end in *s*: words like hostess, princess, Thomas, James, Keats, Burns, etc. The general
rule nowadays is to treat such nouns in the same way as any other singulars and
write the princess's children, St Thomas's Hospital, St James's Square, John Keats's
poetry, Robert Burns's cottage, etc.

Some writers qualify this general rule, saying that the use of a final *'s* depends
on whether or not a pronounceable final syllable is formed (as it is in all of the
foregoing examples); if no final pronounceable syllable is formed, the apostrophe is retained but no *s* is added. So they would write Saint Saens' music,
Socrates' philosophy, for righteousness' sake. They would also treat various biblical and classical names in this way (Achilles' heel, Aristophanes' plays, Xerxes'
army, Ulysses' voyages, Moses' journey, Jesus' example).

Note in passing that the apostrophe has dropped out of some (but not all)
place names. St Albans, St Andrews, St Helens, St Neots, Earls Court and Golders
Green are all spelt without the apostrophe. But Land's End, St Michael's Mount,
Lord's Cricket Ground and St John's Wood all retain it. There is a trend at work
here, illustrated by the village of St Abbs in Berwickshire (apostrophe dropped)
and the nearby cliffs at St Abb's Head (apostrophe retained). Another example is
St Andrew's Church (with apostrophe) in the town of St Andrews (no apostrophe); but note St Andrews University (no apostrophe).

One other problem occasionally associated with ownership involves groups
of nouns (sometimes called the **group genitive**). This need not give trouble.
Only the last member of the noun group takes the apostrophe. Thus:

Tom, Dick and Harry's aunt
William and Mary's joint reign
Gilbert and Sullivan's light operas
***Some Experiences of an Irish RM* is Somerville and Ross's most famous book.**

Some units of measure, time or quantity also show a form of the possessive with
an apostrophe:

in a week's time
a six months' trip to Australia

twenty years' loyal service
I want my money's worth

Contractions

I don't, I can't and I won't do it.
It's a nice day, isn't it?
Here's something for you, and there's something for John.

These example sentences all contain shortened forms. Other common short-ened forms are *I've, you've, we've, they've, I'll, you'll, we'll, they'll, you're, we're, they're, mustn't, oughtn't, shouldn't, didn't, she's, he's, one's.* In this context the word *it's* needs special comment; it always indicates a shortened version of *it is*; it never indicates a possessive pronoun. The possessive pronouns – *mine, yours, his, hers, its, theirs* – do not use the apostrophe, with the sole exception of *one's*.

Omissions

Apostrophes here sometimes indicate the use of non-standard or dialect English:

A man's a man for a' that (a' = all)
ne'er-do-well (ne'er = never)
one o' clock, will o' the wisp (o' = of the)
a trip to Jo'burg (= Johannesburg)

Plurals

You sometimes find the apostrophe used to indicate a plural in the following contexts:

Before 1789 France was ruled by four Henry's, sixteen Louis's and two
**   Francis's.**
How many I's are there in parallel?

Apostrophe: punctuation check-up

Make a note of all the words needing apostrophes in the following sentences. Some will be apostrophes for ownership, some will indicate contractions. Check your answers with the list on page 222.

(a) I cant help it if youve lost money on the purchase.
(b) Its not fair to blame Rita. Shes had a hard time recently. Im sure Johns had a hand in the whole affair.
(c) The cars brakes are very squeaky. Itll need to go to the garage.
(d) The trains driver was arrested after the accident. Im afraid hed been drinking.
(e) Its a bit ridiculous to me, but babies early speech patterns are said to be very significant. Whats your opinion?

(f) Womens clothes are a lot less conservative than mens – or so Im told.

(g) It was a full days walk to the campsite, and wed just about had enough.

(h) The firms business is thriving and theyve just won a Queens Export Award.

(i) Marks new car is a Mini and his dads got his old one, so everyones happy.

(j) The schools library annex has been destroyed by the vandals mindless rampaging. Its a shame that a few thugs can cause such havoc.

Brackets ( )

Sometimes called parentheses, these always come in pairs. (The Greek word *parenthesis* means 'an insertion beside'.) The main use of brackets is to cordon off or enclose supplementary or explanatory information that otherwise would interrupt the basic drift of a sentence or longer piece of writing. The bracketed (or cordoned-off) material may be removed without changing the overall sense or completeness of the text. This chapter focuses mainly on ordinary or round brackets ( ). It makes only passing reference to square brackets [ ], angle brackets < > and brace brackets { }.

Pairs of brackets, commas or dashes may all be used to place text in parentheses. The choice of which to use depends to some extent on house style, personal preference and also on the style of the material. Dashes, for example, make a text look more informal than brackets.

Brackets are a convenient way of marking off subordinate information within a text. They keep the words they enclose out of the way, as it were, leaving the reader free to concentrate on the main text preceding and following the bracketed material. They are used:

1 to isolate supplementary information (more effectively than commas or dashes), as in:

Applications for the vacant post (six copies) should be lodged with the Vice Chancellor by 1 October.

The result of the election (a 40% swing against the government) was decisive.

The result of the election was decisive. (There was a 40% swing against the government.)

It costs 10 euros (roughly £7).

2 to present additional or explanatory (but subordinate) details about the main information provided in the text:

Robert Louis Stevenson (1850–94) is still a popular children's author.

See separate order form (yellow cover) for more information.

Some of the little *bastides* (country houses) of Provence are quite charming.

The syllabus is devised by the National Curriculum Council (NCC).

3 as an economical way of indicating options:

Any candidate(s) for the post of Club Secretary must be formally proposed and seconded.

4   for numbers written within a sentence:
Thirty (30) days settlement is required.
He has to (1) write the essay, (2) deliver the talk, (3) defend his arguments,
**   and (4) answer any questions.**

Brackets are easy to use properly. The main abuse of brackets in punctuation
occurs when a writer needlessly interpolates one independent sentence within
another, for example:

A full statement of accounts (six copies of this statement are enclosed for
**   members of the Board) is to be issued to the whole of the senior manage-**
**   ment team.**

Two separate sentences would be better here, each starting with a capital letter
and ending with a full stop.

Square brackets have two functions. Firstly, they are sometimes used for parentheses within parentheses. Secondly, they indicate an editorial comment (often
drawing attention to a spelling or grammatical mistake).

Stevenson's stepson (Lloyd Osbourne [1868–1947]) collaborated in some of
**   the master's later work.**
He wrote: 'I aint [sic] going.'
Or as James Joyce once put it: 'My patience are [sic] exhausted.'

Angle brackets are only used in scholarly work to show that a piece of text is
missing, defective or otherwise suspect.

Brace brackets are used in mathematics and in tabular material. They are sometimes called curly brackets.

Brackets: punctuation check-up

Parts of these sentences need to go in brackets. Can you write them out properly? You may also need to add a few commas. Check your answers with those on
page 222.

(a) Edward his best friend ignored Roger in the street.
(b) Mrs Crawford a woman I have always admired is coming to our party tomorrow.
(c) We were still are happy to see her settled in a regular job.
(d) No one in our house according to my young sister knows how to cook properly.
(e) The Royal Family pictured left flew to Brazil this afternoon picture on page 3
    for a state visit.
(f) His collection of wild flowers anemones primroses orchids is world famous.
(g) Precious metals gold silver platinum etc are best kept locked up in the bank.
(h) Edinburgh population 450,000 is more than twice as big as Aberdeen popula-
    tion 210,000 and half as big as Dublin population 900,000.
(i) We spent 45 euros about £30 sterling for a trip to explore the caves.

(j) He's a complete eccentric eats snails it's said so his neighbours tend to keep an eye on his movements.

Capital letters

Capital letters are used for two purposes in English punctuation. Firstly, they mark the beginning of a new sentence. Secondly, they indicate a proper noun. The main conventions are summarised below.

Capitals after a full stop (or at the beginning of a sentence)

Capital letters follow full stops. They invariably signal the beginning of a sentence, just as full stops (or equivalents) invariably signal the end of a sentence:

She is a clever woman. What is her name? And where does she come from? That was no lady. That was my aunt!
The king was working in the garden. He seemed very glad to see me. We walked through the garden. It was very jolly. (Ernest Hemingway)

Capitals at the beginning of direct speech

This rule is an extension of the rule regarding capitals at the beginning of sentences. Capitals are not always required following interruptions to direct speech:

The Prime Minister said to his Cabinet colleagues, 'There is no alternative.'
'There is no alternative,' said the Prime Minister to his Cabinet colleagues, 'to fighting our corner.'

Capitals after other punctuation marks

Very occasionally, capitals are used after other punctuation marks – for example after a comma to introduce a very direct thought, or after a colon to introduce a quotation. Thus:

She was thinking, Tomorrow morning I shall know my fate.
Pope put it nicely: To err is human, to forgive divine.

Capitals at the beginning of lines of poetry

Traditionally, the first word of a line of poetry was capitalised, whether or not the punctuation of the poem required it:

The bustle in a house
The morning after death
Is solemnest of industries
Enacted upon earth . . . (Emily Dickinson)

This rule no longer applies in much modern poetry. Today the printer has to follow the preference of individual poets in the layout of a poem.

Capitals for personification

Another traditional poetic use of capitals is in the representation of abstractions and personifications. Thus:

To Mercy, Pity, Peace and Love
All pray in their distress . . . (William Blake)

Capitals for proper nouns and proper names

With the exception of quirky writers like E E Cummings (who famously styled himself e e cummings), the rule for capitalising proper nouns is invariable. It covers people's names and initials (*Seamus Heaney, J K Rowling, Annie Proulx, Rudyard Kipling*), days of the week (*Tuesday, Saturday*), months of the year (*January, May*), other special calendar days (*Easter, Ramadan, Hanukkah, Thanksgiving, Good Friday, Diwali*), placenames, countries of the world and their nationals (*Nottingham, Weston Super Mare, Canada, Lithuania, Ghana, Spaniards, Brazilians*), historical periods and events (the *Thirty Years War*, the *Depression*, the *Renaissance*, but the *eighteenth century*, the *nineteen fifties*). Capitals are also used to refer to *God*, the *Prophet Muhammad, Buddha*, and to the various scriptural books – the *Bible*, the *New Testament*, the *Talmud*, the *Holy Koran*, the *Apocrypha* and other religious works.

Occasional confusion arises over whether a reference is general or specific. Only specific proper names are capitalised:

the Orkney Islands *but* the islands of the Mediterranean
the River Thames *but* the river systems of the Home Counties
Berkeley Square *but* the squares of London
the Ritz Hotel *but* the best hotels

Compass points are capitalised if they are part of a specific geographical region or entity, not if they are part of a general direction:

Northern Ireland   **South Africa**
a westerly gale   **the east coast of Sweden**

Capitals for specific names and titles

Honorific titles joined to proper names require a capital letter if they precede the names, not always if they follow the names:

Her Royal Highness the Duchess of Cornwall
President Bush and Prime Minister Blair
Director General of the BBC
Colonel Davitt of the US Marines *but* Jim Davitt, a colonel in the US
   Marines

Epithets are usually capitalised: Eric the Red, the Iron Duke, John the Baptist, William the Conqueror, Alfred the Great.

Capitals are also used for the titles of books, poems, movies and plays, as in *Whitaker's Almanac*, Gibbon's *Decline and Fall of the Roman Empire, The Merchant of Venice, The Oxford Companion to Sport, Gone with the Wind.* There are two other points to note about titles. Firstly, the usual convention in print is to italicise titles. And secondly, it is only the key words that are capitalised, thus: *The Old Man and the Sea,* or *Across the River and into the Trees.*

The names of specific trains, ships, spacecraft and aircraft are spelt with an initial capital letter: the Orient Express, the Brighton Belle, the Spirit of St Louis, Apollo 8. They are also often italicised, but it is not normally necessary to capitalise the definite article.

Capitals for proprietary or trademark names

These are normally capitalised. So: Martini, Xerox machine, Apple Mac, Microsoft Windows, Kodak camera, a Dyson carpet cleaner, a game of Scrabble.

Capitals and local names

This area sometimes causes slight confusion, because some terms have so completely entered general circulation that the capital letter has been dropped. So we tend to get Yorkshire pudding, Welsh rarebit, Russian roulette; but venetian blinds, wellington boots, brussels sprouts, french windows and scotch eggs.

Capitals for abbreviation

Various countries and political groupings are nowadays written in full capitals (without stops), thus: EU, UK, UN, USA. This tendency also extends to academic institutions, international agencies and companies, for example BBC, TUC, UNESCO, IBM, BP, MIT, SUNY. Many acronyms come under this heading (see p. 81).

Capitals for pronouns

The only pronoun to take a capital letter is normally the first-person singular *I*:

I am the master of my fate, I am the captain of my soul.

Sometimes in religious writing, pronouns and determiners referring to God are capitalised:

God in His mercy will comfort us.

Capital letters: punctuation check-up

Capital letters, apostrophes, commas, question marks and full stops have been left out of these sentences. See if you can rewrite them properly. Answers on pp. 222–3.

(a) im reading philip larkins *collected poems* again its to be returned to the library by 1 september

(b) the english cricket team will visit pakistan in december on their way back from australia

(c) will the bbc or itv or sky tv cover the arsenal v crystal palace game on saturday

(d) im afraid im no expert on french or spanish writing you should speak to professor healey he teaches french and his wife is from argentina i think

(e) they used to tell us in our geography classes that america was the land of opportunity britain was the workshop of the world and the nile delta was the breadbasket of Egypt thats how old I am

(f) admiral nelson was killed at the battle of trafalgar and sir john moore fell at corunna

(g) the 24 bus normally goes up tottenham court road to camden town but yesterday there was a diversion because of a huge tuc anti-war procession along euston road

(h) the gaelic language survives in parts of wales, scotland, ireland and brittany, but it has died out in galicia cornwall and the isle of man

Colon [:]

This punctuation mark has an anticipatory effect: it may precede an explanation or an amplification, or it may introduce an alternative to what has preceded it. The main uses of the colon are as follows.

Colons introducing explanations and amplifications

This use of the colon indicates a fairly close interdependence between the units that it separates. It often provides a certain balance to a sentence. Normally, a capital is not required after the colon in this context.

Guess what: John has won the lottery.
One thing is certain: the best man doesn't always win.
He said he could do it: and he did.
There was only one thing to do: jump.
Knowledge is one thing: the opportunity to use it is quite another.

Colons introducing lists, quotations and letters

Please send the following items: your passport, a completed visa application form, the fee of £30 and a recent photograph.
You will need these ingredients: minced beef, onions, garlic, mushrooms, tomatoes and seasoning.
The cup final was between two old rivals: Rangers and Celtic.
As the poet Robert Burns said: A man's a man for a' that.
She told the children: 'Under no circumstances are you to open the door.'
He was muttering quietly but audibly: 'Some people are never happy.'

In the last four examples, the colon provides a more emphatic alternative than a comma.

The American usage in formal letter writing is to start with *Dear Sir:* or *Dear Madam:* or *Ladies and Gentlemen:* instead of the British practice of using a comma or no punctuation at all.

Colons in numerals, titles and book references

In a straightforward carry-over from mathematical notation, the colon is used to indicate ratios:

In this class, girls outnumber boys in the proportion of 3 : 2.

Colons are often used to separate a book's title from its subtitle, as in:

Goethe's Faust: A New Translation
Classics and Commercials: A Literary Chronicle of the Forties

They are also used to cite a reference:

Today's text was Isaiah 65: 13–25.

It may be a good idea to read this section in conjunction with the section on semi-colons, since the two punctuation marks have a number of similarities. Both parts of speech occupy a position roughly midway between a comma and a full stop.

Colons: punctuation check-up

The following sentences are incompletely punctuated: all lack a colon and/or some commas. Can you provide the missing punctuation? Check your answers on p. 223.

(a) Work fascinates me I can sit and look at it for hours.
(b) We climbed four peaks last week Lochnagar and Broad Cairn on Friday Ben Macdui and Cairngorm on Saturday.
(c) There were lots of boats in the harbour yachts catamarans speedboats fishing boats etc.
(d) He is exactly what people say he is a bore and a fool.
(e) The doctor told him the worst he was not likely to recover.
(f) The following items were stolen a purse a ring a diary and some cheque cards.
(g) The view from the hilltop is splendid the Castle the Old Town and the spires and monuments are all spread out before you.
(h) It has to be one of the surest signs of increasing age you start notice how young the police have become.

Comma [,]

After the full stop, the **comma** is the second key punctuation mark. It is the commonest and most versatile mark *inside* the sentence. It may be used to separate words, phrases, and some clauses. Some commas are considered essential, while others are considered to be optional aids to clarity.

The main uses of the comma are listed below. If the comma is optional in any of the examples, it is shown in square brackets thus: [,].

Commas in lists

The comma breaks up items in a list of three or more. The items to be broken up may be words, phrases, or clauses – the rules are similar:

It was a cold, wet, windy afternoon.
We played soccer, baseball, rounders[,] and tennis.
He doesn't eat eggs, cheese[,] or butter.
He works constantly, travels frequently, has no private life to speak of, and no obvious outside interests.

The main problem with this rule is whether to use a comma before the last item in the list, which is frequently signalled by the use of a conjunction like *and*. The rule here is not to omit this final comma (as in the sentences below) if that is likely to cause any confusion:

In one morning's shopping spree, she went to Harrods, John Lewis, Waterstone's, and Fortnum and Mason's. In the afternoon, she took in Hatchard's, Selfridges, and Hamley's.

A minor problem with this rule involves expressions like 'the grand old duke [of York]' or 'the pretty little girl'. The adjectives here would normally be used in a single, semi-affectionate sense, with *grand* modifying *old*, and *pretty* modifying *little*. They are not therefore lists of adjectives, and no commas are required.

Another minor problem is caused by lists like the following:

He works in an old, tumble-down, post-war municipal building.
He makes a small, monthly cash payment to his son.

No comma is necessary between *post-war* and *municipal*, unless *municipal* is parsed as the last adjective in a list and not as part of the compound noun *municipal building*. Similarly, *cash payment* is used here as a compound noun.

Commas separating main clauses

Commas are usually used to mark off main clauses, whether or not joined by a co-ordinating conjunction such as *and, but, or*. The longer the sentence, the more helpful the comma is:

They came, they saw, they conquered.
I looked for the book[,] but it was not to be seen.
I looked high and low for my homework book and my class notes, but I'm sorry to say that they were nowhere to be seen.

But see also the comma splice (pp. 68–9).

Commas separating relative and subordinate clauses

Commas often mark off relative and subordinate clauses from the main clauses of the sentence:

The London train, which departs from platform 5, is half an hour late.
We arrived at my son's house[,] where we were made welcome.
The man[,] who was in the process of making good his escape from justice[,]
**   is thought to have been a terrorist.**

Commas separating adverbs and adverbials

Adverbials that precede, follow, or interrupt the main clause are usually marked off by commas:

Finally[,] he came to the point[,] after much humming and hawing.
Meanwhile[,] across Europe[,] the storm clouds were gathering.
The army, after crossing the Tigris, fanned out across the plain.
He will be welcome[,] if he decides to come.

Commas for balance

Commas are often used to balance contrasting or opposing phrases and clauses within a sentence:

She's a lovely girl[,] but not very bright.
He will change his shirt, not his opinions.
The time is half past six, not half past seven.

Commas to mark off direct speech

Commas are used to introduce a direct quotation, or to terminate it. They are also used to split quotations:

The children said, 'Tell us a story.'
'Tell us a story,' said the children.
'Tell us a story,' said the children, 'before we go to sleep.'

Commas are not necessary if the quoted material doesn't represent dialogue:

He told her he would go 'straight to the hospital' and then I think he said he
**   was going to telephone her.**

Commas to mark off parentheses

Modifiers and words in apposition are usually set off by commas from the main part of the sentence:

We visited the Tay Bridge, site of the famous disaster.
The Queen, a keen horsewoman, presented the cup.
His latest novel[,] *No Other Life*[,] has been very well received.

Sometimes the presence or absence of appositional commas can tell us quite a lot:

My brother John is a lawyer. (= I [may] have several brothers.)
My brother, John, is a lawyer. (= I have one brother.)
Snakes which are poisonous are to be avoided. (Some snakes)
Adders, which are poisonous, are to be avoided. (All adders)

It is important to remember that if the parenthesis or apposition falls in the middle of the sentence, you need to use *a pair* of commas – one at the start and the other at the end.

Commas to mark off vocatives and interjections

We usually comma off these minor parenthetical elements from the main part of the sentence:

***Ah,* now I get the picture.**
You, *Mary,* must leave at once.
Now, *sir,* what can I do for you?
I put it to you, *ladies and gentlemen,* we need your support.

As a kind of parenthesis, vocatives and interjections need to be marked off with a pair of commas if they fall within the sentence rather than at the beginning or end of it.

Commas to mark off question tags

Commas separate question tags from the rest of the sentence. This usage is straightforward and more or less invariable:

It's a terrible day, isn't it?
You've missed your bus, haven't you?
She'll be able to come, won't she?

Commas to show omission

A comma is sometimes used to show that a grammatical ellipsis has been admitted to the sentence, and certain words must be supplied to make the construction grammatically correct:

Jones gave a negative, but Bloggs a positive response.
A Riesling is preferred by some experts; by others, a Hock.

But the comma is required only if the meaning of the sentence is unclear without it. The following sentence does not require a comma:

She was in love with him and he with her.

Commas to avoid ambiguity

We need commas to mark off chunks of text, if without them the reader is tempted to miss the separation:

Outside, the car park had been full for hours.
In the morning, rolls are delivered to the house.
I want you to meet my friend Mary, Jane.
I am sick, and tired of studying punctuation.

Without the commas, we will read:

Outside the car park . . .
. . . morning rolls . . .
. . . Mary Jane . . .
. . . sick and tired . . .

Commas with *however, meanwhile, nevertheless*

However, meanwhile and *nevertheless* are three adverbs which are particularly prone to attract gratuitous commas. The following pairs of sentences should remind us not to comma off these words unthinkingly:

However you look at it, theft is not really justifiable.
However, lots of people try to justify it.

But meanwhile a number of steps will have to be taken.
Meanwhile[,] back at the ranch[,] . . .

He slept badly. Nevertheless, he spoke well at the rally.
He slept badly, but nevertheless spoke well at the rally.

Commas with inverted word order

Commas are helpful to the reader if the word order of the sentence has been inverted. They assist the text's readability:

Until the fighting stopped, the UN was helpless to act.
Because of the continuing fighting, the relief operation has had to be postponed.
The Allied Command having discussed strategic aims until well into the night, a declaration of intent was released to the press this morning.

Commas to set off titles, dates, geographical references

Commas usually mark off precise titles, dates, or geographical references from the main part of a text:

The German Chancellor, Angela Merkel, took the salute.
On Saturday[,] 16 September[,] 1979, they were married.

He teaches in Lafayette, Indiana, seat of a large American university.

Commas in numbers

Commas are used with numbers above 10,000. They are not generally used in numbers between 1000 and 10,000:

The population of Ireland is around 5,000,000. (5 million)
Melrose (population 2000) is a picturesque village in the Scottish Borders.
His personal fortune was put at $10,000,000.

Commas misplaced

It is quite common to find commas in the wrong place:

He locked the door, and running across the hall, bumped into the intruders.
A brutal, and on the face of it, a motiveless crime.

These should of course be:

He locked the door and, running across the hall,
A brutal and, on the face of it,

Another common error is the comma in place of the full stop:

I visited her in Suffolk, she was not at home.

These are two sentences, with two different subjects and no conjunction, so they should be separated by a full stop. (See **comma splice**, pp. 68–9.)

Commas missing

We have seen above how the presence or absence of commas can make all the difference to the meaning of a sentence:

They thought of taking a house in Brittany perhaps with the Kellys.

What is the function of *perhaps* here? As it stands, the sentence is ambiguous and could take two interpretations:

They thought of taking a house in Brittany, perhaps with the Kellys.
They thought of taking a house in Brittany perhaps, with the Kellys.

A comma would clear up the sense.

Commas: punctuation check-up

Here are some passages which make little sense without commas and full stops. Add these or other punctuation marks where you think they are necessary, and check your answers on pp. 223–4, where the texts are written out properly.

(a) The opening ceremony took place in the presence of the German economics minister the Spanish culture minister the mayor of Frankfurt the president of the German Publishers' Association and the great and good of the European book trade also present was a gaggle of gregarious authors assorted literary glitterati and of course the ever-watchful omnipresent prosperous well-fed remainder merchants.

(b) To make cucumber soup you need one large cucumber one onion two ounces butter one and a half pints white stock seasoning and a quarter pint of thick cream to cook you need to chop then toss the vegetables in the hot butter for a few minutes taking care they do not brown add the stock a small piece of chopped cucumber peel and a little seasoning simmer for twenty minutes then emulsify in a liquidiser or sieve cool then blend in the cream

(c) As well as Mass on Sundays and her weekly visit to a wayside dance-hall Bridie went shopping once every month cycling to the town early on a Friday afternoon she bought things for herself material for a dress knitting wool stockings a newspaper and paperbacked Wild West novels for her father she talked in the shops to some of the girls she'd been at school with girls who had married shop assistants or shopkeepers or had become assistants themselves most of them had families of their own by now they had a tired look most of them from pregnancies and from their efforts to organise and control their large families (from *The Ballroom of Romance*, by William Trevor).

(d) West of the town centre at 2 De Ruyterlaan is the Natuurmuseum with a collection of rare birds insects reptiles and mammals minerals and fossils nearby stands the Synagogue topped by a somewhat oriental copper dome it dates from 1928 east of here is the Boulevard of the Liberation from which the Langestraat branches off on the left leading into a street called De Klomp on the left-hand side is the Elderinkshuis (1783) the only historic building in the town to have survived the Great Fire of 1862

(e) we invited John and Frances and the Macdonalds for supper and Mary happened to drop in too afterwards we had a long discussion about whether to round off the meal with a cup of tea or coffee with rum in it in the end David took us all out for a drink he ordered a whisky and lemonade a gin and tonic two dry martinis with ice three cokes a lager and lime and a brandy and soda I'm glad I wasn't footing the bill

Dash [–]

A dash is used to indicate a break in the continuity of a sentence, often informally. Generally, it is better to avoid using a dash in formal or academic writing, where a comma or a pair of brackets is usually more appropriate. Try imagining sentence 1 below with a comma instead of the dash, and sentence 2 with brackets around the second part:

Hello, it's me – Twinkletoes.
I've arrived – and to prove it, I'm here.

Without the dashes, the impression of colloquial and slightly breathless informality would be lost completely.

The dash to break the continuity of the sentence

Fancy meeting you here – I thought you were in America!
I don't believe it – champagne!

The dash to introduce an afterthought

I'm Charley's aunt from Brazil – where the nuts come from. (Brandon
Thomas)
We're none of us infallible – not even the youngest among us. (W H
Thompson)

These examples are based on spoken and not written English, the first being from a playscript and the second from a speech.

The dash instead of commas or brackets

I am in earnest – I will not equivocate – I will not excuse – I will not retreat a
single inch – and I will be heard. (Wm Lloyd Garrison)
No sun – no moon!
No morn – no noon –
No dawn – no dusk – no proper time of day. (Thomas Hood)

Again, the writers are contriving to simulate spoken English.

The dash introducing a summary statement

Poor old Daddy – just one of those sturdy old plants left over from the
Edwardian Wilderness, that can't understand why the sun isn't shining
any more. (John Osborne)
Wine, women, and song – it's not a lot to ask for once in a while.

The comments after the dash provide a summary on the words or phrases which preceded it.

The dash in broken sentences

There are nine and sixty ways of constructing tribal lays,
And – every – single – one – of – them – is – right! (Rudyard Kipling)
Can't you understand? You – are – on – the – wrong – train!

This particular use of dashes conveys emphasis. Alternatively, this use of dashes can also convey hesitation or uncertainty in speech accompanied by lots of pregnant pauses:

Oh – um, erm – well, I don't – erm – I don't know what – erm, to say.

The dash for balance or amplification

It takes two to speak the truth – one to speak and another to hear. (H D Thoreau)
The most powerful weapon against ignorance – the diffusion of printed
material. (Lev Tolstoy)
I am not arguing with you – I am telling you. (J McN Whistler)
You should study the Peerage, Gerald – it is the best thing in fiction the
English have ever done. (Oscar Wilde)
Take it from me – he's got the goods. (O Henry)

More formal writers might prefer to use colons here.

The dash for parentheses, repetition or emphasis

It was – on balance – a successful operation. (parenthetical dashes)
Kent, sir – everybody knows Kent – apples, cherries, hops, and women.
(Dickens; dashes for emphasis)
She is come at last – at last – and all is gas and gaiters. (Dickens; dashes for
repetition)

The parenthetic use of dashes – in pairs – marks a break in very much the same
way as brackets. Brackets, however, would look rather strong in the above.

'What's the water in French, sir?' 'L'eau,' replied Nicholas. 'Ah!' said Mr
Lillywick shaking his head mournfully. 'I thought as much. Lo, eh? I don't
think anything of that language – nothing at all.' (Dickens)

Here the dash is used to introduce a lugubrious repetition. Dickens was a writer
who rather liked dashes, and used them to great effect.

Dashes to indicate incompleteness

All summer, he conducted a discreet affair with Miss C –.
Mind your own – business!
'Well, I'll be – !' he exclaimed.

This use of dashes indicates that part of a name has been omitted, or that an ex-
pletive has been deliberately deleted.

Dashes to indicate a series of ranges

In the following examples, the dash is equivalent to the word *to*:

1939–1945   volumes I–VI
pages 77–141   A–Z

Dashes instead of hyphens

Dashes are often used to combine two words into a compound adjective where
neither word modifies the other:

**Indo–Roman archaeology, Graeco–Roman traditions
space–time dimensions
the Sapir–Whorf linguistic hypothesis, the Mason–Dixon line**

The dash: punctuation check-up

All of these sentences would benefit from the simple addition of one or two dashes. Occasional commas would also help. Can you supply them? Check your answers with p. 224.

(a) Walk if you please don't run.
(b) Yes oh dear yes the novel tells a story. (*Aspects of the Novel*, E M Forster)
(c) We know Mr Weller we who are men of the world that a good uniform must work its way with the women sooner or later. (*The Pickwick Papers*, Charles Dickens)
(d) Advice to persons about to marry Don't! (*Punch*, 1845)
(e) The English country gentleman galloping after a fox the unspeakable in full pursuit of the uneatable. (*A Woman of No Importance*, Oscar Wilde)
(f) Go directly see what she's doing and tell her she mustn't. (*Punch*, 1872)
(g) The Common Law of England is laboriously built about a mythical figure the 'Reasonable Man'. (A P Herbert)
(h) It is well that war is so terrible otherwise we would grow too fond of it. (General Robert E Lee)
(i) She's the sort of woman who lives for others you can tell the others by their haunted expression. (*The Screwtape Letters*, C S Lewis)
(j) There is nothing absolutely nothing half so worth doing as messing about in boats. (*The Wind in the Willows*, Kenneth Grahame)

Ellipsis [. . .]

Ellipses (plural) are series of full stops (usually three or four), and sometimes they are referred to as **omission marks**. An ellipsis is used to suggest that something is missing or omitted or withheld from a text, within or at the end of a sentence:

Who the . . . does he think he is?

An ellipsis sometimes also indicates that a sentence is tailing off in an incomplete way – perhaps because it is becoming inaudible to the listener, or because the rest of the sentence is left to the listener's imagination (to indicate a more dramatic break, a dash is used):

**An eerie silence hung over the bay, and we waited and waited . . .
We shall leave them there, Dear Reader, whispering sweet nothings under an autumn moon . . .**

An ellipsis is also often used to indicate an incomplete quotation:

How does it go? 'Cowards die many times before their deaths . . .' I'm afraid I
   forget the next line.
Do you promise to tell the truth, the whole truth and nothing but . . .

If an ellipsis occurs at the end of a sentence, and you are representing it by three
dots, it is not necessary to add a fourth dot to indicate the full stop.

Exclamation mark [!]

Like the question mark, the **exclamation mark** is a specialised version of the full
stop. It signals strong feelings or urgency, and is used at the end of an emphatic
utterance or phrase:

Get out of my house! And don't come back!
How lovely she looked!

An exclamation mark is also usually found after an interjection:

Sh!	**Hey!**
Be quiet!	**Ugh!**
Cheers!	**Ow!**
Encore!	

Multiple exclamation marks are to be avoided in print. They usually indicate a
rather desperate attempt to pep up a tired piece of text and are much loved by
writers of comic strips and tabloid press headlines:

NUDE PRINCESS SCANDAL – EXCLUSIVE ! ! !
Eeeeeek!!!!!!!!!!! Kerplonk!!!!!!!!!!!

Full stop [.]

The **full stop** – or **period** (in American English) – is the first and the basic punctuation mark. It ends all sentences and sentence fragments that are not direct
questions or exclamations:

We arrived home late. Very late. We had just got into bed when we heard the
   milkman on his rounds.
I love you. Honestly. Truly.

Full stops following abbreviations and contractions were also in general use
until very recently. The tendency now is to omit full stops here. So you may find
either:

Wm. Wordsworth	*or*	**Wm Wordsworth**
C.S. Lewis	*or*	**C S Lewis**
Bloggs & Co. Ltd.	*or*	**Bloggs & Co Ltd**
U.K. and U.S.A.	*or*	**UK and USA**
N.A.T.O. and U.N.E.S.C.O.	*or*	**NATO and UNESCO**

Dr. and Mrs. Smith	*or*	**Dr and Mrs Smith**
A.D. and B.C.	*or*	**AD and BC**
i.e. and e.g. and etc.	*or*	**ie and eg and etc**

Full stops are not used for decimal currency (£ and p) or for metric measurements (km, m, cm, kg, g, l, etc.).

The full stop to indicate ellipsis

A succession of full stops (sometimes called omission marks) indicates ellipsis within or at the end of a sentence, suggesting that something is missing or withheld from a text, or that a sentence is tailing off in an incomplete way. In the latter sense, it may also be used to imply a threat. (See under **ellipsis**, pp. 128–9.)

Full stops: punctuation check-up

Make the following texts into sentences, with capital letters at the beginning and full stops at the end. Check your answers for accuracy on p. 225.

(a) the crocodile lives in the mudbanks of rivers in Africa and India his huge body grows to a length of ten metres people sometimes hunt him for his leather skin he has four short legs and can walk reasonably well but water is his chosen element here he can move really fast

(b) one night a great storm broke over the city the thunder rolled and roared the lightning flashed and the rain fell in torrents everyone stayed indoors and hid from the elements suddenly there was a positive eruption of noise and flashes of blinding light the bursts came again and yet again the huddled masses trembled in their shanties all the while

(c) you've heard of the famous Niagara Falls several people have tried to go over these falls in barrels or small boats in nearly every case the barrels were smashed to pieces against the rocks and the men in them killed or drowned the only man who ever succeeded in going over the falls was Captain Webb a few years later he lost his life trying to swim the rapids just below the falls

Hyphen [-]

Hyphens have two main uses: they join certain words together (*father-in-law, X-ray, self-control*), and they divide words at the end of a line of print.

Hyphens at the end of a line of print

Nowadays, when everyone seems to use a word-processor, the subject of word breaks has a renewed importance. Traditional typesetters and compositors were trained in the proper division of words, and followed certain rules. One-syllable words were not broken. Words were never broken immediately before the last letter or after the first letter. Words were not broken in such a way as to mislead the reader: for example, words broken by a hyphen into *leg-ends*, *reap-pear*, *screwd-river*, *the-rapist*, *mans-laughter*, *not-able*, *rein-stall*, *un-ionised*, etc. were considered highly confusing for rapid readers, because the meanings of their components (words in their own right) bear no relation to the meanings of the unbroken words. Words were always split at a syllable, or at a prefix or suffix – these were considered to be the 'natural' breaks. This rule should still be applied, as far as possible, although the 'natural' breaks are now thought to be phonetic rather than etymological. So: *photog-rapher* not *photo-grapher*, *biolo-gist* not *bio-logist*.

Hyphens between some prefixes and root words

Hyphens are used when the prefixed element is a proper noun (*pre-Renaissance*, *anti-Hitler*), a number (*pre-1066*), or an abbreviation (*non-EU countries*).

It is also necessary sometimes to use hyphens to make meanings clear:

re-form ('constitute again') and reform ('turn over a new leaf')
re-bound ('given a new binding') and rebound ('bounce back')
re-cover (a chair) and recover (from an illness)

Hyphens also still tend to be used – in British if not in American English – to avoid sequences of the same vowel or other awkward results:

anti-inflationary	**semi-independent**
infra-red	**time-exposure**
co-opt	**co-ordinate**

Hyphens with certain compound nouns

Most compound nouns have now been run together into single words:

bedroom	**toothbrush**	**password**
horsepower	**doorkeeper**	**laptop**
handmaid	**stepfather**	**website**
wheelbarrow	**bricklayer**	**online**

A few compound words tend to 'look' too long for comfort, and are still commonly spelt with a hyphen:

engine-driver   stomach-pump

It is best to consult a dictionary for these.

The following noun compounds take hyphens:

> noun/adjective compounds:
> | | |
> |---|---|
> | **president-elect** | **secretary-general** |
> | **brigadier-general** | **half-term** |

> noun in apposition:
> | | |
> |---|---|
> | **actor-manager** | **king-emperor** |

> nouns preceded by a letter:
> | **U-turn** | **X-ray** | **e-mail** |
> | **S-bend** | **T-junction** | **g-string** |
> | **Z-plan (castle)** | **v-shape** | |

> reduplicating nouns (where words are repeated; see pp. 87–8):
> | **clip-clop** | **tick-tock** |
> | **topsy-turvy** | **hush-hush** |

> compound nouns containing prepositions:
> | **sister-in-law** | **good-for-nothing** |
> | **jack-of-all-trades** | **hang-up** |

> double-barrel family names:
> | **Armstrong-Jones** | **Bowes-Lyon** |
> | **Sackville-West** | **Douglas-Home** |

> placenames containing prepositions:
> | **Newcastle-upon-Tyne** | **Stratford-on-Avon** |
> | **Southend-on-Sea** | **Weston-super-Mare** |
> | **Berwick-upon Tweed** | **Grantown-on-Spey** |

Hyphens with certain compound adjectives

Hyphenation in compound adjectives is normally only necessary preceding a noun. Compare:

an *oil-based* mixture
a mixture that is *oil based*

Hyphens are used for compound adjectives comprising

> noun/adjective + present participle:
> a *wheat-growing* programme
> a *short-lasting* impact
> a *tanker-loading* terminal

> noun + past participle:
> a *chocolate-coated* cake
> a *rice-based* diet
> a *disease-ridden* beast

> adjective + noun:
> a *used-car* salesman
> a *common-sense* suggestion
> a *high-frequency* occurrence

> phrases:
> a *once-in-a-lifetime* opportunity

a *never-to-be-forgotten* trip
a *couldn't-care-less* attitude

Adjectival compounds are also hyphenated if they begin with:

> self-:
  a *self-evident* truth   a *self-sufficient* economy

> well-/ill-:
  a *well-known* opera   a *well-defined* proposal
  an *ill-judged* investment   an *ill-contrived* strategy

> a numeral:
  a *nine-man* junta   *eighteenth-century* architecture
  a *thirty-gallon* tank   a *twenty-year* lease
  a *third-year* student   a *ten-year* jail sentence
  a *three-year* contract   a *three-pronged* attack

Finally, it is worth noting the results of omitting the hyphen from adjectival compounds such as:

a *little expected* conclusion
egg laying hens
a *long standing* Member of Parliament
a *fair skinned* English gentleman
a magic *walking stick*
a *high handed* autocrat

and pondering the ambiguities of:

a light housekeeper as against *a lighthouse-keeper*

And, as noted earlier, Lynne Truss points out (memorably and appropriately in a chapter called 'A little used punctuation mark' [sic!]) that extra-marital sex (with hyphen) is a very different kettle of fish from extra marital sex (without).

Trailing hyphens

Occasionally two compound adjectives with the same second element are used conjunctively to modify a noun, e.g.:

Long-haired varieties and short-haired varieties . . .

This would normally be contracted, with a trailing hyphen on the first word, to:

Long- and short-haired varieties . . .

Hyphens with compound numbers

All the compound numbers between 21 and 99 take a hyphen: thus *twenty-seven, thirty-one, forty-four,* etc. Compound numbers such as *two hundred, three thousand,* etc. are not hyphenated.

Hyphens in fractions

Words like *three-quarters, seven-eighths, nine-tenths* are normally hyphenated.

Hyphens for special effects

'Please s-p-e-a-k u-p c-l-e-a-r-l-y. I'm rather deaf.'
'I'll b-b-b-break your b-b-b-bloody neck!'

In the first example, the speaker is spelling it out. In the second, he is stuttering.

Hyphens: punctuation check-up

These sentences are short of hyphens. Can you supply the missing ones? Check your answers with p. 225, where the hyphenated words are set out.

(a) In the country of the blind the one eyed man is king. (one hyphen)
(b) Mr Mouse fell off the table. Mrs Mouse gave him mouse to mouse resuscitation. (two hyphens)
(c) A two hundred strong search party of policemen was backed up by some thirty odd tracker dogs. (three hyphens)
(d) Guess what happened to my shock proof, corrosion resistant, anti magnetic, waterproof pocket calculator. It caught fire! (three hyphens)
(e) The visitors were impressive in the warm up game: the scrum half and stand off managed some perfect mid run dummies and kicks of hair raising accuracy, while the full back's up and unders kept them well pinned back in the cul de sac of their own goal line. The half time whistle didn't come a moment too soon. (eleven hyphens)
(f) The conference was a very made up affair of off the peg socialism and back of the envelope idealism. The make up team had a field day as did the ice cream sellers at the entrance to the building. Nobody paid any attention to the out patients' department across the carpark. (nine hyphens)
(g) Prominent at last night's meeting were the vice chancellor of the university, the ex president of the students' union, the non executive chair of the schools' liaison committee, and the director of the fund raising event for this year's Charities Week. Their aim was to orchestrate a two thirds increase in student participation. (five hyphens)

Paragraph

Paragraphing is one of the important conventions of written English, and was devised as a visual aid for drawing the reader's attention to the organisation of a piece of extended text. Commas and colons and dashes are punctuation marks inside the sentence. Full stops are punctuation marks signalling the ends of sentences. Paragraphs are punctuation marks showing how sentences are grouped together.

The sentences within a paragraph usually deal with one specific theme or topic or idea which can stand alone. A new paragraph indicates that a new theme or topic or idea has been introduced. Paragraphs may be long or short; they represent a unit of thought not a unit of length. Paragraphs should also be sequenced; they should offer a series of steps towards a conclusion.

A well-paragraphed text is a well-planned text, and user-friendly. It shows its organisation beyond the sentence in clearly demarcated chunks of meaning.

A new paragraph is marked in two ways: firstly, by a new line; and secondly, by indenting the first word from the left-hand margin. Instead of indenting, a recent alternative has been to leave a line space between paragraphs. (If you follow this alternative, you do not also need to indent.)

In an essay, the opening and closing paragraphs are of special importance. The opening paragraph is used to introduce the subject or to state the problem, perhaps with some brief comments about how it will be treated in the body of the essay. The closing paragraph sums up the points covered, offers a conclusion, and perhaps expresses the writer's own opinions on the matter.

Sequential structure of a text

It is important that your paragraphs encapsulate a unity of thought which the reader can identify. If each new paragraph draws attention to a new topic (or scene or argument), the drift of your text will be clear and coherent. Try not to jettison this coherence, for example by combining within a single paragraph short passages that lack any inherent unity of thought; such a presentation will easily mislead the reader.

Writers used to be trained to build each paragraph round a key sentence. That was the sentence which contained the central idea of the paragraph. And students trying to produce a summary or précis of an extended text were trained to hunt out the key sentences of the paragraphs they had to scan. The key-sentence strategy is still a valid one, especially when you are at the planning stages of writing an essay. Your rough list of main topics for the draft essay may well provide you with a paragraph sequence of key sentences for your finished essay.

Particularly important for a good essay are the introductory paragraph and the closing paragraph. The subject of the essay is often laid out in the opening paragraph. It may offer a statement of the problem, and perhaps some brief comments on how it is to be treated in the body of the essay. The last paragraph is an opportunity for the writer to sum up the main conclusions reached in the body of the essay, to offer a conclusion, and perhaps to express the writer's own views, opinions or decisions.

If you are writing fiction, a new paragraph often indicates a change of speaker (see following section), the passage of time, or a scene change.

Paragraphing dialogue in fiction

In fiction, each speaker's dialogue usually starts a new paragraph. Paragraphing in dialogue may therefore be viewed as representing new speakers (and, by implication, new perspectives and points of view), rather than the new themes or ideas or topics of the essay or non-fictional text. An example follows:

> Something about him made her leap into *non sequiturs*. 'I'm so worried about Nick,' she said. 'Suppose his ankle is broken, like he said?'
> 'Suppose it is; another hour won't make any difference. He's on his second drink and feeling no pain. What about you?'
> 'Me?' Her thoughts were still aimed at wiping those [wet marks on the table-top].
> 'All summer my wife's been raving to me about what a terrific figure this woman has down at the beach.'
> 'If you're looking for your wife, she's in the dining room talking to somebody.'
> 'Don't I know it. What can I get you, Katie?'
> 'Get me?' He was one of those men whose chest hair comes up very high; above the neck of his sweatshirt there was a froth the colour of pencil shavings.
> 'G-and-t, whiskey. Bloody Mary . . .' 'Just a white-wine spritzer,' she said. 'Very weak.'
> 'I might have guessed,' he said, with cheerful disgust, and did not follow her into the dining room . . .
>
> (from 'Getting into the Set', in *Trust Me*, by John Updike, 1987)

There is more information on setting out dialogue under **quotation marks** (p. 138).

Paragraphing: punctuation check-up

Here is a passage of dialogue which has not been set out properly. Can you re-organise it so that each new speaker gets a new paragraph? Check with pp. 225–6 afterwards and see if you got it right.

> 'I wonder who did it?' asked Steve. 'I can't imagine,' answered Lem brokenly. 'Did they get much?' 'All I had in the world . . . A little less than thirty dollars.' 'Some smart leather must have gotten it.' 'Leather?' queried our hero, not understanding the argot of the underworld with which the train boy was familiar. 'Yes, leather – pickpocket. Did anyone talk to you on the train?' 'Only Mr Wellington Mape, a rich young man. He is kin to the Mayor of New York.' 'Who told you that?' 'He did himself.' 'How was he dressed?' asked Steve, whose suspicions were now aroused.
>
> (from *A Cool Million*, by Nathanael West)

Here is another passage lacking in paragraphs. Can you put them in? Check your version with p. 226.

> At eight o' clock came the doctor. He would allow only a word or two to be uttered, and his visit was brief. Reardon was chiefly anxious to have news of the child, but for this he would have to wait. At ten Amy entered the bedroom. Reardon could not raise himself, but he stretched out his hand and took hers, and

gazed eagerly at her. She must have been weeping, he felt sure of that, and there was an expression on her face such as he had never seen there. 'How is Willie?' 'Better, dear, much better.' He still searched her face. 'Ought you to leave him?' 'Hush, you mustn't speak.' Tears broke from her eyes, and Reardon had the conviction that the child was dead. 'The truth, Amy!' She threw herself on her knees by the bedside, and pressed her wet cheek against his hand. 'I am come to nurse you, dear husband,' she said a moment after, standing up again and kissing his forehead. 'I have only you now.'

(from *New Grub Street*, by George Gissing)

Question mark [?]

This is a specialised version of the full stop. It is used to end an interrogative sentence or sentence fragment:

Who is Sylvia? What is she?
Have you paid your rates and taxes?
He looks tired, doesn't he?

The last sentence, however, may also be viewed as a statement, and appear without a question mark.

When a direct question is being reported, the question mark is not required:

Where are you going? (direct question)
She asked me where I was going. (reported speech)

Question marks sometimes punctuate a list of question elements:

By Friday morning, can you give me a list of key customers? tell me their current level of debt? and indicate the dates when their payments become due?

Only the punctuation marks at the end of the following sentences tell you which sentence is a statement, which a question, and which an exclamation:

There is a body in the library. (Fetch a doctor at once.)
There is a body in the library? (I don't believe it – you must be joking.)
There is a body in the library! (Help! Murder! Police!)

Sometimes a question mark is used to indicate that a fact is unverified.

She lectures on the poetry of William Dunbar (?1460–?1520) and the Scottish Chaucerians.

Sometimes multiple question marks are found in print to indicate strong feelings, but these, like multiple exclamation marks, are not to be encouraged in formal writing.

What the hell do you think you're doing???

Question marks and exclamation marks: punctuation check-up

See if you can replace the numbers in these sentences with appropriate punctuation – question marks, exclamation marks or full stops. Answers are on p. 226.

(a) It's a painting by Renoir, isn't it (1)
(b) Just look at it – it's ghastly (2)
(c) Where's John's ball (3) Give it back at once (4)
(d) 'What's the time (5)' asked John (6)
(e) Have you change for a pound coin please (7)
(f) 'What is truth (8)' asked Jesting Pilate, but did not stop for an answer (9)
(g) Help me (10) I'm drowning (11)
(h) Who is that lady (12) That's no lady – that's my wife (13)
(i) You'll never, never guess (14) He's won the lottery (15)
(j) She asked me how old I was (16)

Quotation marks [single: ' ' double: " "]

Quotation marks are sometimes called **quotes** or **inverted commas** or **speech marks**. They come in pairs, one to open and one to close the quotation. They may be single or double, with British usage favouring single quotation marks, and American usage favouring double. They are used to mark off direct speech; to show that a word or phrase has been highlighted; and to indicate the title of a short story, an article, or a short poem.

Direct speech

Direct speech is always enclosed within quotation marks:

'Where are you going?' he asked the child. 'And where is your coat?'
'I'm going to the circus,' was the reply, 'to see the clowns. I don't need a coat – I'm not cold.'

Highlighting

Quotation marks are used to highlight particular words and phrases:

When we were children, we called the verb a 'doing word'.
She called herself a 'psychometrist', whatever that is.
He loved the puppy dearly, even though he called it his 'daft wee dug'.
The word *polycentric* means 'having more than one centre', according to my dictionary.
Schools used to talk about certain children as being 'slow learners'; nowadays we define them as having 'special needs' and we provide them with 'positive discrimination' in the allocation of funds.

In the second example, there is a suggestion that the writer disagrees with the use of the highlighted word. In the third example, the use of dialect is effectively quarantined. In the final example, educational jargon is brought under the spotlight. Although highlighting is a useful device, it becomes invalid when it is abused, as when some writers use it instead of seeking out the right word or phrase:

She's 'no oil painting', it is true, but then she has a 'heart of gold'.

Here the quotation marks are saying: I know these are clichés, but I can't be bothered to find my own words.

Titles

Titles of short stories, shorter poems, chapters, articles, essays, lectures, etc. are usually enclosed in quotation marks. This is in contrast to titles of books, long poems that have been published in their own right, plays, newspapers and movies, which in print are usually set in italics:

He read us the poem called 'Anthem for Doomed Youth'. (Short poem)
He studied Milton's *Paradise Lost* for the exam. (Book-length poem)
**Chapter XXI of R L Stevenson's novel *St Ives* is called 'I Become the Owner of
   a Claret-Coloured Chaise'.**
The title of this year's Dimbleby Lecture is 'The Monarchy – What Price?'

Quotes within quotes

As stated earlier, British preference is for single quotes, while American usage favours double. For quotes within quotes, the preferences are reversed – double quotes for UK and single quotes for US usage. British usage:

**'The key witness said, "I saw the whole thing," and looked at the judge for en-
   couragement.'**
'Kindly refrain from calling me your "sweetie pie",' she remarked icily.

Reported speech and direct speech

If you want to use quotation marks to signal direct speech, you must use them only to enclose the speaker's actual words and not a reported version of those words. It is an error to introduce inverted commas into reported speech. Thus:

**She timidly asked him, 'Do you still plan to go home tomorrow morning?'
   (Direct speech)**
**She timidly asked him if he still planned to go home the following morning.
   (Reported speech)**

There follow two versions of the same longer passage, the first using direct speech (Text A) and the second using reported speech (Text B). Study and compare the two versions.

Text A

'Girl number twenty,' said Mr Gradgrind, squarely pointing with his square forefinger, 'I don't know that girl. Who is that girl?'

'Sissy Jupe, sir,' explained number twenty, blushing, standing up and curtseying.

'Sissy is not a name,' said Mr Gradgrind. 'Don't call yourself Sissy. Call yourself Cecilia.'

'It's my father as calls me Sissy, sir,' returned the young girl in a trembling voice, and with another curtsey.

'Then he has no business to do it,' said Mr Gradgrind. 'Tell him he mustn't. Cecilia Jupe. Let me see. What is your father?'

'He belongs to the horse-riding, if you please, sir.'

Mr Gradgrind frowned, and waved off the objectionable calling with his hand. 'We don't want to know anything about that, here. Your father breaks horses, don't he?'

'If you please, sir, when they can get any to break, they do break horses in the ring, sir.'

'You mustn't tell us about the ring, here. Very well, then. Describe your father as a horsebreaker. He doctors sick horses, I dare say?'

'Oh yes, sir.'

'Very well, then. He is a veterinary surgeon, a farrier, a horsebreaker. Give me your definition of a horse.'

(Sissy Jupe thrown into the greatest alarm by this demand.)

                                        (from *Hard Times*, by Charles Dickens)

Text B

Mr Gradgrind hesitated at the twentieth girl, pointed at her with his square forefinger, and asked her name. When the girl had blushed, stood up, curtseyed, and had given her name as Sissy Jupe, Mr Gradgrind stated that Sissy was not a name and ordered her to call herself Cecilia. In a trembling voice and with another curtsey, the girl replied that it was her father who called her Sissy. Mr Gradgrind was having none of that, repeating that her name was Cecilia Jupe, and then asking her what her father did. When the girl explained that her father belonged to the horse-riding, Mr Gradgrind frowned, waved off the objectionable calling with his hand, and assured her that they didn't want to know anything about that *there*, in the schoolroom. Once it had been established, after further questioning, that Mr Jupe was a horsebreaker and a horse doctor, Mr Gradgrind then asked the child for her definition of a horse – a demand which threw her into the greatest alarm.

Obvious differences in the presentation of texts A and B are the use of quotation marks and new paragraphs in text A and their absence in B. There are changes in tense between A and B – with present becoming past; and the word *here* in A becomes *there* in B. And so on.

There is a further note on the paragraphing of direct speech on pp. 135–6.

Punctuation in relation to quotation marks

Writers often seek guidance on where to place punctuation marks such as full stops, commas and question marks in relation to quotation marks. Should they go before or after? The answer is that their position depends on their function in the sentence. If the punctuation relates primarily to the matter within quotation marks, it goes before the closing quotation mark; if it relates to the broader sentence as a whole, then it goes after. For example:

John said to her, 'I beg your pardon?'
Why did you say to her, 'I beg your pardon'?

Note carefully the position of the question mark in these two examples.

Quotation marks: punctuation check-up

Write out these sentences with appropriate punctuation – quotation marks, commas, full stops, question marks, capital letters, etc. Check your sentences with those printed on p. 227.

(a) Is this the road to the seashore asked the motorist
(b) Im not sure replied the young lady im a stranger here myself
(c) I told you to buy a map said his wife but now its too late and all the shops are shut
(d) My favourite reading this year has been district and circle seamus heaney's new book of poems and a very funny collection of bits and pieces called lost worlds by michael bywater
(e) In the end she said we took the umbrella to the lost property office it was too good an article to leave lying in the street she added by way of explanation
(f) But this said angela is murder we need to phone the police she added her voice growing ever more shrill
(g) The chances of a serious accident began the professor are probably greater than theyve ever been in history whoever thought kamikaze pilots would deliberately set out to crash their planes into busy office buildings

Semicolon [;]

The **semicolon** has two main punctuational uses within the sentence: it is used in complex lists, and it is used as an alternative to the overuse of conjunctions.

Especially in long or complex sentences, some lists may already use lots of commas, so the semicolon is brought into use as a refinement:

She sent an e-mail to their branches in Toronto, Canada; Tokyo, Japan; and Wiesbaden, Germany.
Candidates require a good degree, preferably in Spanish; a knowledge of current events in Argentina, Chile and Uruguay; and the ability to work long hours, travel long distances, and keep colleagues at head office briefed on relevant developments.

Semicolons are also useful in sentences with two (or more) main clauses not joined by a coordinating conjunction:

Some people are excellent public speakers; others are not.
She may have been brought up in America; she may have had a strong New York accent; she may have told us kids to 'keep to the sidewalk'; yet she considered herself as British as John Bull.

Sometimes – but by no means invariably – phrases such as *however, nevertheless, hence, furthermore, moreover, also, that is to say*, are preceded by a semicolon:

The Chinese are an ingenious and industrious people; hence the powerful development of their economy.
These exercises are recommended; however, they are not obligatory.

Some writers might prefer to use full stops in place of the semicolons in the following:

We liked John; we disliked his politics.
Churchill was a great man; moreover, he had a fine sense of history.
Hate her, you may; despise her, you cannot.

Stylistically, the effect of full stops is to separate the parts of these statements more completely than semicolons do. To do this is slightly to change the meaning of the sentences. For, as Gowers well puts the matter in *Plain Words*, the semicolon here is saying, 'Here is a clause or sentence too closely related to what has gone before to be cut off by a full stop.' A semicolon is a sort of halfway house.

Semicolons: punctuation check-up

Here are some sentences that lack semicolons and, in some cases, commas. Try to punctuate them suitably, and then compare your answers with those on p. 227. Study the punctuated sentences carefully in order to appreciate the function of the semicolon within them.

(a) This is my umbrella that is yours.
(b) She insisted on giving us the whole story it went on and on for ages.
(c) I don't think that's fair you don't know the whole story.
(d) They looked everywhere but couldn't find her she must have left the office.
(e) The doctor did her morning rounds of the wards at nine she was accompanied by two nurses a physiotherapist and a consultant.
(f) The last chickens had gone it seemed clear that the fox had again entered the hen-house during the night.
(g) The judge passed sentence the defendant passed out the press corps sprinted off to relay the verdict to a waiting world.

Slash [/]

The **slash** is sometimes called the **oblique mark**, and – by the Americans – the **virgule**. It has become common in recent years, and has acquired several punctuational uses.

Slashes to show alternatives

Dear Sir/Madam
You will need a passport and/or visa.
Dinner jacket/lounge suit to be worn.

Modifications of this use are common in advertisements:

advanced/proficiency courses in Russian
two-room flat in the Islington/King's Cross/Clerkenwell area

and in 'politically correct' non-sexist language constructions:

s/he
Everyone must do his/her best.

Slashes to indicate periods of time

These are particularly common in fiscal and academic contexts:

Costs for 2007/8 are not yet fixed.
He's claimed the new allowance in his 2006/7 tax form.
She spent the academic year 2005/6 at the University of Leeds.

Slashes in itineraries

This use is now quite common in the travel trade:

Lufthansa flight 321 Frankfurt/Nairobi/Johannesburg
The New York/Memphis/New Orleans bus leaves at noon.

Slashes marking off lines of verse

When for reasons of space a poem is not properly laid out line for line, the line breaks are shown by a slash.

Up the airy mountain,/Down the rushy glen,/We daren't go a-hunting/For
**   fear of little men.**

Slashes for abbreviation

Several abbreviations commonly incorporate a slash:

I'm staying c/o Beattie, 49 Bentinck Drive. (c/o = care of)
Charge to my a/c. (a/c = account)

Major Macmillan is the officer i/c this unit. (i/c = in charge of)

Per is generally shown by a slash:

60 ft/sec   100km/hr

The slash abused

Many people seem nowadays to prefer using the slash to the comma. This is a worrying development that many teachers (who should know better) appear to have endorsed by themselves flocking to it. The following examples are taken from a recent government educational programme:

The poem should contain a clear sense of the writer's imaginative/emotional/intellectual involvement with the topic.
Responses should recognise ways in which aspects of the language/style contribute to the meaning/effect/impact.
Discussion of ideas/themes/texts/approaches with peers/lecturers/teachers is encouraged.

What's wrong with writing 'Discussion of ideas, themes, texts or approaches . . .'?

It may be something to do with society's increasing confidence at the laptop keyboard; we found how to do bullets, and lo, there were more bullets flying about than in a bloody war; then we discovered the slash, and what fun that was – such a stylish and dramatic marker that made the comma appear very old hat, especially to people who were never all that sure about punctuation anyway. Or was the slash perhaps just more visible than the comma? Whatever: it appears to be here to stay awhile. But note that it raises its own little keyboarding niggles. The biggest of these is the problem of what to do with a long list when it goes into a second line of text. If the list is punctuated with commas, there isn't a problem; but if it is split by slashes, the keyboard will be unable to impose an automatic line-break.

The creative use of the slash

The following passage from the novel *Metroland*, by Julian Barnes, is the sort of virtuoso performance not perhaps to be held up as a model. But it shows us how the slash may be successfully exploited for its punctuational potential; and it also shows us that it's not going to go away.

I suppose I must be grown-up now. Or would 'adult' be a better word, a more . . . adult word? If you came and inventoried me, I'd have ticks in all the appropriate boxes. I'm surprised how well camouflaged I seem.
Age: Thirty/ Married: Yes/ Children: One/ Job: One/ House: Yes/ With mortgage: Yes/ (Rock solid so far.)/ Car: Arguable/ Jury service: Once, finding accused not guilty after long discussion of 'reasonable doubt'/ Pets: No, because they mess up/ Foreign holidays: Yes/ Prospects: Bloody better be/ Happiness: Oh, yes; and if not now, then never.

Five

Figures of speech and literary devices

allegory
alliteration
anacoluthon
analogy
anticlimax
antithesis
apostrophe
assonance
bathos
catch phrase
clerihew
cliché
colloquialism
dead metaphor
doubles
epigram
euphemism
haiku
hyperbole
idiom
innuendo
irony
limerick
litotes
malapropism
meiosis
metaphor
metonymy
metre
onomatopoeia
oxymoron
palindrome
paradox
personification
proverb
pun
rhetorical question
simile
spoonerism
syllepsis
synecdoche
zeugma

He understood ... Walt Whitman who laid end to end words never seen in each other's company before outside of a dictionary, and Herman Melville who split the atom of the traditional novel in the effort to make whaling a universal metaphor.

David Lodge, *Changing Places*, 1975

Oft on the dappled turf at ease
I sit, and play with similes,
Loose types of things through all
*   degrees ...*

Wordsworth, 'To the Daisy', 1802

One simile, that solitary shines
In a dry desert of a thousand lines.

Pope, 'Satires and Epistles of Horace Imitated', 1738

All slang is metaphor; and all
*   metaphor is poetry.*

G K Chesterton, *The Defendant*, 1901

Figures of speech and literary devices

Few people nowadays seem able to identify **figurative language**, although of course we all use it as much as ever. In classical times, various types of figurative language were identified by grammarians, and many of the terms they coined remain extant to this day. There is not complete agreement on the definition of the various figures of speech, but the foregoing list gives the main devices; these are amplified below with examples and comments.

Metaphor, or figurative language, is everywhere. Indeed, according to I A Richards it is 'the omnipresent principle of language' (*Practical Criticism*, 1929). But we use it to best effect when we are aware we are using it. This chapter is therefore about awareness raising (in the interest of improving your writing style).

When writing the first edition of this book in 1992, I was in some doubt about whether to discuss **tautology** in this chapter (as a figure of speech) or in the next (as a common error): for it is both. In the end, I forgot to include the subject in either place.

In rhetoric and poetry, tautology is frequently a feature of powerful writing:

Alone, alone, all, all alone,
Alone on a wide wide sea . . . (Coleridge, 1798)

I have nothing to offer but blood, toil, tears and sweat. (Churchill, 1940)

Birds do it, bees do it,
Even educated fleas do it,
Let's do it, let's fall in love. (Cole Porter, 1954)

It is not wrong to make skilful and deliberate use of repetition: as used above, tautology has excellent rhetorical and poetic justification and precedent. However, nowadays we tend to use the term in its other, pejorative sense of redundancy, verbosity, verbal flatulence; and of course this kind of tautology is better avoided.

Many everyday catchphrases are tautological: *all well and good, at this precise point in time* (= now), *in close proximity, in this day and age, limited only to, new innovation* . . . (Is there ever an *ancient* innovation?) How often does *an armed gunman* feature on our TV news? How often are we asked to *repeat that again*, instead of simply *to repeat that* or *say that again*? How often do we hear about *free gifts* and *true facts*, not to mention *actual facts* and *added bonuses*, or *fully comprehensive* life insurance, no doubt against our *final demise*? All of these verbose phrases are tautologies. And if good style is 'the right word in the right place', they are examples of bad style. If you find them in your draft essays, letters or other writing, it might be a good idea to take a red pen to them. Because unintentional tautology is no more than verbiage.

Verbs, verb phrases and phrasal verbs are also tautologically productive. Look at:

abolish completely
build up
circle around
continue on
enter into
join/mix together
plan ahead
raze to the ground
reduce down
repeat again
rise above

Much redundancy – and waffle – is built into such expressions. They are best handled with care in formal writing.

Another potential minefield is **mixed metaphor**. But again, if we are aware of the literal meaning of language that we use metaphorically, we are better prepared to avoid the more ludicrous pitfalls of inappropriate, discordant or mixed metaphors. To be avoided are following kinds of sentence:

The two football teams have a common goal.
The deep rift that had never healed between these two men came home to roost last week.
The problem of global warming has been in the pipeline for some time.
The party leadership quickly went over the top and took up a variety of deeply entrenched positions.
The nuts and bolts of the package will have to be digested before we reach a verdict on it.

These are all example of bad journalese, of a sort we read daily. They occur when people use figurative language insensitively. That is why this chapter is justified in a grammar book. If you study the various devices that are listed here, you will be more alert to their possibilities and pitfalls. Consider the use of **euphemism**, for example (p. 155), but also ask yourself when it shades into mere jargon: what are they trying to hide? And is **syllepsis** (p. 168) a price worth paying for political correctness? These are **rhetorical questions** (p. 166).

Allegory

An **allegory** is a form of story which operates on more than one level – it has a surface significance, and a deeper significance below the surface. The characters in an allegory usually personify or represent a vice or virtue (see **personification**, pp. 164–5), with common nouns capitalised to give characters' names – *Sloth, Lust.* Allegory was popular in the Middle Ages, and the best-known English allegories are *The Faerie Queene*, by Edmund Spenser (1552?–99), and *Pilgrim's Progress*, by John Bunyan (1628–88). More modern allegorists include authors such as Nathaniel Hawthorne (1804–64), C S Lewis (1898–1963), and George Orwell (1903–50).

Alliteration

Alliteration is the repetition of initial sounds or letters in a sequence of words; or, in verse, of stressed syllables:

Round and *round* the *rugged rocks*, the *ragged rascal ran*.
Peter Piper picked a *peck* of *pickled peppers*.
sing a *song* of *sixpence*
the *wild* and *woolly west*
I hear *lake* water *lapping* with *low sounds* by the *shore* . . . (Yeats)

In poetry, alliteration is often used as a phonetic device to unify the passage in which it occurs, so in that context it may be regarded as a form of **rhyme**. Much medieval English poetry was written according to a variety of alliterative schemes:

In a *somer season* when *soft* was the *sonne* . . . *(Piers Plowman)*

A *fair field full* of *folk found* I between
Of all *manere men*, the rich and *meane*
Working and *wandering* as the *world* asketh . . . *(Piers Plowman)*

A more modern poet much given to alliteration was Swinburne:

When the hounds of spring are on winter's traces,
The *mother* of *months* in *meadow* or plain
Fills the shadows and windy places
With *lisp* of *leaves* and *ripple* of *rain*. *(Atalanta in Calydon)*

Now all strange hours and all strange loves are over,
Dreams and *desires* and *sombre songs* and *sweet*. ('Ave atque Vale')

Alliteration is much loved by modern advertisers:

Graded grains make *finer flour*.
Tetley tea totally tantalises tastebuds.
P-p-p-pick up a *Penguin*.

Anacoluthon

This is a figure of speech, often inadvertent, in a sentence where a fresh construction is adopted before the original is complete. It is often employed to convey interruption and indecision. The Greek word means 'lacking sequence':

You really ought – well, do it your own way.
I'd like to introduce – I don't think you are listening to me.

Analogy

An **analogy** is a kind of **simile** (see pp. 166–8) in which there is an inference of resemblance between two items which are equated or compared:

Time is like the tide – it waits for no man.
The child is the analogy of a people at the dawn of history.

Anticlimax

An **anticlimax** is a figure of speech consisting of a sudden descent from the lofty or sublime to the trivial or ridiculous. Deliberate anticlimax has a comic or satiric effect in good writing. (See also **bathos**, p. 150.)

A better cavalier ne'er mounted horse,
Or, being mounted, *e'er got down again*. (Byron)

Not louder shrieks to pitying heaven are cast,
When husbands *or when lapdogs* breathe their last. (Pope)

A man, a master, a marvel . . . *a mouse*.

Antithesis

A figure of speech in which there is a striking opposition or contrast of ideas. Although the words are opposed, they are balanced. An **antithesis** may be quite succinct – *Action, not words* – or it may be longer:

My words fly up, my thoughts remain below. (Shakespeare)
Better to reign in hell than serve in heaven. (Milton)
To err is human, to forgive, divine. (Pope)
Marry in haste; repent at leisure.
Hair today, bald tomorrow!
One small step for man; one giant leap for mankind. (Neil Armstrong)

Apostrophe

In addition to being a punctuation mark (see pp. 110–113), the **apostrophe** is a figure of speech. It is a kind of rhetorical address or speech to an absent listener:

O Liberty, what things are done in thy name! (Carlyle)
O Romeo, Romeo! wherefore art thou Romeo? (Shakespeare)

In the sense that no answer is expected, the apostrophe is often a form of **rhetorical question** (see p. 166).

Assonance

Assonance is a repetition of two or more identical vowel sounds, as in f*ee*t/ st*ee*r/st*ea*m; sp*i*n/sk*i*p/gr*i*d; or r*e*d/h*e*n/h*e*ld. It is always involved in rhyme, as in s*ee*/fl*ee*; or r*e*d/d*ea*d. Poetic examples of assonance are found in:

R*e*nd with tr*e*mendous sound your *e*ars as*u*nder
With g*u*n, dr*u*m, tr*u*mpet, bl*u*nderbuss, and th*u*nder . . . (Pope)

We shall *see*, while above us
The *wa*ves roar and whirl,
A *cei*ling of amber,
A *pa*vement of pearl. (Arnold)

Fair daffodils *we wee*p to *se*e
You haste away so soon. (Wordsworth)

And a *grey* mist on the sea's *fa*ce and a *grey* dawn brea*k*ing. (Masefield)

Between my finger and my thu*mb*
The squat pen rests; sn*ug* as a g*un*. (Heaney)

Bathos

The term for a passage that is meant to be solemn and impressive, but which fails
to live up to its intention because of some textual incongruity. The result is often
a ludicrous **anticlimax** (see p. 149).

The piteous news, so much it shocked her
She quite forgot to send the doctor. (Wordsworth)

Along the wire the electric message came:
He is no better, *he is much the same.*
    (Alfred Austin, Poet Laureate 1896–1913, on the illness of the Prince of Wales)

Catch phrase

A term for a slogan or quotation (often a misquotation), usually from an actor or
politician or an advertisement, and popularised by much use. Popular catch
phrases of their day were:

You've never had it so good. (Harold Macmillan)
A week is a long time in politics. (Harold Wilson)
There is no alternative. (Margaret Thatcher)
Guinness is good for you. (advertisement)
Come up and see me some time. (Mae West)

Clerihew

A **clerihew** is a humorous, four-line, light verse form that rhymes AABB. It was
popularised in the late 1920s by Edmund Clerihew Bentley (1875–1956) and is
named after him. The distinctive feature of the clerihew is that it usually deals
with a person named in the first line, and then goes on to describe that person in
a fanciful way.

Sir Christopher *Wren*   A
Said, 'I am going to dine with some *men*.   A

If anyone *calls*   **B**
Say I am designing St *Paul's.*'   **B**

Sir Humphrey Davy
Abominated gravy.
He lived in the odium
Of having discovered sodium.

John Stuart Mill
By a mighty effort of will
Overcame his natural bonhomie
And wrote 'Principles of Political Economy'.

Cliché

A **cliché** is a stereotyped, or hackneyed, or trite phrase or expression. Clichés often serve as courtesy fillers or formulas in polite, unrehearsed conversation. In a harsh judgment, George Orwell attributed clichés to speakers making appropriate noises in the larynx, but whose brains were not involved in choosing their words for themselves.

Clichés may be words (*nice* used to be held up as a cliché adjective), or phrases (*at this point in time, part and parcel, intents and purposes, conspicuous by its absence, tender mercies, from time immemorial*), or figures of speech (*come hell or high water, at death's door, swing of the pendulum, thin end of the wedge, white elephant, as old as the hills*), or formulas (*have a nice day, how do you do?*). They are often confusing to non-native English speakers.

One of the most fertile fields for the creation of British clichés is politics: *the war against inflation, stand on our own feet, light at the end of the tunnel, the green shoots of economic recovery, the war on terror, roll out an initiative* (preferably one that is *fit for purpose*), may be among the current crop, but each parliament spawns its own. Many of them are quotations, repeated like a mantra by followers, bureaucrats, etc.

It is pointless to draw up a list of clichés with some sort of health warning: cliché – keep off. Context determines whether the word or phrase is used merely as a cliché or because it is the best way of expressing a meaning. See also **dead metaphor** (pp. 152–3).

Part of the appeal of Oscar Wilde was his knack of reversing clichés:

Nothing succeeds like excess.
Work is the curse of the drinking classes.
Her hair has gone quite gold with grief.

Beside this kind of innovative sparkle the hackneyed geek-speak phraseology of our bureaucrats and politicians is pallid brain-rotting stuff. Try reading a typical NHS or local-authority social work report, where we're forever 'revisiting issues' – usually 24/7 – and 'singing from the same hymn-sheet'. These maddening mantras are today's code words: they tell your peers that you are 'in the loop', to quote another grating cliché. And who can forget that when John Birt left the BBC he was recruited by Tony Blair to do some 'blue-sky thinking'? This would almost certainly have involved 'thinking outside the box', not to mention 'pushing the envelope'. Aaargh.

The message is simple: stick to plain speaking or straight talking any day. And avoid cliché in written English. Today's clichés are usually tomorrow's gobbledygook.

Colloquialism

A **colloquialism** is a figurative expression used in informal everyday speech, including slang. Colloquialisms are often inappropriate in essays or in a piece of serious writing. Examples include:

at a loose end nothing to do
at the double very quickly
chew the fat with someone chat with someone
come a cropper fail
dead beat exhausted
down in the mouth dejected, in poor spirits
face the music confront the worst
get cracking hurry up
have a heart be reasonable
hold your horses wait a minute
keep one's powder dry be ready to cope with surprises

lead up the garden path fool someone
play the game act fairly
put the cart before the horse start at the wrong end
smell a rat suspect something
take forty winks take a short sleep
take the bull by the horns confront an adversary
under a cloud in trouble or disfavour
a wet blanket a discouraging person

Idioms trawl the language of colloquialism for some of their most memorable lines (see pp. 156–7). But they need to be used with care in writing, especially academic writing.

Dead metaphor

There are two types of *dead metaphor*. Firstly, there are the figurative expressions that are no longer recognised as such. They have entered the language as literal terms. Examples are everyday items like *the arm of a chair, the leg of a table, to foot the bill, break of day, nightfall, blueprint,* etc. In a more specialist context – in this case the world of economics – terms like *targets, ceilings, backlogs,* and *bottlenecks* tend no longer to be used with any awareness of their metaphoric origin; so they too are dead metaphors.

The other kind of dead metaphor is perhaps better termed an overworked metaphor. Like a **cliché** (see pp. 151–2), it is an overused expression which has lost all freshness, and is used mainly for convenience. It is often a form of jargon. Examples from equestrianism are terms like *he has taken the bit between his teeth*, *she's flogging a dead horse*, and the very widespread *the situation is in hand*. Other metaphors one might like to see dead include *the lower income bracket*, *exploring every avenue*, and *leaving no stone unturned*.

With any luck, some of the following recent idioms and clichés have probably now entered this category. They sound like a bad hangover, or at least as if they have gone off the boil:

carbon-copy killings When did anyone last see a carbon copy of anything? Even serial killers use word processors nowadays.

the feel-good factor Like many others, no doubt, I continue to feel bad about the feel-good factor.

player Often found in the same context as 'in the frame'. For a period, these expressions indicated that someone was in the running for something. 'Is John Reid still a player for the top job?' 'Oh no, I think he's right out of the frame now.'

up to speed Once ubiquitous, this simply meant the speaker was conversant with something. An office update meeting might have concluded with: 'Well, that's us up to speed for another fortnight.'

weather conditions When the weather turned bad, it ceased to be weather and became a condition.

white-collar workers From the good old days of heavy industry when the little woman stayed at home to wash and iron the shirts (and no doubt bleach them).

Doubles

Doubles are pairs of words that habitually go together. They are sometimes called dyads, from Greek *dyo*, 'two'. They are formed in various ways:

> Repetition of the word:

again and again	**out and out**
by and by	**so and so**
neck and neck	**such and such**
over and over	

> Repetition of the meaning:

goods and chattels	**rant and rave**
hale and hearty	**hue and cry**
stuff and nonsense	**bawl and shout**
fast and furious	**aided and abetted**

> Alliteration:

kith and kin	**alas and alack**
humming and hawing	**rough and ready**

might and main   rack and ruin
part and parcel   time and tide

> Opposites:
  this and that   ancient and modern
  on and off   here and there
  great and small   come and go
  give and take   ups and downs

> Rhyme or assonance:
  high and dry   wear and tear
  fair and square   out and about

Epigram

Originally, an **epigram** was a short inscription (often on a tomb). Nowadays, it is a pithy saying, effective by its wit, ingenuity, brevity and balance. In true epigrammatic form, Coleridge defined it thus:

What is an epigram? a dwarfish whole,
Its body brevity, and wit its soul.

The French writer François de La Rochefoucauld (1613–80), in his *Maximes*, was a source of many epigrams based on Roman and Greek writers:

The glory of great men must always be measured by the means they have
**   used to obtain it.**
Hypocrisy is the homage that vice pays to virtue.
We are almost always bored by the very people whom we must not find
**   boring.**
Everyone complains of his memory; no one of his judgment.

More modern attempts at epigrams include:

A self-made man is forever praising his creator.
We learn from history that we do not learn from history.
A life of idleness is hard work.
When a man kills a tiger, he calls it sport; when a tiger kills a man, he calls it
**   vicious.**
A lawyer is a wise man who rescues your estate from your enemies and keeps
**   much of it for himself.**
Poor folk want food for their stomachs; rich folk want stomachs for their
**   food.**

Oscar Wilde (1854–1900) was a master of the epigram:

A cynic is a man who knows the price of everything and the value of nothing.
Men can be analysed, women merely adored.
Experience is the name everyone gives to their mistakes.

Euphemism

In **euphemism**, an accurate but explicit word is substituted with a gentler and less distasteful term. Its use is justified when the cold truth is inappropriate, e.g. to avoid giving offence or causing distress. It is not the same thing as **meiosis** or **litotes** (see p. 159).

For example, many people avoid direct reference to death, preferring terms like *the departed, pass on, pass away, terminally ill*. Rather than say *When I die . . .*, they prefer, *If anything should happen to me . . .* Other contexts prone to euphemism include illness, mental handicap, old age, obesity, poverty, dishonesty, and sex. Hence:

She's a little confused. (= She's mentally disturbed.)
He's a senior citizen/getting on in years. (=He's old.)
She has a full figure. (= She's fat.)
Terminological inexactitude. (= a lie)
He's been economical with the truth. (= He lied.)
They're sleeping together. (= They're having sexual intercourse.)
His clothes have seen better days. (= They're shabby.)
A Third World country (= a poor country)

Euphemism sometimes goes to ludicrous or even to wicked lengths, as in:

A terminal episode (= death, in American jargon)
Schedule overrun (= late/overdue, in business jargon)
Ethnic cleansing (= mass displacements of populations)
The final solution (= Nazi term for the extermination of the Jews)

A special variety of euphemism is 'nukespeak', where acronyms are cunningly deployed to gloss over the obscenities to which they refer – an ICBM or a MIRV looks so much friendlier than an Inter-Continental Ballistic Missile or a Multiple Independently-Targetable Re-entry Vehicle; and carefully devised positive-sounding terms like 'clean strike', 'surgical strike', and 'collateral damage' are dreamt up by the official thought police of Western capitalism to make the unthinkable thinkable. Here euphemism melts into George Orwell's 'mind control'.

Another set of euphemisms derive from the current notion of 'political correctness'. Nowadays we are told not to call someone 'small' (even if he is): he is 'vertically challenged'. Similarly, sex-change operations have become 'gender realignment'.

Another sensitive area in contemporary life is getting the sack from work, or losing one's job; so this topic has produced a predictably huge flowering of euphemisms: *decruitment, degrowing, dehiring, destaffing, downsizing, executive culling, negotiated departure, outplacement, redeployment, personnel surplus reduction, reducing headcount, release, rightsizing, schedule adjustment, skill-mix adjustment, vocational relocation, voluntary severance,* and *workforce imbalance correction* are among the thirty-odd modern jargon terms used to describe the problem of coping with redundancy.

Haiku

The **haiku** is a short Japanese poetic form, in three unrhymed lines, with an exact number of syllables per line. The syllable pattern is usually 5–7–5. The traditional subject matter is usually something out of nature. Haiku are often thoughtful and rather haunting word-pictures:

Cat stretching slowly   O fan of white silk,
Pads outside to the garden.   Clear as frost on the grass-blade,
Shiver, small creatures!   You also are laid aside. (Ezra Pound)

Hyperbole

Hyperbole is overstatement. As a figure of speech, it consists of an extravagant statement or exaggeration. It is used to emphasise the importance or extent of something. It is in use when Lady Macbeth says: 'Here's the smell of blood still: *all the perfumes of Arabia* will not sweeten this little hand.' Or when the deposed Richard II says: '*Not all the water in the rough rude sea* can wash the balm from an anointed king.'

More prosaically, we employ hyperbole if we say we are *dying of hunger* if we merely wish to go for lunch; or if we say there were *millions of people* on the train this morning merely to indicate that it was very busy. Other colloquial examples:

He ran like lightning.
He ran me off my feet.
She was boiling hot.
He embraced her a thousand times.
He snapped my head off.

From hyperbole comes the sales/marketing term **hype**, a form of extravagant promotion designed to publicise a product or event. (The word is formed by **clipping**; see pp. 85–6.)

Idiom

An **idiom** is an expression whose meaning cannot easily be worked out from the words it contains. For example, the expression *to let the cat out of the bag* has nothing to do with cats or bags in the usual sense of those words. It is an idiom, meaning 'to reveal a secret'. Idioms have the potential to cause foreign learners of a language some difficulty. If you say to a native speaker visiting a place for the first time, 'How did you *find* Stratford?' you will get the response, 'Great – I loved it,' or, 'I didn't like the place at all.' But if you ask a non-native speaker the same question, the response may be blank puzzlement. 'How did I *find* Stratford? The train took me there.' Here, *find* is used idiomatically.

Where there is no resemblance between the meaning of the individual words and the meaning of the idiom, it is called **opaque.** If part of the phrase retains a literal meaning, the idiom is **semi-opaque.** Where the meaning of the whole can be guessed from the meaning of the parts, the idiom is **transparent.**

> Opaque idioms:

sacred cow
straw that breaks the camel's back
to jump the gun
to give the show away
to pull the wool over someone's eyes
to score a hat trick
to pass the buck
to lead someone up the garden path
a shot in the arm

> Semi-opaque idioms:

to come down on someone like a ton of bricks
to lay down the law
to force someone's hand
keen as mustard
to leave someone to his own devices

> Transparent idioms:

to keep a straight face
to stand shoulder to shoulder
to be a devil/angel

Many idioms are used only in colloquial English. Some are more or less acceptable in formal English: for example, *to be the life and soul of the party*. But they should always be used with great care in formal writing.

The form of many idioms is fixed, while others permit slight rearrangement of their component parts. It is possible to 'cut a *sorry/fine/handsome* figure'. But you can only '*bite* the dust' (= die); idiomatically you cannot '*chew/suck/lick* the *earth/soil/ground*'.

Innuendo

Innuendo is a type of **irony** (see below), where something is hinted at, but not stated openly. It works by implication rather than by direct statement. It often involves a veiled allusion or insinuation, sometimes malicious or equivocal, reflecting on a person's character:

Frank Harris is invited to all the great houses of England – once. (attr. Oscar Wilde)
He was quite a good singer – he managed to sing in tune at least some of the time.

Irony

Irony is a figure of speech where the speaker says one thing but implies the opposite. Compare the following:

That will fetch a good price.
A good price *that* will fetch!

The words may be the same, but the second sentence means the opposite of the first. It is an ironical way of saying, 'That will not fetch a good price.' Similarly, with suitable emphasis, for these expressions:

***That's* a great help (I don't think)!**
Much good *that* will do!
***You're* a fine cook/A fine cook *you* are!**

Dramatic irony occurs when the audience/reader understands the implications of a situation or a dialogue on stage, but the characters (or some of them) do not. Tragic irony is a refinement of this.

There is dramatic irony in Sheridan's classic comedy *School for Scandal* (1777) when Sir Peter Teazle speaks movingly about his flirtatious young wife, unaware that she is hiding behind the screen. This situation enables the audience to anticipate an outcome contrary to that expected by Sir Peter.

Had Queen Marie Antoinette of France said in 1789, 'The King and I have not the slightest intention of losing our heads over these silly popular revolutions!' she would have uttered an ironic statement, albeit unintentionally.

Limerick

The **limerick** is a humorous, five-line, light verse form rhyming AABBA. There are usually three stressed beats in the A lines and two stressed beats in the B lines. The form became popular after the 1846 publication of *The Book of Nonsense*, by Edward Lear (1812–88). Examples of the form include:

There was an old man of Darjeeling	A
Who got on a train bound for Ealing.	A
It said on the door,	B
'Please don't spit on the floor.'	B
So he got up and spat on the ceiling.	A

There was a young lady from Twickenham
Whose boots were too tight to walk quick in 'em.
So after a while
She sat down on a stile.
And took off her boots and was sick in 'em.

There was a young bard of Japan
Whose limericks never would scan.

When they said it was so,
He replied, 'Yes, I know.
But I make a rule of always trying to get just as many words into the last line
   as I possibly can.'

Litotes

Litotes is a special kind of understatement, in which a positive statement is achieved by denying something negative – i.e. something is expressed by denying its opposite:

He's *not a bad* swimmer. (= He's quite a good swimmer.)
This is *no easy* task. (= It's a difficult task.)
Her life was *no bed of roses*. (= She had a hard life.)
no mean city (= a great city, in St Paul's remark about Rome)

Other common expressions involving litotes:

by no means negligible
in no small measure

Malapropism

This term denotes the incorrect use of a word, often a scholarly word. It derives from Mrs Malaprop, an amusing character in *The Rivals* (1775), the classic comedy by R B Sheridan (1751–1816). Mrs Malaprop's name is from the French *mal à propos* (= 'not apt or apposite, inappropriate'), and she is much given to the sorts of utterances for which the term was coined – the misapplication of long words. She confuses words such as *alligator* and *allegory, allusion* and *illusion, hydrostatics* and *hysterics*. Some of her memorable throwaway lines include:

She's as headstrong as an *allegory* on the banks of the Nile.
An aspersion upon my parts of speech . . . Sure, if I *reprehend* anything in this
   world, it is the use of my *oracular* tongue, and a nice *derangement of
   epitaphs*.

Meiosis

Meiosis is deliberate understatement, for the sake of effect. The aim of meiosis is to emphasise the size, importance, etc. of what is apparently belittled. It is a colloquial and quintessentially English figure of speech, indicated by the use of words like *rather*. **Litotes** (see above) is a form of meiosis:

She's *rather* nice. (= I like her very much.)
He made a *decent* contribution. (a generous one)
This is *some* game. (It's a wonderful or amazing game.)

Metaphor

Metaphorical language is not the same as the classical view of language, according to which words are thought of as 'labelling' things in the 'real' world. **Metaphors** express a way of conceptualising, a way of seeing and understanding one's surroundings. We often forget how pervasive metaphorical language is. But as C S Lewis said, 'Human beings are incurably metaphorical'; and I A Richards has called metaphor 'the omnipresent principle of language'.

Metaphor is a way of wording the world. It reminds us that language constructs as well as reflects, and that it is not always a transparent vehicle. It is a figure of speech in which A is identified with B. It is based on substitution and comparison. The process of comparison yields a **simile** (see pp. 166–8), while the process of substitution yields a metaphor. So:

The law is *an ass*. (Dickens)
The waves were *soldiers* moving. (Wallace Stevens)

These utterances are not to be understood literally – they are to be taken as pictures of the author's (or speaker's) meaning.

Metaphors come in all shapes and sizes. They can be examined from the point of view of their grammatical construction. We may identify:

> appositional metaphors:
My wife, a *rose* among *thorns*.

> vocative, or apostrophic metaphors:
My *flower*, my darling!

> verbal metaphors:
The minutes *crept by* slowly.
She *was rooted* to the spot in terror.
Their blows *rained down* on the innocent victim.

> prepositional metaphors:
The *apple of* my eye
The *knife of* pain and betrayal

> adjectival metaphors:
With *leaden* feet
A *flaming* temper
A *stony* silence

> adverbial metaphors:
He was caught *red-handed*.
A *grief ago*. (Dylan Thomas)

Metaphors can also be analysed for the kind of work they do. So we can identify:

> animistic metaphors, in which inanimate nouns receive animate qualities:
A good book is the *best of friends.*

> concretive metaphors, in which abstractions are given substance:
Music is the *brandy* of the damned! (G B Shaw)
Liberty's a glorious *feast*! (Burns)

> humanising metaphors, in which non-human nouns are given human attributes:
A *babbling* brook
An *angry* sky
April is the *cruellest* month . . . (T S Eliot)

(See also **personification**, pp. 164–5)

> dehumanising metaphors, in which people are given non-human characteristics:
Christ the *tiger* (Blake)

> deifying metaphors, in which divine qualities are attributed to people or things:
The *almighty* dollar
The *eternal* triangle

> more broadly – paradoxical metaphors, in which qualities associated with one
thing are attributed to another:
To a *green* thought in a green shade. (Andrew Marvell)
Thoughts of a *dry* brain in a dry season. (T S Eliot)

(See also **paradox**, p. 164.)

Metonymy

Metonymy is a figure of speech which refers to someone or something via an associated item. For example, *the Crown* and *Downing Street* are terms often used
in the UK when speaking about the monarchy and the Prime Minister. Other
metonymic expressions are:

King of the *ring* (= boxing)
He has taken to the *bottle*. (= alcoholic liquor)
She was called to the *Bar*. (= the profession of a barrister)

Compare **synecdoche**, p. 169.

Metre

Metre means 'measure', and may be defined as any form of measured, or regulated,
rhythm. All language has stressed and unstressed syllables, and in English poetry
metre is the technical term for the rhythmic arrangement of those syllables. Just as
English grammar was based on Latin grammar, so too English poetic metre was
based on Latin. The basic measure of Latin verse was the **foot**, and four popular
types of poetic foot in regular English verse are:

> **iambic** (unstressed + stressed, shown as x/):

God gives all men all earth to love,	x/x/x/x/ (= 4 iambic feet)
But, since man's heart is small,	x/x/x/
Ordains for each one spot shall prove	x/x/x/x/
Belovèd over all. (Kipling)	x/x/x/

> **trochaic** (stressed + unstressed, shown as /x):

Beauty, midnight, vision dies:	/x/x/x/ (= 3.5 trochaic feet)
Let the winds of dawn that blow	/x/x/x/
Softly round your dreaming head	/x/x/x/
Such a day of sweetness show . . . (Auden)	/x/x/x/

> **anapaestic** (2 unstressed + 1 stressed, shown as xx/):

At the corner of Wood Street, when daylight appears,	xx/xx/xx/xx/ (= 4 anapaestic feet)
Hangs a thrush that sings loud, it has sung for three years . . . (Wordsworth)	xx/xx/xx/xx/

> **dactylic** (1 stressed + 2 unstressed, shown as /xx):

Fast they come, fast they come;	/xx/xx (= 2 dactylic feet)
See how they gather!	/xx/x
Wide waves the eagle plume,	/xx/xx
Blended with heather . . . (Scott)	/xx/x

Particular names were given to lines with a certain number of feet. So a line with five feet is a **pentameter**, a **hexameter** has six feet, a **heptameter** has seven, etc. An **iambic pentameter** has five iambic feet.

Onomatopoeia

Onomatopoeia is a kind of sound symbolism. Words are onomatopoeic if the sound of the word suggests its sense. They are sometimes called **mimic words**, and obvious examples are:

babble, bubble, burble, buzz
crack, click, clack, clatter, crunch, clang, croak
fizzle, flutter, flicker, flash
gurgle, grate, grunt, gleam, glow, glisten
hiss, hush, hum, hurly-burly
lullaby
plop, plonk, patter
rustle, rattle
shush, slush, slap, slime, slink, slither
twang, tinkle, twinkle, twitter

From the above list, it can be deduced that in English certain sounds particularly lend themselves to onomatopoeia. Many words beginning with *sl*- seem to have unpleasant connotations, while various words beginning with *gl-* are associated with light.

A form of writing that has created its own range of onomatopoeic terms is the comic strip with its special effects: *wham, zap, kerplonk, splat!*

Sometimes onomatopoeic words imitate a person or an animal's sound: *yum yum, yuk, bow-wow, cock-a-doodle-doo, cuckoo, peewit, curlew.*

There was much poetic use of onomatopoeia, often with alliteration thrown in for good measure:

Over the *c*obbles he *c*lattered and *c*lashed . . . (Browning)

There was never a sound beside the wood but one,
And that was my long scythe whispering to the ground. (Robert Frost)

Then I heard the boom of the blood-lust song
And a thigh-bone beating on a tin-pan gong. (Vachel Lindsay)

Keeping time, time, time,
In a sort of Runic rhyme,
To the tintinnabulation that so musically wells
From the bells, bells, bells, bells. (Edgar Allan Poe)

Oxymoron

The **oxymoron** is a kind of **paradox** (see p. 164) – a combination of contradictory or incongruous words, like *deafening silence, bitter-sweet, sublimely bad, cruel kindness,* or *devoted enemies.* It is a figure of speech mainly employed to make a special impact, either in poetry or for humorous effect:

His *honour* rooted in *dishonour* stood,
And *faith unfaithful* kept him *falsely true.* (Tennyson)

Evil, be thou my *good.* (Milton)
There's no *success* like *failure.* (Bob Dylan)
Include me *out.* (Sam Goldwyn)
A *verbal contract* isn't worth the *paper it's written on.* (Sam Goldwyn)
I'll give you a *definite maybe.* (Sam Goldwyn)
Silence is wonderful to *listen to.* (Sam Goldwyn)
He'd make a *lovely corpse.* (Dickens)
Poverty and oysters always seem to go together. (Dickens)

Oxymorons may be used cynically, as when *military intelligence* or the *United Kingdom* are called contradictions in terms.

Palindrome

The arrangement of numbers, words, or lines of text to give the same message backwards as forwards is called a **palindrome**. The word is from Greek *palin* *dromo*, 'to run back again'. They have also been called **Sotadics**, after their reputed inventor, Sotades, a Greek poet of the 3rd century BC. Examples of palindromic words are *madam, radar, bib, level,* and *noon* and numerals like 1991 or 2002. Longer examples are:

Madam, I'm Adam. (Adam's greeting to Eve)
Was it a cat I saw?
Lewd did I live, and evil I did dwel. (Philips, 1706)
Able was I ere I saw Elba. (attr. Napoleon)
A man, a plan, a canal – Panama!

One of the longest palindromes in English is:

Dog as a devil deified/Deified lived as a god.

A **word palindrome** is one in which only the complete words are reversed:

What? So he is dead, is he? So what?

The village of *Glenelg* in Scotland is a **placename palindrome**.

Paradox

A **paradox** is a statement that appears contradictory or contrary to common sense, and yet is true in some other sense:

Nowadays we know the price of everything and the value of nothing.
    (Wilde)
The child is father of the man. (Wordsworth)
He who would save his life must lose it. (Bible)

Personification

Personification is a special kind of metaphor. It is a figure of speech in which some abstraction or inanimate thing is represented as a person, or is given human qualities. **Allegory** (see p. 147) makes special use of personification. Giant Despair, in Bunyan's *Pilgrim's Progress*, is an example of a personification: the abstract concept of despair represented as a person. Other examples:

Truth sits upon the lips of dying men. (Arnold)
Riches are a good handmaid, but the worst mistress. (Bacon)
Prudence is a rich ugly old maid, courted by incapacity. (Blake)
Time, the great healer . . .
Can Honour's voice provoke the silent dust/Or Flatt'ry soothe the dull cold
    ear of Death? (Gray)
Slowly, silently, now the moon/ Walks the night in her silver shoon. (De la
    Mare)
Ol' man river, he just keeps rolling along . . . (Hammerstein)

Other 'humanising' **metaphors** (see pp. 160–61), by giving an adjective normally associated with a person to a non-human noun, are also a sort of personification:

a *babbling* brook
Come, *friendly* bombs, and fall on Slough . . . (Betjeman)

Proverb

A **proverb** is a popular saying memorably expressed:

Once bitten, twice shy.
Easy come, easy go.

Proverbs tend to encapsulate traditional or accepted wisdom, and to be anonymous or unattributable. Common stylistic devices used in proverbs include:

> Rhyme or assonance:
Early to bed, early to rise,
Makes a man healthy, wealthy and wise.

Birds of a feather flock together.

A stitch in time saves nine.

Red sky at night – shepherds' delight.
Red sky in the morning – shepherds' warning.

> Alliteration:
Love laughs at locksmiths.
A cat may look at a king.
A miss is as good as a mile.
Every dog has his day.

Some proverbs betray their age by retaining linguistic archaisms:

Pride goeth before a fall.
He goes a-sorrowing who goes a-borrowing.
Shoemakers' wives are worst shod.

Proverbs is the name of a book of the Old Testament, containing, as the name indicates, quantities of proverbial utterances. Many of them were originally attributed to King Solomon.

The fear of the Lord is the beginning of knowledge.
Hope deferred makes the heart sick.
He that has knowledge spares his words.
A good name is rather to be chosen than great riches.
A fool utters all his mind.
Where there is no vision, the people perish.

Pun

A **pun** is a figure of speech that uses words in such a way as to convey – and make a play on – their double meaning. Puns were popular in the nineteenth century and in earlier periods, but are nowadays regarded by many as rather childish:

Ask for me tomorrow, and you shall find me a *grave* man. (= dead,
    Shakespeare, *Romeo and Juliet)*
When is a door not a door? When it's *ajar.* (= a jar)
Drilling holes is *boring.*
King Kong was the original urban *guerrilla.* (= gorilla)
'His sins were scarlet but his books were *read.'* (= red, Belloc, 'On His Books')
The Egyptians received a *check* on the bank of the Red Sea which was *crossed*
    by Moses. (cheque)
Marriage isn't a word – it's a *sentence*! (King Vidor)

Examples appearing on notices in, respectively, a chemist's shop window, a photographer's shop window, a gents' toilet, and the back window of a bridal limousine:

WE DISPENSE WITH ACCURACY
OUR BUSINESS IS DEVELOPING
WE AIM TO PLEASE – YOU AIM TOO. PLEASE
AISLE ALTAR HYMN

Then there was the unfortunately ambiguous newspaper headline:

TRAIN ON FIRE – PASSENGERS ALIGHT

and the old favourite school report-card comment:

Your son is *trying.* (making an effort/exasperating)

Rhetorical question

A **rhetorical question** is asked for effect, and requires no answer. Often it is the equivalent of an emphatic statement:

Was I hungry? (i.e. I was extremely hungry.)
Do you take me for an imbecile? (i.e. I'm an intelligent person.)

Sometimes it is intended as a passing observation:

What are things coming to?

Simile

A **simile** is a figure of speech in which one thing or person is explicitly compared with another, and is said to be *like* another. It is used for explanatory, illustrative, or ornamental purpose. The word is from Latin *similis*, 'like', and the words *like* or *as* are usually found in similes:

I wandered lonely *as* a cloud . . . (Wordsworth)
My love is *like* a red, red rose . . . (Burns)
Money is *like* muck, not good except it be spread. (Bacon)
Float *like* a butterfly, sting *like* a bee. (Muhammad Ali)
Squat *like* a toad he sat . . . (Milton)

Poetic simile is often extended over several lines:

Thick *as* autumnal leaves that strow the brooks
In Vallombrosa, where th' Etrurian shades
High over-arched embow'r . . . (Milton, *Paradise Lost*)

And we are here *as* on a darkling plain
Swept with confused alarms of struggle and flight,
Where ignorant armies clash by night. (Arnold, 'Dover Beach')

Some similes or comparisons are very well established and widely used. Others have almost become clichés and are to be used with care:

as agile as a cat
as bald as a coot
as black as soot/a boot
as bold as brass
as cheap as dirt
as cool as a cucumber
as dead as a doornail
as deep as the sea
as dull as ditch water
as fast as light
as fit as a fiddle
as frisky as a colt/lamb
as good as gold
as happy as a lark
as heavy as lead
as hideous as the witch of Endor
as hungry/ravenous as a wolf
as keen as mustard
as mean as a miser
as obstinate as a mule
as plain as a pikestaff
as pleased as Punch
as pretty as a picture
as quiet as a mouse
as sharp as a razor

as ambitious as the devil
as big as a whale
as blind as a bat
as brown as a berry
as cheerful as the day is long
as crafty/cunning as a fox
as deaf as a post
as dry as dust
as false as Judas
as fidgety as an old maid
as flat as a pancake
as game as a fighting cock
as grim as death
as hard as nails
as helpless as a baby
as hollow as a drum
as innocent as a lamb/baby
as mad as a March hare
as naked as the day (one) was born
as pale as death/Banquo's ghost
as playful as a kitten
as poor as a church mouse
as proud as a peacock
as restless/ruthless as the sea
as sick as a dog

as simple/easy as ABC
as sly as a fox
as stealthy as a cat
as stubborn as a mule
as swift as an arrow/lightning
as tough as nails
as uncertain as the weather
as warm as toast
as wet as a drowned rat
as young as the morning

as slow as a snail
as sober as a judge on circuit
as stiff as a ramrod
as sure as fate/death
as thick as thieves
as ugly as sin
as vast as the ocean
as weak as water
as wise as Solomon

Spoonerism

A **spoonerism** is an accidental transposition of initial sounds in two or more words, as in *sons of toil* for *tons of soil*. It is named after the Rev W A Spooner (1844–1930) of Oxford University, who was said to be given to this form of linguistic confusion. To a student, he is reputed to have said: 'You have *hissed* all my *mystery* lectures', instead of 'You have *missed* all my *history* lectures.' Other often-quoted spoonerisms:

Let us drink to the *queer* old *Dean*. (proposing the loyal toast)
***Kinkering kongs* their titles take. (announcing hymn in chapel)**

A popular, latter-day dilution of the spoonerism is the transposition of two words:

Take that silly *face* off your *expression*!
Did you get a nice *flight* on the *meal* out?
Excuse my *pig* – he's a *friend*!

Syllepsis

Syllepsis is a stylistic device in which a number of words depend on, or relate to, one word, but this word does not agree with all of them in number or in gender:

I don't think Mrs Brown or the children *know*.
James and Alice *each have their* duties.

Sometimes syllepsis is used as a synonym for **zeugma** (see p. 169).

Much evidence of 'degenerative' syllepsis in the language arrived in the wake of feminism. It was better to be politically correct than grammatically correct. So we got – and continue to get – things like:

We do not have the caller's number to return *their* call. (BT recorded message)
**You need to remember one main thing about contracts: the person with
    more muscle uses *theirs*.**
**The novel's main character is the reader *themself*. (Review, Waterstone's
    New Books)**

Synecdoche

Synecdoche is the figure of speech that puts the part for the whole (as 'fifty *sail*' for 'fifty *ships*', or 'ninth *bat*' for 'ninth *batsman*'); or the whole for the part (as in '*Parliament* voted to . . .' for '*A majority of the members of Parliament* voted to . . .'). Other examples:

Britannia rules *the waves* (= the sea)
All hands on deck (= seamen)
an estate belonging to *the Crown*
Such matters need the authorisation of *the Foreign Office*.
He made his career on *the boards*.
Hampshire won the toss and opened the batting.
Two heads are better than one.

It is common for the term 'England' to be used as a synecdoche for the 'United Kingdom', giving endless offence to the Scots, Welsh and Northern Irish; and for Canadians and Mexicans to be called 'Americans'. Compare **metonymy**, p. 161.

Zeugma

Zeugma is a stylistic device in which a word, usually a verb, is followed by two words which in conventional language would not be found together. The result is an unexpected coming together of constituents, often deployed for humorous effect. It is a form of **ellipsis** (see p. 78).

Mr Pickwick *took* his hat and his leave. (Dickens)
See Pan with flocks, with fruits Pomona crowned. (Pope)
She *arrived* in a bikini and a flood of tears. And now she's *lost* her coat and her temper.
He *plays* with verve and with Sheffield Wednesday.
John *left* Mary in the library and in a hurry.
Her mother and the fish stew *upset* Alice.
She *filed* the papers and her nails.
They *opened* their door and their hearts to the orphan boy.

Six

Common errors and confusibles

The English Language

*Some words have different meanings
  and yet they're spelled the same.*
*A cricket is an insect, to play it – it's a
  game.*
*On every hand, in every land, it's thor-
  oughly agreed,*
*The English language to explain, is very
  hard indeed.*

*Some people say that you're a dear, yet
  dear is far from cheap.*
*A jumper is a thing you wear, yet a
  jumper has to leap.*
*It's very clear, it's very queer, and, pray,
  who is to blame*
*For different meanings to some words
  pronounced and spelled the same?*

*A little journey is a trip, a trip is when
  you fall.*
*It doesn't mean you have to dance
  whene'er you hold a ball.*
*Now here's a thing that puzzles me:
  musicians of good taste*
*Will very often form a band – I've one
  around my waist!*

*You spin a top, go for a spin, or spin a
  yarn maybe –*
*Yet every spin's a different spin, as you
  can plainly see.*
*Now here's a most peculiar thing, 'twas
  told me as a joke –*
*A dumb man wouldn't speak a word,
  yet seized a wheel and spoke!*

*A door may often be ajar, but give the
  door a slam*
*And then your nerves receive a jar –
  and then there's jars of jam.*
*You've heard, of course, of traffic jams,
  and jams you give your thumbs.*
*And adders, too, one is a snake, the
  other adds up sums.*

*A policeman is a copper, it's a nick-
  name (impolite!)*
*Yet a copper in the kitchen is an article
  you light.*
*On every hand, in every land, it's thor-
  oughly agreed,*
*The English language to explain is very
  hard indeed!*

Harry Hemsley, in *Verse That Is Fun*,
ed. Ireson (Faber, 1962)

Hints on Pronunciation for Foreigners

*I take it you already know
Of tough and bough and cough and
dough?
Others may stumble, but not you
On hiccough, thorough, laugh and
through,
Well done, and now you wish perhaps
To learn of less familiar traps?*

*Beware of heard, a dreadful word
That looks like beard and sounds like
bird.
And dead: it's said like bed, not bead –
And only Scotsmen call it deed!
Watch out for meat and great and
threat.*

*They rhyme with suite and straight and
debt.*

*A moth is not a moth in mother,
Nor both in bother, broth in brother,
And here is not a match for there
Nor dear and fear for bear and pear,
And then there's dose and rose and
lose –
Just look them up – and goose and
choose.
And cork and work and card and ward,
And font and front and word and
sword,
And do and go, and thwart and cart –
Come, come, I've hardly made a start!
A dreadful language? Man alive –
I'd mastered it when I was five.*

Herbert Farjeon

Common errors and confusibles

There are two A–Z listings in this section of the book – neither of which is exhaustive. The first list is a selection of words which writers commonly confuse, for one reason or another. Sometimes the words are **homonyms** (i.e. they sound the same, as *alter* and *altar*, *meter* and *metre*, *serial* and *cereal*). Generally, the entry shows the two (or more) words in the contexts in which they frequently appear, by means of example sentences or phrases. The confusible word is usually then explained by a synonym.

The second list is of commonly misspelled words. If there is a word that is almost invariably misspelled, that is highlighted in bold type to bring the problem to the reader's attention. The words are arranged in groups of ten, in the hope that bad spellers will work their way through this section, group by group, practising their spelling.

The best way to practise spelling is to follow the **look/cover/write/check** procedure. That is to say: **look** at the shape of the word and how it is formed; **cover** it over; **write** it down on a sheet of paper; and finally **check** your written version with the version in the book.

Speaking more generally, the best way actively to develop your spelling and to guard against misspellings and confusibles is to make a regular and routine habit of checking words (spellings, etymologies, usage) in a good dictionary. This habit is no longer very widespread, and does not seem to be very actively encouraged and developed by schools.

A list of confusibles

abdicate, abrogate, arrogate

King Edward VIII *abdicated* the British throne in 1936. (= relinquished)

He *abrogated* his traditional responsibilities. (= formally annulled)

The prime minister has *arrogated* to herself numerous responsibilities which were traditionally the responsibility of the Cabinet. (= assumed)

abuse, misuse

Patients were sometimes physically *abused*. (= improperly used, mistreated)

The crowd shrieked *abuse* at the prime minister. (= insults)

Misuse of one's time, *misuse* of a word (= incorrect use)

accede, exceed

To *accede* to this request would set a dangerous precedent. (= agree, submit)

It is dangerous to *exceed* the speed limit. (= go over)

accept, except

She *accepted* a gift of food and clothes. (= took)

Everyone was sick *except* me. (= apart from)

acerbic: see **acid**

acetic, ascetic

Acetic acid is the main substance in vinegar. (Latin *acetum*, 'vinegar')

His face was pale, thin, *ascetic*. (= austere)

acid, acrid, acerbic

He spilled a solution of weak *acid*. (= chemical substance)

The room was filled with an *acrid* smoky smell. (= pungent)

There was an *acerbic* sharpness to her voice. (= bitter)

acknowledgement, acknowledgment

Either spelling is acceptable.

acrid: see **acid**

activate, actuate

He quickly *activated* the spacecraft's retro-rockets. (= set in motion)

Most of his work is *actuated* by selfish motives. (= motivated)

adherence, adhesion

This country's *adherence* to a treaty, *adherence* to communism/Islam (= attachment/obedience to)

This glue gives a very strong *adhesion*. (= sticking power)

adjacent, adjoining

A bedroom with bathroom *adjacent* (= nearby, but not with direct access)

A bedroom with bathroom *adjoining* (= with direct access)

adverse, averse

He received an *adverse* report on the proposed takeover. (= unfavourable)

I am not *averse* to the occasional whisky. (= disinclined)

advice, advise

He needs some paternal *advice*. (noun)

I *advise* you to see a doctor. (verb)

aesthetic, ascetic

Aesthetic means appreciative of, or relating to beauty. *Ascetic* means austere or monastic, practising self-denial.

affect, effect

What is the *effect* of putting acid on wood? (= result)

He *effected* his getaway under cover of darkness. (= made)

His death has badly *affected* us all. (= distressed)

He has an *affected*, lisping accent. (= unspontaneous, artificial)

afflict, inflict

He is *afflicted* with Parkinson's disease. (= suffers from)

Rangers *inflicted* a 6:nil defeat on the visiting team. (= imposed)

ageing, aging

Either spelling is acceptable.

aggravate, exacerbate, exasperate

Aggravate means to annoy or irritate, and *exasperate* also means to annoy, while *exacerbate* means to make matters worse. The original meaning of *aggravate* too was to make something worse: scratching would *aggravate* a chilblain; *exacerbate* is used more of a moral dilemma than of a physical problem.

all ready, already

We were *all ready* for the visitors long before they arrived. (= prepared)

I've *already* had some tea. (= previously)

all right, alright

All right is still felt to be more correct, though *alright* is now widely accepted in a sentence such as 'Are you feeling *alright*?' On the other hand, a sentence such as 'Are your test answers *all right*?' (meaning all correct) would not run these two words together.

allusive, elusive

He made an *allusive* speech, with numerous echoes from the writings of his favourite Classical authors. (= full of references)

The owl is an *elusive* nocturnal bird. (= difficult to find or see)

altar, alter

The minister stood before the church *altar*. (= communion table)

The ship *altered* course to avoid the iceberg. (= changed)

alternately, alternatively

Alternately means one after another; *alternatively* means one instead of another.

altogether, all together

He didn't *altogether* trust his boss. (= entirely)

The prisoners assembled *all together* in the yard. (= all of them in one place)

ambiguous, ambivalent

The words 'light house keeper' are *ambiguous*. (= have more than one meaning)

Most people are *ambivalent* about the value of antiquated institutions such as the Royal Family. (= in two minds)

amend, emend

Amend means to improve; *emend* means to correct.

amiable, amicable

He had an *amiable*, chatty manner. (= friendly)

They made an *amicable* decision to separate. (= in a spirit of friendliness and goodwill)

among, amongst

Among is preferable; *amongst* is old-fashioned. Similarly, *amid* is better than *amidst*, while than *whilst*.

among, between

The cash was divided *among* the members of the gang. (many people)

The votes were divided evenly *between* Mr Black and Mr White. (two people)

amoral: see immoral

annex, annexe

There was a short war in 1990 when Iraq tried to *annex* Kuwait. (verb)

John works in the science *annexe*. (noun)

antagonist, protagonist

Hitler was a formidable *antagonist*. (= enemy)

He was the leading *protagonist* in the anti-abortion lobby. (= champion)

arbiter, arbitrator

Arbiter is the more general term, and includes *arbiters* of taste and fashion as well as people with the general power to mediate in or control a situation. An *arbitrator* is a more specific term for a person who is appointed to settle a dispute.

Arctic, Antarctic

The *Arctic* is the region around the North Pole, the *Antarctic* being the region around the South Pole.

arrogate: see abdicate

artist, artiste

An *artist* is a person who draws, paints, sculpts, etc. as a job or as a hobby; or who is very skilled at something. A music-hall or circus *artiste* is a popular professional entertainer.

ascetic: see acetic and aesthetic

assure, ensure, insure

She was not *assured* till she saw him safe and unhurt. (= persuaded that all was well)

The state's duty is to *ensure* the safety of its citizens. (= guarantee)

Is the house *insured* against fire? (= covered against loss)

astonished, astounded, dumbfounded

These words express various and increasing degrees of surprise, with *astounded* implying a temporary inability to react, and *dumbfounded* implying not only inability to act but also inability to speak – because struck dumb.

astronomy, astrology

Astronomy is the scientific study of the stars and planets in the galaxy. *Astrology* is the non-scientific study of the same subject, in the belief that it can foretell things about your future.

atheist, agnostic

An *atheist* denies the existence of God or of divine things. An *agnostic* takes the view that God's existence cannot be proved or disproved, and is therefore sceptical on the subject.

averse: see **adverse**

aural, oral

Aural concerns the ear, while *oral* concerns the mouth. An *oral* exam is therefore a spoken exam (for example in French), while an *aural* exam tests listening (for example in music).

authoritative, authoritarian

To make an *authoritative* comment implies that the speaker is a genuine authority on the subject. An *authoritarian* person, on the other hand, is dictatorial – the father in a Victorian family was said to be *authoritarian*, for example.

backward, backwards

The adjective is *backward*, as in 'a rather *backward* pupil'. The adverb can be spelled either way: 'The train started going *backwards / backward*.'

bail, bale

They *bailed* out the leaking dinghy. (= empty of water)
The court set his *bail* at $20,000. (= security)
The barn was full of *bales* of hay. (= stacks)

baited, bated

The bears were cruelly *baited*. (= teased)
He stood with *bated* breath. (= held, from 'abated')

bale: see **bail**

bath, bathe

She gave the baby its evening *bath*. (= noun, wash)
The sea was too stormy for a *bathe*. (= noun, swim)
He was advised to *bathe* the wound daily. (= verb, cleanse)

bereaved, bereft

She has recently been *bereaved*. (= lost a member of her family through death)
The trees are now *bereft* of leaves. (= devoid)

beside, besides

Oh, I do like to be *beside* the seaside. (= near)
Besides us, only John is here. (= in addition to)

between: see **among**

biannual, biennial

Biannual means twice yearly. *Biennial* has two meanings: (1) every two years; (2) used of plants, means lasting for two years, flowering in the second year.

biased, biassed

Either spelling is acceptable.

born, borne

She was *born* in Edinburgh in 1943. (= had her birth)
She has *borne* five children. (= carried, given birth to)
She has *borne* her troubles with fortitude. (= put up with)

break, brake

Don't *break* the speed limit. (= exceed)

There was a squeal of *brakes* and a smell of burning rubber. (= device for slowing down a vehicle)

brothers, brethren

These are the two plurals *of brother*, and *brothers* is the one generally used.

Brethren is archaic and biblical, and now limited to religious or poetic uses.

burned, burnt

The adjective is usually *burnt*, as in '*burnt* toast', '*burnt* ochre'. For the verb, *burned* is usually preferable, as in 'He *burned* his finger.'

burst, bust

The balloon *burst* with a loud pop. (= punctured)

The company went *bust* in the 1990s recession. (= collapsed)

She is a statuesque woman with a very large *bust*. (= chest)

callous, callused

A *callous*, heartless act (= cruel)

Hard, *callused* hands (= with thick, horny skin)

cannon, canon

The warship bristled with heavy *cannon*. (= big guns)

He is a *canon* of Westminster Cathedral. (= senior priest)

The *canon* of 20th-century classic fiction (= authoritative list, corpus)

canvas, canvass

They were sleeping in the garden under *canvas*. (= in a tent)

A fine, oil on *canvas* painting (= on cloth)

The candidates have been *canvassing* support far and wide. (= soliciting)

capital punishment, corporal punishment

The former means 'removal of the head' (*caput*, in Latin), or execution.

The latter is a physical punishment of the body (*corpus, -oris*, in Latin), such as beating, flogging, etc.

carat, carrot

A 200-*carat* diamond, 24-*carat* gold (= measurement of weight or purity)

A dish of boiled beef and *carrots* (= orange-coloured root vegetables)

censor, censure, censer

The mail of all prisoners is *censored*. (= officially inspected)

The Opposition has strongly *censured* the Government's handling of the issue. (= criticised)

Incense is burned in a *censer*. (= specially made container)

cereal, serial

Wheat, oats, and barley are *cereal* crops. (= grain producing)

He was watching an Australian TV *serial*. (= episode in a series)

ceremonial, ceremonious

Millions of viewers watched the Trooping the Colour *ceremonial*. (= traditional ritual)

He addressed us in a *ceremonious* and flamboyant manner. (= slightly theatrical)

childish, childlike
She decided to punish his *childish* tantrums. (= immature)
He never lost a somewhat *childlike* faith in human goodness. (= innocent)
chord: see cord
classic, classical, Classics
Traditionally, if you studied Latin and Greek you were called a student of *Classics*, and had received a *classical* education. Down the years, other writers (such as Milton and Scott and Dickens) have come to be described as *classic* writers of British literature. More recently and more narrowly, Agatha Christie, P D James or Ian Rankin could be said to have written *classics* of detective fiction, i.e. masterpieces of their genre. *Classical* architecture was inspired by the Ancients. *Classical* music is from the canon of great European music – Haydn, Mozart, Bach, Beethoven, etc.
clench, clinch
She muttered angrily through *clenched* teeth. (= tightly fixed)
A trade deal has at last been *clinched*. (= finalised, agreed)
climactic, climatic
The *climactic* finale was an operatic tour de force. (adjectival form of *climax*)
Favourable *climatic* conditions (= pertaining to the weather)
cloths, clothes
Factories make *cloth*, which tailors and dressmakers then make into *clothes*. We have dish*cloths*, floor*cloths*, table*cloths*, altar *cloths*, etc., but we go out each morning in our working *clothes*, cut the hedge in our gardening *clothes*, and sleep under bed*clothes*.
coarse: see course
commitment, committal
He has a strong *commitment* to the cause. (= loyalty)
The *committal* ceremony was private. (= burial, committing of the body to the ground)
complement, compliment
She prepared an excellent salmon dish *complemented* by a fine hock wine. (= enhanced)
May I *compliment* you on an excellent speech. (= congratulate)
contemptible, contemptuous
His lack of courage was *contemptible*. (= despicable)
He addressed us in haughty tones of *contemptuous* disdain. (= scornful)
continually, continuously
The former suggests a succession of occurrences, with the possibility of short breaks in the sequence. *Continuously* describes something that never stops; it does not admit of breaks in the sequence.
comic, comical
A *comic* actor's job is to make you laugh. (= deliberately funny)
His attempt to appear sober was *comical*. (= unintentionally or unexpectedly funny)

cord, chord

The term for a length of rope etc. is *cord*, as in 'dressing-gown *cord*', 'umbilical *cord*', 'spinal *cord*'. The musical or emotional term is *chord*, as in the '*chord* of C sharp', the 'lost *chord*', or 'His speech struck the right *chord*.'

corporal punishment: see capital punishment

correspondent, co-respondent

He is the Far East *correspondent* for the *Independent*. (= journalist, writer)

He was cited as *co-respondent* in the Duchess of Argyll's divorce proceedings. (= adulterous lover)

council, counsel

There is a monthly meeting of the town *council*. (= elected body)

Never take *counsel* from such an unreliable person. (= advice)

They were well *counselled* by the Citizens' Advice Bureau. (= advised)

course, coarse

'An eighteen-hole *course*', 'a *three-course* meal', 'a difficult *course* of study'; here *course* means a 'sequence or progression'.

'*Coarse* cloth', '*coarse* language', and '*coarse* fishing' means 'rough or basic'.

credible, creditable, credulous

His story is not quite *credible*. (= believable)

His exam result was very *creditable*. (= worthy of credit)

It was a trick to convince only the most *credulous*. (= gullible)

crevice, crevasse

The rock face was full of little *crevices* for footholds. (= cracks, gaps)

The glacier is broken up by several deep *crevasses*. (= large fissures)

criterion, criteria

Criterion is singular, *criteria* is plural. So it is wrong to say, 'He has only one *criteria*.'

currant, current

The *currant* is a small dried grape, and the black*currant* and red*currant* are berries. *Current* means (1) a steady flow, as in 'Swimming against the *current*' or an 'electric *current*'; (2) the present time, as in '*current* affairs/ events'.

deadly, deathly

His French classes are *deadly* dull. (= extremely)

Cyanide is a *deadly* poison. (= lethal)

Her face was *deathly* white. (= as white as in death)

decidedly, decisively

A person of *decidedly* anarchist opinions. (= emphatically)

The election results *decisively* settled the matter. (= conclusively)

deduce, deduct

What can we *deduce* from this evidence, Watson? (= conclude, infer)

Tax is *deducted* from your salary. (= taken away)

defective, deficient

The car's brake was found to be *defective*. (= faulty)

Old people are often *deficient* in vitamins. (= lacking, short of)

definite, definitive

I'll give you a *definite* answer tomorrow. (= certain, clear)

Richard Ellmann's is the *definitive* biography of James Joyce. (= ultimate, best)

defuse, diffuse

The bomb was *defused* by an army expert. (= neutralised)

A *diffused* glow of orange light hung over the darkened landscape. (= spread out)

delivery, deliverance

Delivery for a letter, a baby, a speech, etc. *Deliverance* from evil, danger, a fate
worse than death, etc.

delusion: see illusion

dependent, dependant

In British English, in the days when spelling was drilled, these spellings used to
cause endless heart-searching and dictionary-hunting. *Dependent* is the adjective and *dependant* the noun. Nowadays, there is a tendency to copy our
American cousins, drop the heart-searching – and use only the word *dependent*.

deprecate, depreciate

The whole village *deprecated* such a wanton act of hooliganism. (= deplored)

His investment is certain to *depreciate*. (= decline in value)

His comment was sensible. There is no need to *depreciate* it. (= disparage)

deprivation, depredation

It was an inner-city area suffering from multiple *deprivation*. (= poverty)

The *depredations* of the locusts have wiped out the crop. (= attacks)

derisive, derisory

'*Derisive* laughter' mocks something or someone. 'A *derisory* proposal' is one
which deserves derision.

desert, dessert

They were lost in the Sahara *desert*. (= dry region)

He promised never to *desert* her. (= leave)

He took strawberries and cream for *dessert*. (= pudding)

despatch, dispatch

Either spelling is acceptable.

detract, distract

Poor weather *detracted* from the success of the holiday. (= diminished)

Don't *distract* the driver. (= take the attention of)

device, devise

His office is full of labour-saving *devices* and contraptions. (= gadgets)

We have *devised* a new method of sending urgent messages. (= invented)

diffuse: see defuse

disc, disk

He is suffering from a slipped *disc*. (= the cartilage between spinal vertebrae)

Musical tapes and compact *discs* (= records)

Computer *disk*, floppy *disk* (= information store)

discreet, discrete

She watched the proceedings from a *discreet* distance. (= safe, cautious)

The company operates world-wide as a number of small, *discrete* units.
   (= autonomous, not overlapping)

disinterested, uninterested

I try to be a *disinterested* observer. (= objective)

She was totally *uninterested* in current events. (= without interest)

disoriented, disorientated

More or less interchangeable, with British English favouring the longer version
   and American favouring the shorter.

dominate, domineer

A church spire may *dominate* a townscape, a loquacious person may *dominate* a
   conversation, and a brand leader will *dominate* a certain market. A *domineer-
   ing* person is overbearing, and tries to control others at any price.

doubtful, dubious

The building's safety is *doubtful/dubious*. (= uncertain)

His business contacts are very *dubious*. (= shady, potentially dishonest)

draft (US), draught (UK)

A money *draft* (= order)

A *draft* outline/proposal (= preliminary)

Many *draft* dodgers were imprisoned. (= military conscription)

A howling *draught* (= current of air)

Draught beer (= from the barrel)

A *draughtsman* (= one who makes drawings)

dual, duel

Dual carriageway, *dual* purpose (= double)

A *duel* with swords, a verbal *duel* (= contest between two people)

dubious: see doubtful

dumbfounded: see astonished

dying, dyeing

Dying of hunger/old age, *dying* to see you, etc.

Indigo is used for *dyeing* cloth blue. (= colouring)

earthly, earthy

This *earthly* life (= worldly)

An *earthy* smell (= of the earth, unrefined)

eatable, edible

Eatable means merely fit to be eaten; while *edible* means suitable for eating, or
   able to be eaten.

These carrots are so dried up that they are hardly *eatable* – better buy some fresh
   ones. (= they won't contain much nourishment)

These mushrooms don't look *edible* to me. (= safe to eat)

effect: see affect

e.g., i.e.

Two common abbreviations which indicate that more information follows.

e.g. (Latin *exempli gratia*, 'for sake of an example') means 'for example'.

i.e. (Latin *id est*, 'that is') means that an explanation follows.

Reasonable expenses, *e.g.* train fares, meals away from home, will be reimbursed.
Crustaceans, *i.e.* sea creatures with legs and a hard shell, are the staple diet.

elder: see **older**

elusive: see **allusive**

emend: see **amend**

emigrant: see **immigrant**

eminent, imminent

An *eminent* physicist (= distinguished, famous)
An *imminent* attack (= about to happen)

emotional, emotive

She was in a state of physical and *emotional* exhaustion. (= psychological, mental)
Abortion is an *emotive* issue in Catholic countries. (= people are not objective about it)

enquiry, inquiry

He made a polite *enquiry* about my health. (= he asked after . . .)
The police have set up an *inquiry*. (= formal investigation)

ensure: see **assure**

equable, equitable

Britain has an *equable* climate. (= not extreme, without great variation)
We are looking for an *equitable* court decision. (= just, well balanced)

exasperate, exacerbate: see **aggravate**

exceed: see **accede**

except: see **accept**

exceptional, exceptionable

She is an *exceptional* teacher. (= of rare quality)
His *exceptionable* behaviour has ostracised him from society. (= objectionable)

exercise, exorcise

He's a fitness fanatic and takes lots of *exercise*. (= gymnastic training)
The ghost of the former owner of the house was *exorcised* by means of a special ceremony. (= expelled, eradicated)

exhausting, exhaustive

The climb to the summit was *exhausting*. (= very tiring)
The police conducted an *exhaustive* inquiry. (= comprehensive)

faint, feint

She fell down in a dead *faint*. (= collapse)
There was a *faint* smell of ether in the air. (= slight)
It was a contest of *feint* and counter-*feint*. (= dummy move)

farther: see **further**

fatal, fateful

Another *fatal* accident on the A74 (= deadly)
A *fateful* decision (= momentous)

fearful, fearsome

She is very *fearful* of the dark. (= frightened)
A *fearful* mess, a *fearful* argument (= very bad)
An angry bear is a *fearsome* beast. (= causes fear)

ferment: see **foment**

fiancé, fiancée

These words follow French spelling conventions, with *fiancé* the masculine and *fiancée* the feminine version.

fictional, fictitious

Sherlock Holmes and Dr Watson are a famous *fictional* pair. (= existing only in fiction)

He bought the weapon under a *fictitious* name. (= false, invented)

flare, flair

She has a really bad temper which *flares* up from time to time. (= erupts)

He has a *flair* for cooking. (= aptitude)

flaunt: see **flout**

fleshy, fleshly

A *fleshy* person, *fleshy* legs (= fat, plump)

Fleshly desires and pleasures (= carnal, of the flesh)

flounder, founder

The Government *flounders* from crisis to crisis. (= struggles)

The ship *foundered* on the rocky shore. (= broke up)

George Heriot, the *founder* of a famous school. (= person who founded)

flout, flaunt

Where the law is an ass, we must *flout* it. (= disregard)

She likes to *flaunt* her huge wedding ring. (= show off)

foment, ferment

She goes about *fomenting* distrust. (= stirring up)

The country is in a political *ferment*. (= upheaval)

forage, foray

He *foraged* in the kitchen for some food. (= rummaged about)

He went on a *foray* round the junk shops. (= excursion)

forceful, forcible

He was a *forceful*, competent leader. (= powerful)

There has been a *forcible* imposition of military control. (= by force)

forebear, forbear

His *forebears* are all from the west of Ireland. (= ancestors)

She will *forbear* to ask for financial support. (= forswear, abstain)

forever, for ever

She is *forever* interrupting the conversation. (= endlessly)

She has left him *for ever*. (= permanently)

foregone, forgone

The outcome of the election was said to be a *foregone* conclusion. (= obvious, inevitable)

She has *forgone* her holiday as a result of the fire. (= gone without)

formally, formerly

He was *formally* introduced to the Princess Royal. (= officially)

He dressed *formally* for the occasion. (= smartly)

St Petersburg was *formerly* called Leningrad. (= previously)

fortuitous, fortunate
We met *fortuitously* in George Street. (= by chance)
He made a *fortunate* escape from his captors. (= lucky)

fulfil, fulfill
Fulfil is British spelling, *fulfill* is American. The past tense of both versions is *fulfilled*.

further, farther
Further seems to be the norm nowadays, with *farther* confined to sentences specifying physical distance, like 'Glasgow is *farther* from London than it is from Dublin.' Thus: 'Until *further* notice' or '*Further* to your recent letter' or 'Any *further* questions?' or '*further* education'.

gamble, gambol
He *gambled* all his savings on that horse. (= bet)
The lambs *gambolled* about in the spring sunshine. (= skipped and jumped)

gaol: see jail

gipsy, gypsy
Both spellings are accepted.

gorilla, guerrilla
The *gorilla* is the largest of the apes.
The army was attacked by well-armed *guerrillas*. (= insurgents)

gourmand, gourmet
He was a famous *gourmand* and bon viveur. (= person who enjoys food and drink)
He was a *gourmet* of good cheeses. (= person who knows a lot about food and drink)

graceful, gracious
Graceful describes elegant physical movement, forms, shapes: as in 'a *graceful* colonnade', 'a *graceful* pas de bas'.
Gracious means kind, courteous, well mannered: as in '*gracious* living', 'ladylike and *gracious*', 'a *gracious* tribute'.

grey, gray
British spelling favours *grey*, while Americans prefer *gray*.

grisly, gristly, grizzly
A *grisly* murder (= nasty, gruesome)
A *gristly* lamb chop (= tough, full of gristle)
A *grizzly* infant (= crying, whingeing). Also a *grizzly* bear.

gypsy: see gipsy

hale, hail
Hale and hearty (= healthy)
Sleet and *hail* (= frozen rain)
Hail a hackney (= call a taxi)

handiwork, handwork
She stood back and admired her *handiwork*. (= skill, efforts)
Lace-making used to be a very labour-intensive form of *handwork*. (= work with the hands)

hanged, hung

The regular past tense of the verb *hang* is *hung*, as in 'He's *hung* up his coat and hat.' *Hanged* is used only in the context of an execution: 'You will be *hanged* by the neck until you are dead.'

hanger, hangar

Clothes are hung on a *hanger*. Planes are kept in a *hangar*.

hereditary, heredity

A *hereditary* illness, a *hereditary* title (= inherited; an adjective)

Your *heredity* is your genetic inheritance (= genetics; a noun)

histrionics: see hysterics

holy, holey, wholly

Holy books, *holy* scripture, *holy* Jesus (= sacred)

Holey socks, *holey* cheese (= full of holes)

Wholly innocent, *wholly* convincing (= entirely)

hoofs, hooves

Either plural spelling is acceptable.

horde, hoard

She was surrounded by *hordes* of shrieking children. (= multitudes)

A *hoard* of Viking treasure has been uncovered. (= secret collection)

hull, hulk

A ship's *hull* is its body; a ship's *hulk* is its dismantled or sunken frame.

human, humane

Human beings, the *human* race, the *human* body (= concerning people)

We wish to see a more *humane* and civilised society. (= decent, considerate)

hung: see hanged

hysterics, histrionics

She went into a fit of sobbing *hysterics*. (= an uncontrolled fit, in this case, of crying)

He's full of *histrionic* gestures. (= over-dramatic)

idle, idol

He sits there, bone *idle*, watching others work. (= lazy, useless)

The shrine was full of statues of strange *idols*. (= gods)

illegal, illicit

He was jailed for *illegal* possession of marijuana. (= forbidden by law)

His *illicit* association with a certain actress was well known. (= secret, not approved by society)

illegible: see unreadable

illusion, delusion

She had no *illusions* about his intentions. (= false ideas)

He suffers from *delusions* that the world is about to end. (= erroneous ideas)

immigrant, emigrant

An *immigrant* has come into a country, while an *emigrant* has gone out of it.

imminence, immanence, eminence

They sat by the shore, unaware of the *imminence* of disaster. (= something about to happen)

Even Dr Johnson was struck by the *immanence* of Iona's piety. (= inherent atmosphere)

The islanders were unaware that the visitor was a person of great *eminence*. (= celebrity)

immoral, amoral

An *immoral* person has bad or low moral standards, while an *amoral* person has no moral standards.

imply, infer

Her comment *implied* that he was stupid rather than lazy. (= hinted)

It is fair to *infer* that the car will not go if the engine is not switched on. (= deduce)

impractical, impracticable

He may be a brilliant academic, but he's completely *impractical* about the house. (= useless, not handy)

The idea was quite *impracticable*. (= impossible to achieve)

incredible, incredulous

In its day, running the four-minute mile was an *incredible* achievement. (= not believable)

He stood there with an *incredulous* expression on his face. (= disbelieving)

inflict: see afflict

infringe, impinge, impugn

I have no wish to *infringe* the rules of the game. (= break)

His work *impinges* heavily on his family life. (= overlaps into)

He is *impugning* my professional reputation. (= challenging)

ingenious, ingenuous

The film's plot was extremely *ingenious*, and the final scene came as a surprise to everyone. (= clever)

He made a frank and *ingenuous* apology for the error. (= obviously honest)

inimitable, inimical

He spoke in his own *inimitable* manner. (= not to be imitated)

The desert is *inimical* to most forms of life. (= unfavourable, hostile)

inquiry: see enquiry

insure: see assure

intense, intensive

Intense heat, *intense* effort, *intense* pain, *intense* excitement (= acute)

Intensive care, *intensive* agriculture, *intensive* study, *intensive* training (= thorough, rigorous)

inveigle, inveigh

She was *inveigled* into donating £20 to the charity. (= cajoled, persuaded)

People like to *inveigh* against the taxman. (= attack, rail against)

its, it's

The dog licked *its* paws. (= belonging to it)

It's a long way to Tipperary! (= It is)

jail, gaol

The first spelling is commoner, though either is acceptable in British English. Americans do not use the second spelling.

judgment, judgement

Either spelling is acceptable.

judicial, judicious

There is usually a *judicial* enquiry into financial scandals. (= legal)

The *judicious* use of EU investment grants has stimulated the local economy. (= careful)

knit, knitted

When *knitting* needles and wool are involved, the past tense is *knitted*, e.g. 'She *knitted* me a pair of socks.' In other contexts, *knit* is commoner, e.g. 'He *knit* his brows.' Past participles are similar, e.g. 'a *knitted* hat' but 'a *close-knit* community'.

leeward, windward

These words are opposites, *leeward* meaning in the lee of the wind, or sheltered from it; *windward* meaning exposed to the wind.

licence, license

Do you have an international driving *licence?* (noun)

A ship's captain is *licensed* to perform marriages and burials. (verb)

lie, lay

Three confusible verbs are *lie/lying/lay/lain* (intransitive), meaning to rest or stretch out in a horizontal position; *lie/lying/lied* (intransitive), meaning to tell untruths; and *lay/laying/laid* (transitive), meaning to put down, or prepare, or produce.

Come *lie* with me and be my love. (= sleep)

The body *lay* in state. (= was reposing)

The dog was *lying* stretched out on the hearth. (= resting)

Don't *lie* to me – I want the truth. (= tell untruths)

Please *lay* the table. (= set)

I wouldn't so much as *lay* a finger on you. (= put)

The shipyard is *laying off* a hundred riveters. (= sacking)

The goose that *laid* the golden eggs (= produced)

lighted, lit

Both past tense/participle forms are used, but *lit* is commoner as a verb, *lighted* as a participle in use as an adjective, e.g. 'We *lit* the bonfire'; 'a *lighted* match'.

liquidate, liquidise

He has *liquidated* his assets. (= made them liquid, or saleable)

Al Capone *liquidated* his opponents. (= eliminated, killed)

Liquidise the mixture in a blender. (= make it into a liquid)

liquor, liqueur

Liquor is any alcoholic drink. A *liqueur* is a sweet alcoholic drink taken after a meal as a digestif.

Popular *liqueurs* are Drambuie, Cointreau, Benedictine, and Kummel.

literal, literate, literary

I need a *literal* translation. (= word for word)

He was the first *literate* member of the family. (= able to read and write)

Paris in the 1920s was a base for many *literary* Americans. (= involved in literature)

livid, lurid

His expression was *livid* with rage. (= furious)

A *livid* bruise (= black and blue)

She wore a *lurid* pink and orange coat. (= garish)

He's full of *lurid* stories about his girlfriends. (= shocking)

loathe, loath, loth

He *loathes* the smell of cigarettes. (= hates)

He was *loath/loth* to sell his sports car. (= reluctant)

lose, loose

He tends to *lose* things rather easily. (= mislay; verb)

She has gone to the dentist about a *loose* tooth. (= wobbly; adjective)

lurid: see livid

luxuriant, luxurious

He was sporting a *luxuriant* moustache. (= abundant, growing vigorously)

We dined in a *luxurious* restaurant. (= expensive, comfortable)

madam, madame

Madam is the English spelling of this French word. *Madame* is the French spelling. English stresses the first syllable, French the second.

magic, magical

A *magic* wand, a *magic* carpet (= with magic qualities)

A *magical* experience, a *magical* visit (= delightful, enchanting)

malevolent, malignant

He spoke in *malevolent* tones. (= wishing someone ill)

The cancer was *malignant*. (= fatal, not medically controllable)

A witch with a *malignant* power (= able to do evil)

masterly, masterful

A *masterly* analysis, a *masterly* performance (= brilliant, excellent)

There was a *masterful* tone to his voice. (= authoritative, determined)

maybe, may be

Maybe I will and *maybe* I won't. (= perhaps)

The bus *may be* late.

medieval, mediaeval

The first spelling is commoner. It is standard in American English.

medium, media

A *medium* (from Latin *medius*) was something 'in the middle'. It soon came to mean an 'intermediary' or 'means of communication' between the earthly world and the spirit world. Nowadays we talk about 'the *media*' (plural of *medium*) when referring to the various means of mass communication, including the press, radio, television, etc.

melted, molten

Melted is the general form, both as verb and adjective. *Molten* is used only as an adjective, and only of substances which melt at very high temperatures: thus '*molten* lava' or '*molten* iron', but '*melted* chocolate'.

metal, mettle

Brass is a good-looking *metal*. (= hard mineral substance)

The new recruit was on his *mettle*. (= on the alert)

meter, metre

A measuring instrument (e.g. for parking, water, gas, etc., as well as a speedo-meter, thermometer, etc.) is a *meter*. A unit of length is a *metre*, thus *kilometre*, *centimetre*, etc. (unless you are American, in which case you spell it *kilometer*, *centimeter*, etc.). The poetic measure is also spelled *metre*.

militate, mitigate

The drought is *militating* against effective self-help farming initiatives. (= hindering)

The Government is endeavouring to *mitigate* the people's distress. (= alleviate)

misuse: see **abuse**

molten: see **melted**

moral, morale

The *moral* is clear: don't marry for money. (= lesson)

The victory gave a great boost to *morale*. (= feelings of confidence)

motive, motif

I question the Government's *motives*. (= reasons for action)

Her dress was blue with a white *motif*. (= pattern)

mucus, mucous

Mucus is the noun, *mucous* is the adjective.

naturist, naturalist

A *naturist* is a nudist, or a person who tries to go back to nature. A *naturalist* is a person who studies nature; zoologists, entomologists, ornithologists are all *naturalists*.

naval, navel

Hornblower was an eighteenth-century *naval* officer. (= in the Navy)

Some people are said to contemplate their *navels*. (= belly buttons)

nicety, niceness

Let's forget the *niceties* and get to the point. (= quibbles, finer details)

Her *niceness* smiled out of her face at you. (= pleasantness)

no one, no-one

The two-word version is preferable, but the hyphenated version is also common. The one-word version *noone* is to be avoided.

notable, noticeable

Robert the Bruce was a *notable* Scottish king. (= famous)

His right eye had a *noticeable* squint. (= conspicuous)

nutritional, nutritious

What is the *nutritional* value of peanut butter? (= dietary)

Honey is said to be highly *nutritious*. (= nourishing)

obsolete, obsolescent

The steam engine has long been *obsolete*. (= outmoded, out of use)

Nuclear weapons have reduced most other armaments to *obsolescence*. (= uselessness, i.e. they are becoming obsolete)

of, off

The grand old Duke *of* York

Keep *off* the grass.

official, officious

The prime minister's office will be putting out an *official* statement. (= formally authorised)

She's an *officious* old busybody. (= bossy, interfering)

older, elder

The adjective *old* has comparative and superlative *older/elder* and *oldest/eldest*, with *older* and *oldest* being the standard forms. *Elder* and *eldest* occur only within the family to describe seniority, e.g. 'an *elder* brother', and in certain specific usages, e.g. 'an *elder* statesman'.

onward, onwards

Onward is commoner nowadays. *Onwards* is almost confined to British English, and is used only as an adverb.

oral: see **aural**

ordinance, ordnance

There used to be various *ordinances* prohibiting Sunday trading. (= regulations)

Weapons and other *ordnance* were issued to soldiers. (= military supplies)

The *Ordnance* Survey is the British agency that is charged with the production of detailed maps of the country.

outdoor, outdoors

Outdoor is the adjective, *outdoors* is the adverb.

outward, outwards

Outward is the adjective, *outwards* is the adverb.

partly, partially, partiality

He is by background *partly* French, *partly* American. (= not completely)

A *partially* clothed body, a *partially* blind person (= semi-)

He spoke very *partially* in our favour. (= in a biassed way)

He has a well-known *partiality* for dry sherry. (= liking)

passed, past

We *passed* you in the street. Have you *passed* the exam?

It's five *past* two. She has a colourful *past*.

Many years *passed*. (= many years went by)

Many years *past* (= many years ago)

patent, patient

He's a quack, and talks a lot of *patent* nonsense. (= manifest, obvious)

Sorry to keep you – you've been very *patient*. (= forbearing, calm)

perceptive, percipient, perspicuous, perspicacious

A *perceptive* remark, a *perceptive* biography (= observant)

She was an unusually *percipient* person who could pick up all sorts of vibrations in a gathering, well outside the normal range of the senses. (= almost telepathic)

The judge gave a clear and *perspicuous* summing-up of the case.

(= precise, comprehensible)

A *perspicacious* student of human foibles would notice this trait in her make-up.
(= keenly observant)

perfunctory, peremptory

We exchanged a *perfunctory* greeting in the foyer. (= cursory, casual)

I was shown out in a most *peremptory* manner. (= imperious, brusque)

perpetuate, perpetrate

People who fail to learn from history *perpetuate* its mistakes. (= preserve and/or repeat)

Terrorist organisations sometimes *perpetrate* appalling crimes. (= commit)

persistence, perseverance, pertinacity

The *persistence* of her illness was a measure of its seriousness. (= continuation)

He showed great *persistence* in the dogged pursuit of his case. (= determination)

Only the *perseverance* of the crew saved the ship. (= effort against the odds)

The battle was waged with courage and *pertinacity*. (= doggedness)

perspective: see prospective

perspicuous, perspicacious: see perceptive

pertinacity: see persistence

phenomenon, phenomena

Phenomenon is singular, *phenomena* is plural.

pigeon, pidgin

The well-fed *pigeons* of Trafalgar Square (= birds)

The Lagos traders speak an interesting *pidgin*. (= mixture of colloquial languages)

plane, plain

He smoothed the surface of the wood with his *plane*. (= a tool)

The *plane* has landed. (= aircraft)

The rain in Spain falls mainly in the *plain*. (= flat ground)

She is a *plain* Jane. (= lacking in beauty)

plate, plait

A *plate* of food, a photographic *plate*, a metal *plate* (= dish or slide)

She wore her hair in two long *plaits*. (= pigtails)

poignant: see pungent

politic, political

His decision was not *politic* and offended many. (= wise)

I am not a very *political* animal. (= interested in politics)

pour, pore

The rain *pours* down, and tea is *poured*. (= flows)

He *pored* over the document. (= studied carefully)

The skin is full of tiny *pores*. (= holes)

practical, practicable

She's very *practical* and methodical. (= handy, businesslike)

Pollution has been eliminated as far as is *practicable*. (= feasible)

practice, practise

A medical *practice;* a quaint Japanese *practice* (noun)

Hamish *practises* his bagpipes every evening. (verb)

pray, prey

The congregation *prayed* for peace. (= asked God for)

The kestrel is a bird of *prey*. (= predator)

precede: see proceed

precipitate, precipitous

We tried to avoid any *precipitate* decisions. (= abrupt, hasty)

There was a *precipitous* drop of a thousand feet to the sea. (= sheer, like a precipice)

predict, predicate

I *predict* a win for Arsenal. (= prophesy, foresee)

The plan is *predicated* on these assumptions. (= based on)

prescribe, proscribe

The doctor has *prescribed* rest. (= ordered, recommended)

He has *proscribed* physical exertion. (= banned, forbidden)

presumptive, presumptuous

The *presumptive* diagnosis looks bad. (= probable)

It is *presumptuous* to intercede between spouses. (= forward)

principle, principal

Dishonesty is against his *principles*. (noun = code of conduct)

Tourism is one of our *principal* industries. (adjective = main)

The college *principal* is called Mr Nackyball. (noun = head)

proceed, precede

He *proceeded* to ask lots of questions. (= went on)

Let us go back to the *preceding* chapter. (= the one before, previous)

prodigy, protégé

Mozart was one of the best-known child *prodigies*. (= marvels)

Leicester was one of Queen Elizabeth's *protégés*. (= acolytes)

program, programme

The former is the US spelling, the latter is British English. The one exception, where the American spelling is always used in British English, is 'computer *program*' and its various 'computerspeak' spin-offs.

prophecy, prophesy

Noah knew the *prophecy* of the Flood. (noun)

People are forever *prophesying* the end of the world. (verb)

proscribe: see prescribe

prospective, perspective

He is a *prospective* Member of Parliament. (= would-be)

You can look at the problem from a number of *perspectives*. (= points of view, positions)

prostrate, prostate

He lay *prostrate* before her. (= stretched flat on the ground, helpless)

The *prostate* gland is an organ beside the male bladder.

protagonist: see antagonist

protégé: see prodigy

psychology, psychiatry

Psychology is the scientific study of the mind and of human behaviour.

Psychiatry is the branch of medicine which studies and treats mental disorders.

pungent, poignant

A *pungent* smell of bonfires filled the autumn air. (= sharp)

She gave a *poignant* description of her own deprived childhood. (= moving)

purposely, purposefully

She *purposely* tried to antagonise him. (= intentionally)

He walked *purposefully* towards the gate. (= resolutely)

rebound, re-bound

He hit the ball on the *rebound*. (= when it bounced back)

The family Bible was *re-bound*. (= given a new binding)

recipe, receipt

He had a marvellous *recipe* for fruit loaf. (= list of ingredients)

I got a *receipt* for each purchase. (= printed record)

recount, re-count

He *recounted* his story with humour. (= told)

The vote was so close that there had to be a *re-count*. (= further count)

recover, re-cover

She *recovered* very well from her illness. (= got better)

She stumbled but *recovered* herself. (= regained her balance)

She has *re-covered* the armchair beautifully. (= put on a new cover)

regal, royal

Burlington Bertie's bearing was so *regal* that neighbours called him His Majesty.
 (= splendid, king-like)

She may be a member of the *royal* family, but her conduct is less than *regal*.

reign, rein

Queen Victoria's glorious *reign* (= rule)

Give your horse free *rein*. (= straps for controlling a horse)

remittance, remission

Your *remittance* is now overdue. (= payment)

The *remission* of sins, of a jail sentence, of an illness (= forgiveness, reduction)

repetitive, repetitious

His job is routine, *repetitive*, mechanical. (= characterised by repetition)

She has written a very *repetitious* account of her childhood. (= it contains unnecessary repetitions)

reversal, reversion

He suffered *reversal* after *reversal*. (= setback)

. . . a *reversion* to his former barbarous ways (= return)

review, revue

A *review* of progress, a *review* of the troops, a salary *review*, a book *review* (= critical study, assessment, inspection)

A Christmas *revue* (= show)

role, roll

What was the *role* of the prime minister in the affair? (= part)

Four buttered *rolls*, a *roll* of wallpaper, a *roll* of honour, a drum *roll*

royal: see **regal**

saccharin, saccharine

I've no sugar but can offer you a *saccharin*. (= sugar substitute)

He flashed me a *saccharine* smile. (= artificially sweet, less than sincere)

sarcastic, sardonic

Sarcastic remarks tend to be positively cutting or sneering in intention, whereas a *sardonic* remark is more laid back and generally scornful.

sceptic, septic

Doubting Thomas was the original *sceptic*. (= person with lots of doubts)

Wounds are cleaned to prevent them turning *septic*. (= infected)

seasonal, seasonable

Seasonal greetings are greetings of the season. *Seasonable* weather is the sort of weather to be expected at a certain time of year.

sensitivity, sensibility

Calling *sensitivity* merely sense, Jane Austen wrote a whole novel to articulate the differences between these two words. By her book, *sensitivity* is the better characteristic, because it means 'good judgment, awareness of others' feelings, and respect for them'. *Sensibility*, on the other hand, is a slightly more public characteristic, implying an emotional delicacy which is impressionable and perhaps too easily – or too visibly – affected.

sentiment, sentimentality

He expressed little *sentiment* or emotion. (= feeling)

The whole affair was a display of mawkish and wallowing *sentimentality* whipped up by the popular press. (= emotionalism)

septic: see **sceptic**

serial: see **cereal**

sew, sow

She *sewed* a lace border round the wrists and hem. (= stitched)

The farmer *sowed* a crop of early grass. (= planted)

singing, singeing

They are *singing* their hearts out. (= making vocal music)

Drake is remembered for *singeing* the Spanish king's beard. (= scorching)

social, sociable

I've met him at *social* and business functions. (= communal)

She's an outgoing and *sociable* type. (= friendly)

sometime, some time

Come up and see me *sometime*. (= at some future but unspecified period)

I may be gone for *some time*. (= a little while)

speciality, specialty

The first spelling is British English, the second is American.

stalactite, stalagmite

Icicle-shaped formations in limestone caves produced by a mixture of dripping water and lime. *Stalactites* hang down from the ceiling, and *stalagmites* grow up from the ground. (Remember: there is a *c* in *stalactite* and in 'ceiling', and there is a *g* in *stalagmite* and in 'ground'.)

stationary, stationery

Do not leave the bus until it is *stationary*. (= not moving)

He buys his office *stationery* from Smith's store. (= paper, envelopes, etc.)

story, storey

Tell me a scary *story*. (= fictional tale)

A multi-*storey* car park (= floors or levels of a building)

straight, strait

The car came *straight* at me. (= directly)

Your tie is not *straight*. (= hanging in a line)

The organisation is in desperate financial *straits*. (= circumstances)

The *straits* of Gibraltar (= narrow sea)

Note spellings of *strait*jacket and *strait*laced.

straightened, straitened

He *straightened* his tie. (= made it straight)

They live in very *straitened* circumstances. (= impoverished, restricted)

struck, stricken

The verb *strike* has two past participles. *Struck* is the general term, as in 'The clock *struck* three' or 'The car was *struck* by lightning.' *Stricken* is confined to sickness and distress, as in 'panic-*stricken*', 'poverty-*stricken*', '*stricken* with fever', etc.

suit, suite

You wear a dinner *suit*, business *suit*, etc. (= matching jacket and trousers)

A *suite* is a set of furniture, or rooms, or a piece of music with a set of movements: a dining-room *suite*, a honeymoon *suite*, Bach's *Suite* and Variations.

swap, swop

Either spelling is acceptable.

swatted, swotted

He *swatted* the flies on the windowpane. (= hit at and squashed)

She *swotted* hard for her final exam. (= studied)

temerity, timidity

He had the *temerity* to ask for a pay rise. (= boldness)

His social *timidity* means he is terrified of company. (= shyness)

tense, terse

He looks worried and *tense* and taut. (= edgy, anxious)

His poems are *terse* little word pictures. (= spare, brief)

their, there, they're

The children were joined by *their* parents. (= belonging to them)

We went *there* on the way home. (= to that place)

They're on their way. (= they are)

theirs, there's
The blue towels are *theirs*, not ours. (= belonging to them)
There's not much time. (= there is)
timidity: see temerity
to, too, two
Oh, *to* be in England . . . (infinitive)
Push the door *to*. (adverb = 'shut')
He's gone *to* Paris. (preposition, 'in the direction of')
Try some vegetables *too*. (= also)
That's not *too* bad. (= very)
Two eyes can see better than one. (= number 2)
tortuous, torturous
The old city was a maze of narrow, *tortuous* alleys. (= winding)
The prisoners were subjected to *torturous* conditions. (= painful)
troop, troupe
A *troop* of mounted police, cavalry, artillery, etc. (= armed force)
A *troupe* of entertainers, acrobats, performers, trained animals (= company)
towards, toward
Both forms are correct, with British English favouring the -*s* ending and American
    English favouring the ending without -*s*.
two: see to
unaware, unawares
He was *unaware* of the danger. (adjective)
The bandit crept up on them *unawares*. (adverb)
unexceptional, unexceptionable
He is the author of several *unexceptional* novels. (= not very remarkable or interesting)
His behaviour was quite *unexceptionable*. (= blameless, i.e. there was nothing
    about his behaviour to which one could have taken exception)
uninterested: see disinterested
unreadable, illegible
The book was so verbose it was virtually *unreadable*. (= too wordily dull to read)
My doctor's handwriting is almost *illegible*. (= indecipherable)
unwanted, unwonted
She feels very unloved and *unwanted*. (= not wanted)
He suffered a sudden, *unwonted* attack of panic. (= unaccustomed, untypical)
urban, urbane
Urban unemployment is a major problem. (= in cities)
He is the soul of *urbanity* and wit. (= sophistication)
venial, venal
The priest heard the confession of a variety of *venial* sins. (= trivial, forgivable)
Many local politicians are *venal* and unscrupulous. (= open to bribes)
vicious, viscous
The shark can be a *vicious* killer. (= brutal)
The oil slick left a *viscous* black mess along the shoreline. (= glutinous, thick and sticky)

wave, waive, waver

They *waved* goodbye at the station. (= gestured with the hand)

... splashing about in the *waves* by the shore (= ripples of sea)

The formal application procedures were *waived*. (= not enforced)

Britannia rules the *waves* ... and often *waives* the rules.

His faith has never *wavered*. (= faltered, hesitated)

whether, weather

I wonder *whether* it will rain. (= if)

The *weather* was very hot and humid. (= climate)

whose, who's

He was a man *whose* main hobby was music.

Who's been eating my porridge? (= who has)

wholly: see **holy**

windward: see **leeward**

wright, write

A *wright* is a craftsman (e.g. *wheelwright*, *shipwright*). The chief confusable between these two spellings is the word *playwright*, the name for a craftsman who makes plays. Many people make the mistake of spelling it 'playwrite', thinking of a *writer* rather than a craftsman.

yoke, yolk

The colonial *yoke* was lifted in the 1960s. (= burden)

The *yolk* of an egg (= the yellow part)

Commonly misspelled words

abbreviate

abscess

abundance

abyss, abysmal

accelerate

accept, acceptable

access, accessible

accident, accidental

accommodation

accompany, accompaniment

accumulate

achieve, achievement

acknowledge

acquaintance

acquiesce

acquire, acquisition

acquit

actual

address

adequately

adieu

adjacent

admission, admittance

adolescent

advantageous

advertisement

advice (noun)

advise (verb), advisable

aerial

affect

aggravate
aggregate
aggressive
agreeable
aisle
alcohol
allege, allegation
allocate
allotted
almighty

alms
already
altar
alter
altogether
amateur
amount
analyse, analysis
ancillary
anecdote

ankle
annihilate
Antarctic
anticipate
anxious, anxiety
apology, apologise
apostle, apostolic
appal, appalling
apparatus
apparently

appearance
appendix
appreciate
approach
appropriate
approximate
arctic
argument
arrangement
ascend, ascent

aspirin
assassinate
associate, association
asthma
atheist
athlete, athletic
atmosphere
attempt
attendance, attendant
attitude

audible
audience
author
authority
autumn, autumnal
auxiliary
available
aviation, aviator
awkward
bachelor

bailiff
ballet
balloon
bankrupt
banjo, banjoes
bargain
basically
battalion
bayonet
bazaar

beauty, beautiful
becoming
begin, beginning
believe, belief
benefit, benefiting, benefited
besiege
bicycle
bigger, biggest
biscuit
bizarre

borough, burgh
boundary
bouquet
breath (noun), breathe (verb)
brief
brilliant
Britain
buccaneer
buffet
bulletin

buoyant
bureau
burglar, burglary
bury, burial
business
calendar
calibre
camouflage
campaign
canoe

career
careful
caricature
carriage
cashier
catarrh
catechism
category, categorical
caterpillar
caustic

cavalier
cedar
ceiling
cemetery
centre
challenge
champagne
changeable
chaos
character, characteristic

chasm
chassis
chauffeur
chocolate
choir
chorus, choral
Christian
chronic
cigarette
circuit

cite, citation
cocoa
collaborate
colleague
college
colonel
colonnade
colour, colourful
column
commemorate

commercial
commission, commissioner
committee, committed
comparative, comparison
compatible
competent
computer
concede, concession
conceit
conceivable

concentrate
concern
condemn
confectioner, confectionery
connoisseur
connotation
conscience, conscientious
conscious
consensus
consistent, consistency

conspiracy
contemporary
continuous
controlled
controversy
convenient, convenience
coroner
corps
corpse
correlate

correspondence
corroborate
council, councillor
counsel, counsellor
counterfeit
coupon
courteous, courtesy
criticism, critical
cruel
cupboard

curious, curiosity
curtain
cynic, cynicism
dairy
debris
debt, debtor
deceive, deceit
decision
defence, defensive
definite

degradation
democracy
dependent
depot
descend, descendant
describe, description
design
despair, desperately
detach
develop, developed

device (noun), devise (verb)
diaphragm
diarrhoea
diary
different, difference
difficult
digestible
dilapidated
dilemma
dining

diphtheria
diphthong
disappear
disappoint
disastrous
discern
disciple, discipline
disease
disillusioned
dissatisfied

dissolve
dominant
donor
dough
duly
dungeon
dynamo, dynamos
dysentery
earnest
eccentric

eclipse
ecstasy
eczema
edible
eerie
efficient
eight, eighth
eliminate
embarrass, embarrassment
embezzle

emperor
emphasise
encyclopedia
endeavour
enough
enthusiasm, enthusiastic
entrance
envelope (noun), envelop (verb)
environment
equipped

estuary
etiquette
exaggerate
exceed, excessive
excellent
except
excite, excitement
excusable
exercise
exhaust

exhibition
exhilarating
existence
expense
experience
experiment
extraordinary
fallacy
family
fantasy

fascinate
fashion
fatigue
favour, favourite
feasible
February
fibre
field
finance, financial
focus

forcible
foreign
fortunately
forty
four, fourth
fourteen
freight
friend
fulfil, fulfilled
fundamental

gaiety
gallop, galloping
gauge
genius
gigantic
gnat
gnaw
government
grammar
grieve, grief, grievous

grotesque
guarantee
guard
guide, guidance
guitar
haemorrhage
handkerchief
handled
happen
happiness

harass
hearse
heaven
heifer
height
heinous
heir, heiress
heretic
hero, heroes, heroic
hiccup

hindrance
hippopotamus
hoe, hoeing
honour, honourable
hopeful, hoping
humour, humorous
hydraulic
hygiene
hymn
hypocrite

icicle
ignorant, ignorance
illegible
illiterate
imaginary
immediately
impair
impertinence, impertinent
importance, important
incidentally

indefinitely
independence, independent
indispensable
inevitable
influenza
ingenious
ingredient
initiative
innocence
inoculate

inseparable
install, installation, instalment
instinct
intelligent
intention
interest
interference
interpretation
interrupt
irrelevant

irreparable
irresistible
irritate
island, islet
isosceles
jealous, jealousy
jeopardy
jewellery
jubilee
juice, juicy

keenness
kernel
khaki
kiln
knowledge, knowledgeable
knuckle
laboratory
laborious
labour
labyrinth

ladle
laugh, laughter
laundry
leisure
lettuce
liaison
library
licence (noun), license (verb)
lieutenant
lightning (thunder and)

liquor
listen, listener
literary
lively
luscious
mackerel
magnificent
maintain, maintenance
maize
malicious

manageable
manifesto, manifestos
manoeuvre
mantelpiece
marriage, marriageable
martyr
marvellous
matinee
meant
measles

mechanic, mechanical
medicine
medieval
Mediterranean
melancholy
messenger
mileage
miniature
minuscule
miscellaneous

mischief, mischievous
mistletoe
monastery
mortgage
mosque
mosquito
motor
motto, mottoes
moustache
move, movable

muscles
myrrh
mystery, mysterious
naive
necessary
negligent
neigh
neighbour
niece
ninety

ninth
no one
note, notable
notice, noticeable
nuisance
occasion, occasional
occur, occurrence
offered
omit, omission
operate, operator

opponent
opportunity
opposite
ordinary, ordinarily
pageant
pamphlet
paraffin
parallel, paralleled
paralysis, paralytic
parcel

parliament
patience, patient
pavilion
peace
pencil
perceive
perennial
permanent, permanence
permissible
persecute

persistent
personal
personnel
persuade, persuasion
pharmacy, pharmaceutical
phenomenon, phenomenal
phlegm, phlegmatic
photo, photos
physical
physician

physique
piano, pianos
picnic, picnicking
picturesque
piece
pigeon
plague
plateau
playwright
pleasure, pleasant, pleasurable

plough
plumber
pneumatic
pneumonia
poisonous
pomegranate
Portuguese
possess, possession
potato, potatoes
practice (noun), practise (verb)

precede
prefer, preferred
prejudice
preliminary
prevent, preventable
privilege
proceed
profess, professor
programme (unless computer
    program)
pronounce, pronunciation

propaganda
propeller
prosecute, prosecutor
psalm
psychology
punctual, punctuality
puncture
pursue, pursuit
quarrel, quarrelled
quay

queue
quiet
quite
radius
raspberry
realise
really
realm
rebel, rebellion
receipt

receive, receiving
recipe
recognise
recommend
refer, referring, referral, referee
refrigerator
reign
rein
relative
relieve, relief

reminisce, reminiscence
rendezvous
represent
reservoir
resign, resignation
resistance
responsible
restaurant, restaurateur
rheumatism
rhinoceros
rhododendron

rhythm, rhyme
rogue
sabre
sacrifice
sacrilegious
sanctify, sanctity
satellite
satisfy
sauce, saucy

scenery
sceptre
schism
science
sculptor, sculpture
scythe
secondary
secret, secrecy
secretary
seize, seizure

sentence
separate
sepulchre
sergeant
several
Shakespeare
shepherd
shield
shining
shrewd

siege
sieve
sign, signal
significant
silhouette
sincerely
singe, singeing
skilful
social
solemn, solemnity

solicitor
soliloquy
solo, solos
sombre
sorcery, sorcerer
sovereign
spasm
spectacle
spectre, spectral
sphere, spherical

sponsor
stabilise
stalk
stationary (not moving)
stationery (paper, pens, etc.)
statistics
strategy, strategic
strength
stretch
substantial

subtle, subtlety, subtly
succeed, success
sufficient
suite
summary, summarise
superintendent
supervisor
suppose
suppress
surgeon

surprise
surveyor
susceptible
suspense
sustain, sustenance
syllable
syllabus
symbol
symmetry
synagogue

synonym
syringe
tariff
tarpaulin
technical
teetotal, teetotaller
temperament
temperature
temporary
tendency

theatre, theatrical
thief, thieves
thigh
thorough
thought
through
tie, tying
tincture
tobacco
toboggan, tobogganing

tomato, tomatoes
tongue
tough
tragedy, tragic
transfer, transferred
tremendous
trophy
trousers
truly
tuberculosis

twelfth
typhoid
tyranny, tyrannical
umbrella
unconscious
undoubtedly
unique
unnecessary
until
usury, usurer

vacuum
value, valuable
vault
vegetable
vehicle
veil
vein
vengeance
veterinary
vicious

victuals
vigour, vigorous
villain
virtually
viscount
visible
warrant
weather
Wednesday
weight

weir
weird
wharf
whether
wholly
wield
wilful
withhold, withheld
woollen
wrestle, wrestling

xenophobe
xylophone
yacht
yield
yoke (bond or link)
yolk (of egg)
yours
zephyr
zinc
zoology

Seven

Check-up pages

This selection of exercises should not be taken too seriously. But I believe many readers will welcome the opportunity to make a mechanical check of their language and punctuation skills. If a particular exercise seems particularly difficult, refer back to the relevant earlier section of the book. I take it for granted that most readers will use a good dictionary, where most of the answers may be verified. A set of answer pages follows this section of the book. See pp. 227–38.

1 Number

Change all the **singulars** into **plurals**:

1. I heard the noise in the tree.
2. The ship has struck a rock.
3. The lady's hat was on the peg.
4. The wolf is eating the rabbit.
5. The child ran to the window to see the fox.
6. The thief stole a valuable painting.
7. I kept the rabbit in a cage.
8. The sailor is swimming to his ship.
9. A cat – or a mouse – may look at a king.
10. I took a knife and fork.

2 Verbs

Underline all the **verb phrases** in these sentences:

1. Good King Wenceslas looked out/On the feast of Stephen.
2. John is going home tomorrow.
3. The doctor should have spoken to you.

4. The plane will be landing around ten o'clock.
5. The crew have been safely rescued by a helicopter.
6. Come and see – the job is almost finished.
7. The supermarket was crowded with Christmas shoppers.
8. The sun has risen to its zenith.
9. Drink this medicine.
10. They fought the dogs, and killed the cats, and bit the babies in the cradles.

3 Phrasal verbs

Use suitable verbs from the following list to fill in the **phrasal verbs** in these sentences:

hang, break (used twice), *get, turn* (used twice), *call, give, check, keep* (used twice)

1. He _____ up angrily halfway through the phone call.
2. Some people seem to _____ away with murder.
3. Under prolonged interrogation, she _____ down in tears.
4. He _____ up on Monday and was offered a job.
5. The military police were _____ in to _____ up the demonstration.
6. She found it difficult to _____ up smoking.
7. Conference delegates have to _____ in at this desk.
8. Because of ill-health, he has had to _____ down an excellent job.
9. My neighbour _____ on working into her late 70s
10. She _____ at her piano practice and became a famous pianist.

4 Prepositions

Fill in the **prepositions** in these sentences:

1. He's not accustomed _____ criticism.
2. Are you in charge _____ these dogs?
3. She's too clever _____ me.
4. The team is confident _____ victory.
5. What is their reaction _____ the plan?
6. Why are you talking _____ a whisper?
7. He is a native _____ Birmingham.
8. Please just glance _____ this letter.
9. Books are _____ sale _____ the basement
10. You don't approve _____ him, _____ other words.

5 Parts of speech

What **parts of speech** are the underlined words or phrases?

1. These buns are <u>lovely</u>.
2. Who <u>rang</u> the bell?

3. He's <u>quite</u> a bright child.
4. She <u>leaves</u> by the six o'clock train.
5. He looked <u>beyond</u> the trees.
6. The child <u>seems</u> hungry.
7. She complained, <u>but</u> I ignored her.
8. You ought to consider the matter <u>seriously</u>.
9. <u>It</u> is going to rain.
10. I've got a red car and Fred's got a blue <u>one</u>.
11. The <u>professor</u> will see you now.
12. The choir sang <u>beautifully</u>.
13. <u>Dear me</u> – what has happened to you?
14. The beast in question is <u>an extremely fierce dog</u>.
15. Baghdad, <u>capital of Iraq</u>, has again been under heavy fire.
16. I can see <u>something</u> in the distance.
17. I don't think he'll <u>get away with</u> it.
18. That's quite sensible, <u>isn't it</u>?
19. He walked <u>all the way</u> to the station.
20. He <u>came round</u> two hours after the operation.
21. A dinner <u>is being organised</u> in his honour.
22. He's <u>deliriously happy</u> with the result.
23. They live in a cottage <u>beside the beach</u>.
24. He's <u>been brought up</u> by an uncle.
25. He's eaten the lot. I have <u>nothing</u>.
26. She'll be with us <u>during November</u>.
27. The Taj Mahal is the <u>most beautiful</u> building in the world.
28. Nobody <u>ever</u> agrees with him.
29. My sister has written <u>me</u> a long letter.
30. Hydrogen <u>is mixed</u> with oxygen.

6 Phrases, clauses and sentences

Which are **phrases** and which are **sentences**?

1. A black and white cat.
2. That's quite all right.
3. Once upon a time.
4. Up the road and into the trees.
5. There's nothing wrong.
6. I enjoy a good film.
7. Fish and chips for tea.
8. Not on your life.
9. It's a funny old world.
10. Not in front of the children.

Here are some main **clauses**. Add a second **clause** to each to complete the sentence:

11. I went out into the snow _____.
12. _____ the dog will bark.
13. The cat's been sick _____.
14. Last week I painted the front door _____.
15. _____ the birds all flew away.
16. Lie down on that sofa _____.
17. _____ we got chips on the way home.
18. _____ the gerbil hid in a corner of its cage.
19. The elephants appeared suddenly out of the trees _____.
20. _____ Emma is no good at swimming.

Make these pairs of sentences into one **compound sentence**. Use **coordinating conjunctions** like *and* or *but* or *so*:

21. I like chips best. My brother likes pasta.
22. The rain came on. I put up my umbrella.
23. I offered a small donation. The secretary thanked me for it.
24. Mary went by air. The flight was delayed.
25. The ice cream looks nice. The trifle looks less than fresh.
26. They knew it was a long trip. They ate a good breakfast.
27. There was a loud peal of thunder. The children were frightened.
28. She caught a large salmon. She took it home for tea.
29. The taxi was summoned. Nobody left the party.
30. The college boiler broke down. The students were sent home.

Make these pairs of sentences into one **complex sentence**. Use **subordinating conjunctions** like *who, which, when, while, whereas, if, although, because*, etc. (The pairs can be moved around.)

31. I was angry with George. George was late.
32. How can you hear me? You're not even listening.
33. The boy wore a black tracksuit. He sat on my left.
34. I arrived. You were out.
35. I can't go. It's too expensive.
36. The dog barked. He heard a noise.
37. My brother likes pasta. I like chips.
38. She waited downstairs. I got ready hurriedly.
39. The explosive was found by a security man. It was in a plastic bag.
40. She looked very edgy and worried. Her companion was quite inoffensive.

Here are some **subordinate** and **coordinating clauses**. Add a good **main clause** to complete the sentences:

41. If you go down in the woods today _____
42. Although it was snowing _____
43. When Sleeping Beauty pricked her finger _____
44. While Goldilocks was fast asleep _____

45. Whenever the bell rang _____
46. _____ because I don't feel very well.
47. _____ and I go to bed.
48. _____ but that's the way the cookie crumbles.
49. Unless there's a marked improvement in his conduct _____
50. _____ and then we should see some results.

Underline the **main clauses** in these sentences:

51. Give him some more money, whatever he wants it for.
52. Show me the photos next time you visit me.
53. It's five years since we first met.
54. Suddenly I understood what he meant.
55. I have a dog which I'm very fond of.
56. She lives in Reading and works in London.
57. Sally's gone to Edinburgh but Andrew's gone to Glasgow.
58. When he arrived safe and sound, we were all relieved.
59. If you take the road that turns right at the traffic lights, you'll see a sign-post that will direct you.
60. I was more interested in watching the game and in listening to the commentary than either of my companions seemed to be.

7 Word formation

7.1 Form **nouns** from these (e.g. *able, ability*):

able admire allow anxious arrive beg behave choose civilise create cruel describe enjoy exhaust false famous fierce fragrant grow hate holy injure invite lazy live lose mission move oppose please prosper punish real remember revive secure see serve sick simple speak strong think warm weary wide worthy young

7.2 Form **adjectives** from these (e.g. *accident, accidental*):

accident affection anger attract Bible Britain child continent courage craft critic custom destroy disaster duty exceed faith fashion favour forget giant grace height inform introduce law love meddle metal music neglect north occasion parent pity pride quarrel reason silk star success thirst thought tire union victory voice water wood youth

7.3 Form **verbs** from these (e.g. *beauty, beautify*):

beauty circle civil courage critic dark false fat fertile full glass grief joy large long magnet peril pure rich sharp simple solution speech success trial

7.4 Form **adverbs** from these (e.g. *able, ably*):

able bright courage critic destroy exhaust heavy hero joy just lazy ready resent succeed typical vain weary wise worthy wretch

7.5 Form **compound words** from these (e.g. *ache, headache*):

ache back berry black book cloth day door foot grand heart hedge house life man mill moon news night piece post rain sea school snow sun table water witch work

7.6 Underline the **prefixes** in these words (*e.g. amphitheatre*). Then consult your dictionary and try to say what the words mean, with and without their prefixes:

amphitheatre antibiotic archangel bespectacled biography chronometer counterattack deactivate democrat disconnect downsize ecosystem equivocal forgo hypermarket hypodermic megalopolis metamorphosis millipede misjudge parasol perimeter polygon postdate submarine surcharge surname teleprinter tomorrow unclear unicycle upstream

7.7 Underline the **suffixes** in these words (e.g. *admirable*). Then consult your dictionary and try to say what the words mean, with and without their suffixes:

admirable assistant baker Brazilian bushcraft computerese consultancy cookery damsel digestible dutiful farmhand fortunate girlish gossipmonger government hostess ignition interviewee Japanese kibbutznik letterhead machinery Marxism milkman minority modular narrator notify officialdom parliamentarian piracy privateer singer Spanish stationary threefold washable witchcraft workaholic youngster

8 Figures of speech

Complete these **doubles**:

1. To put on airs and _____
2. Everything is cut and _____
3. They fought tooth and _____
4. To be worn only on high days and _____
5. Membership is open to all and _____
6. The pros and _____ of the situation
7. The garden has gone to rack and _____
8. A danger to life and _____
9. He is at his mother's beck and _____
10. We strove for this outcome might and _____

Complete these **proverbs**:

11. Set a thief _____
12. When the cat's away _____
13. Too many cooks _____
14. One man's meat _____

15. Little children should be seen _____
16. Discretion is the better _____
17. Birds of a feather _____
18. A rolling stone _____
19. Every dog _____
20. Faint heart _____

Complete these contrasting **idioms**:

21. When the wolf attacked them, Steven _____ heels but Andrew _____ ground.
22. If you do that, it will be a feather _____ rather than a blot _____
23. John was offered a promotion and I advised him to strike _____ hot, and not _____ grass _____
24. Sally finds most maths problems plain _____ but Jane tends to find anything like that a very _____ nut _____
25. In a crisis, Dorothy will take her courage _____ hands, but Ann will get cold _____

9 Confusibles

Supply the correct words:

9.1 *practice* or *practise*
There is a football _____ on Wednesday.
_____ what you preach.
_____ makes perfect.
Can we _____ the whole thing tomorrow?
Do you _____ regularly? An hour's _____ a day is all you need to do.

9.2 *advice* or *advise*
What do you _____ me to do?
I _____ you to see a doctor.
Let me give you some expert _____.
The Citizens' _____ Bureau offers a free _____ service.
People love to _____ others, but they seldom follow their own _____

9.3 *all together* or *altogether*
He did less and less work, and has now given up _____.
They were huddled _____ in the climbers' bothy.
Try to keep your tools _____ in one box.
Such methods are not _____ satisfactory.
_____, he has played in 44 international matches.

9.4 ***principal* or *principle***

The _____ character was played by Kenneth Branagh.

   She has abandoned all her left-wing _____.

Do you agree in _____ with the idea?

The _____ will see you in his office now.

The party is organised on Leninist _____

9.5 ***alternate* or *alternative***

We met on _____ Mondays.

We need an _____ source of supply

There was no _____ but to increase the price.

They _____ between hope and black despair.

Can you suggest an _____ ending to the story?

9.6 ***forego* or *forgo***

I was disappointed to _____ my summer holiday.

Please read the _____ paragraph very carefully.

I acknowledge the ideas of Thorstein Veblen in the _____ analysis.

He has _____ smoking and drinking beer in his effort to get fit.

The result is a _____ conclusion.

9.7 ***practicable* or *practical***

This information is of no _____ use.

Noise levels have been reduced as far as is _____.

I try to be more _____ than you.

A white carpet in the kitchen is not exactly _____

His approach is down-to-earth and entirely _____

9.8 ***lay/lie* or *laid/lain* or *laying/lying***

She'll _____ anyone a bet on the Derby.

I _____ down for a short nap.

The leaves have _____ on the grass all winter.

He gently _____ the book down.

They are _____ down a red carpet for the President.

9.9 ***passed* or *past***

He's been in bed for the _____ few days.

The train _____ through Perth at half _____ two.

They say he has a rather murky _____.

She _____ me a copy of the report.

The plane _____ overhead with a roar.

9.10 ***inimical* or *inimitable***

He dresses in a quite _____ manner.

They are as _____ as oil and water.

The Arctic environment is _____ to habitation.

Her attitude is _____ to any form of opposition.

Her _____ voice was audible outside the door.

9.11 *course* or *coarse*

They played golf on a 9-hole _____

The _____ of the war changed after Stalingrad.

The grass by the shore was very long and _____

The wine was gritty and rather _____

I do hope he will stick the _____ .

9.12 *deadly* or *deathly*

He's not joking – he's _____ serious.

She swallowed a _____ dose of the poison.

Her poor face was _____ pale.

There's a _____ hush in the street tonight.

After his outburst, there was a _____ silence in the room.

9.13 Underline **the correct word** of the two words in brackets.

You are not (*aloud, allowed*) in there.

The moon shone (*pale, pail*) across the sleeping town.

The jacket was made of (*course, coarse*) tweed.

Che Guevara was a famous Latin American (*gorilla, guerrilla*).

This murder is one of the (*grizzliest, gristliest*) in police records.

You are always (*losing, loosing*) something.

Large-scale British maps are produced by the (*Ordinance, Ordnance*) Survey.

Her front teeth are fixed to a dental (*plate, plait*).

The runaway horse came (*strait, straight*) at me.

I don't think you've (*all together, altogether*) appreciated the urgency of the problem.

Your good (*advise, advice*) had no apparent (*effect, affect*) on his behaviour.

She was a famous chef and (*restauranteur, restaurateur*).

10 Spelling

10.1 *-able* and *-ible*

There is no easy rule to follow when making adjectives with these **suffixes**, but we know that from *sense* we get *sensible*, while *admire* gives *admirable*. If necessary with the help of a dictionary, complete these:

practic . ble	excit . ble
access . ble	indispens . ble
prevent . ble	invis . ble
convert . ble	neglig . ble
approach . ble	advis . ble
incred . ble	permiss . ble

contempt . ble   cur . ble

respons . ble   irrit . ble

10.2 **Homonyms** are words with the same sound but different spellings and meanings (such as *wave* and *waive, piece* and *peace*, etc.). Confusion often arises with such pairs of words. With the help of a dictionary if necessary, write down a word with the same sound as the following, then define the pairs:

weight	hall
doze	vale
seed	maize
muscle	serial
marshal	sore
peak	threw
teem	grate
gild	stare
sweet	paws
beach	time
board	rite
stake	cheque
hair	fair

10.3 Sometimes it is possible to enlist the help of an easier spelling to help us with a harder one. For example, we all know that *ball* is spelled with two *l*'s. This should help to remind us to spell *balloon* with two *l*'s too. Use the easier words in the following sentences to help you to spell the harder ones correctly:

My birthday is *certified* on my birth _____ cate.

The *bat*_____ of soldiers was ready for *battle*.

A _____ *ette* is a small *cigar*.

On _____ *mas* Day we remember the birth of *Christ*.

The job of a _____ *ment* is to *govern*.

Some _____ *cines* are not recommended by *medical* authorities.

A _____ *ary* sometimes handles confidential and *secret* information.

We *com* _____ certain events and keep them in our *memory*.

Bronchitis is the name for inflamed _____ *al* tubes.

A _____ *ic* explosion is one which fills passers-by with *terror*.

10.4 The **roots** of many derived words are not spelled exactly as the roots of the words from which they are taken. Thus a female *tiger* is not a *tigeress*, but a *tigress*. And a person with a sense of *humour* is not *humourous* but *humorous*. Add the **suffix** shown in brackets to the following words, and change the root appropriately. Check your answer with a dictionary:

wonder (-ous)	exclaim (-ation)
remember (-ance)	carpenter (-y)

sculptor (-ess)	glamour (-ous)
proprietor (-ess)	register (-rar)
winter (-y)	enchanter (-ess)
disaster (-ous)	curious (-ity)
encumber (-ance)	hinder (-ance)
vigour (-ous)	monster (-ous)
enter (-ance)	pronounce (-iation)
waiter (-ess)	repeat (-ition)
labour (-ious)	(de-)odour (-ant)
administer (-ation)	
vapour (-ise)	

11 Punctuation

Here are some exercises for you to try your punctuation skills on. Answers are on pp. 233–8. If you find you are getting the answers wrong, refer back to the relevant section of the book.

11.1 **Full stops**

Write these passages out in proper sentences. Start each sentence with a capital letter and end it with a full stop.

(a) my cousin Lucy is at the University of Sussex she is finding she has to work very hard (two sentences)

(b) mrs Pitman has gone to the garage she'll be back in an hour's time i'll tell her you called (three sentences)

(c) jackdaws look rather like rooks they are sometimes kept as pets with patience they can be taught to mimic human speech but don't forget that jackdaws are mischievous birds they carry off and hide any small glittering object (five sentences)

(d) there are three ways to get a job done the best way is to do it yourself then you can pay someone to do it for you the third way is to tell your children not to do it under any circumstances (four sentences)

11.2 **Exclamation marks and question marks**

These sentences need to be punctuated with full stops, question marks or exclamation marks at the end. Other punctuation may also be needed.

(a) A fine lot of good that will do us

(b) I am asking all of you if you will subscribe a pound to the cause

(c) If only this toothache would stop

(d) How often do you make the round trip to London nowadays

(e) I wonder how that trick is done

(f) Tom and Barbara are coming with us aren't they

(g) Tell me why you asked that question

(h) Get out stay out and don't come back

(i) Question what do you call a budgie that's been run over by a lawn mower answer shredded tweet

11.3 **Commas**

These sentences need to be punctuated with commas and full stops.

(a) I will not detain you ladies and gentlemen any longer than necessary

(b) Beethoven one of the world's greatest composers was stone deaf towards the end of his life

(c) Fill all the cracks with plaster rub down with fine sandpaper apply a first coat of size allow to dry before rubbing down again if necessary and then apply the first coat of paint

(d) After what seemed like ages we found an area of flattish ground unloaded our gear from the car and began to erect our tent in pitch darkness

(e) He told me frankly that he had telephoned the police and that he didn't care when I went where I went or how I went so long as I left his premises at once

(f) According to tradition a bride should carry or wear something old something new something borrowed something blue

(g) They say the unexpected doesn't always happen but when it does it generally happens when you are least expecting it

11.4 **Semicolons**

Put punctuation marks as needed in the following phrases. All of them will need semicolons, among others.

(a) Swallows migrate vast distances a thousand-mile journey is nothing to these amazing little birds

(b) Like alligators crocodiles lay eggs snakes also reproduce themselves in this manner

(c) Friends Romans countrymen lend me your ears I come to bury Caesar not to praise him

(d) The sun sets night falls very suddenly and after the great heat of the day the desert quickly becomes cold this causes the rocks to split and crumble

(e) A gossip talks to you about others a bore talks to you about himself a brilliant speaker talks to you about you

(f) The items which were found on the beach consisted of a particularly grubby tattered old shirt you wouldn't be seen dead in a pair of old shoes made out of rope string and bits of old tyres and finally a torn and grease-stained pair of overalls

11.5 **Colons**

Put punctuation marks as needed in the following passages. All of them will require colons, among others.

(a) We visited many interesting places during our trip to Paris the Eiffel Tower the Champs Elysées the Louvre the Pantheon and the cemetery at Père Lachaise

(b) This is captain steadman speaking first i'll give you the good news the flight-time is a world record now the bad news because of fog at frankfurt we are having to divert to amsterdam

(c) There is only one way to win wars make certain they never happen

(d) We had quite a shock when we reached home the house had been burgled

(e) Take care of the pennies the pounds take care of themselves

(f) Richard II said not all the water in the rough-rude sea can wash the balm from an anointed king

11.6 **Apostrophes**

Here are some newspaper headlines. You have to insert the apostrophes, where necessary.

(a) ALL TODAYS TENNIS RESULTS

(b) NEW ROUTES FOR LONDONS BUSES

(c) FIRE DESTROYS NURSES FLATS

(d) LORRYS BRAKES FAIL ON HILL

(e) SHIPS CREW ADRIFT IN DINGHIES

(f) PENSIONS FOR SOLDIERS WIDOWS

(g) CITY GALLERIES FINANCIAL PROBLEMS

(h) THREE MONTHS RAIN IN TWO WEEKS

(i) CABINET MINISTERS AT ST PAULS

Correct these sentences by putting in the apostrophes and any other missing punctuation.

(j) A smiles the way to start the day thats what id say

(k) Im sorry but youve got the wrong number theres no mike here

(l) She was in the 95 hockey team when last i saw her shes changed a bit since then of course

(m) My cousins hands were badly hurt

(n) Johns watch is five minutes slower than Andrews

(o) The ladies cloakroom is on the left opposite the mens

(p) The childrens books were all left at uncle colins house

(q) There were displays of babies clothes in the shop windows

11.7 **Capital letters**

Put capitals and other punctuation in the following sentences, where needed.

(a) i bought a copy of the daily mail at edgeware road and read it on the underground to kings cross

(b) mr briggs who is irish teaches french and german at st pauls school in hammersmith

(c) camilla duchess of cornwall inspected the guard of honour at st jamess palace before going on the the haymarket theatre to see an afternoon performance of the cocktail party by t s eliot

(d) julius caesar conquered north africa he conquered gaul he conquered britain but before he could take ireland he ran out of conkers

(e) dr barbara holland consultant at the royal hospital for sick children in glasgow is seen in our picture caring for scott stephanie and karen a set of very premature triplets from paisley

(f) this term our english class is studying the poetry of john milton last week we read lycidas and for next week we have to study the poem called on his blindness

11.8 Hyphens

Put hyphens where needed in these sentences, along with any other missing punctuation.

(a) The idea of inter continental air travel would have been considered far fetched three quarters of a century ago.

(b) Telling a hair raising story to a bald headed man is a good example of time wasting.

(c) There are twenty seven people in my french class at the franco british institute.

(d) He had one of those insufferable im better than you and you know it expressions on his silly pompous face.

(e) There was a thirty gallon tank in the attic full of the most evil smelling liquid.

(f) A three ton lorry with a top heavy load bumped into a two door sports car at the crossroads.

(g) They were hiding in a bomb proof shelter in the cellar of that prison like building beside the palace.

Remember that phrases do not need a hyphen usually until you use them as an adjective. Here are some pairs of sentences with words italicised. Which of these words need the hyphens?

(h) Our reporter John Walsh is *on the spot* with the latest news.
Our reporter John Walsh sends us this *on the spot* report.

(i) It was a *never to be forgotten* cup final.
It was a cup final *never to be forgotten*.

(j) The *first night* audience gave the show a good reception.
On the *first night* the audience was enthusiastic.

(k) This timetable is *out of date*, and not to be trusted.
This is an *out of date* timetable, and not to be trusted.

(l) In July, there was a serious crisis in the *balance of payments*.
Things have settled down since the last *balance of payments* crisis.

(m) He is a good person with lots of *common sense*.
   He is a good, *common sense* person.

11.9 Quotation marks

Punctuate these sentences with quotation marks and any other correct punctuation.

(a) The young man asked have you seen my chisel yes replied my brother you left it on the kitchen table

(b) Oh no cried the boy i don't believe in that sort of thing any more

(c) I hope said the child to her father that you will tell me the story of the african pirate king well smiled her father i may do that but not until you've finished your homework

(d) I believe he's gone to the police station said the young lady to the inspector in a very quiet voice i'm afraid i shall have to ask you too for a statement said the inspector taking out his notebook

(e) I asked John if he was angry and he answered not really i'm more annoyed than angry

(f) this said miss johnstone looking out of the window is the most important day of my life

(g) if i see anyone move said elizabeth am i to fire at them

(h) do you know a poem called the raven i asked my mother oh yes i think i do she said it was one of those things we had to learn by heart at school its by edgar allan poe isnt it i haven't the faintest i admitted but it's a clue in todays telegraph crossword do you remember how it went erm once upon a midnight dreary while I pondered weak and weary began my mother with a weary pondering look on her face thats it i interrupted her ive got it now thanks

11.10 Parenthesis

Put brackets, dashes, or commas – as you think best – in the following. Remember to use pairs.

(a) Now and then as though dreaming she smiled in her sleep.

(b) I shall need a rucksack a really big one for all that gear.

(c) Roger tells me I hope he is right that admission to the castle is free.

(d) The following day Bank Holiday Monday we all went down to Brighton to see the sea.

(e) It was at the nearby town Saumur that we had planned our rendezvous with John.

(f) The officer searched the drawers all the cupboards were locked and he unearthed some useful clues.

(g) I have reached the conclusion having considered all the evidence thoroughly that this young man is innocent.

(h) Fife District area 507 sq m has a population of 350,000 Local Authority Statistics 2001.

    (i)   Abou Ben Adhem may his tribe increase awoke one night from a deep dream of peace.

    (j)   People like peaches and pears grow sweet shortly before they begin to decay.

11.11 A final punctuation check-up

Punctuate these sentences:

    (a)   wheres the car asked the mechanic

    (b)   her uncle said heres a cup of tea

    (c)   mrs jones exclaimed what a dreadful storm

    (d)   hes gone to the police station said james in a quiet voice

    (e)   the girl suddenly shouted look

    (f)   oh cried the child ive got no money for the bus

    (g)   come here said the teacher coming replied george

    (h)   the gardener asked have you seen my rake yes replied his mate i put it back in the shed

    (i)   John asked have you time for a coffee sorry not tonight i replied im late for my train

    (j)   when we get home said her father to the girl ill tell you the story of the pirate king oh good she replied are we nearly there

    (k)   lets make a list of the places we want to visit first carthage second tunis third kairouan were going to need a good long holiday

    (l)   he said that andrew who usually went fishing at weekends had gone to london instead

    (m)   a tall woman walked into the shop removed her hood laid down her umbrella and handbag on a chair and drummed her fingers on the counter id like to buy a pair of black flat heeled shoes she announced to the shop at large glancing round briskly for an assistant

    (n)   in a climate like ours blue comparatively speaking is one of the coldest most unfriendly colours one can use to decorate a room or at least that is my opinion

    (o)   as the presidential motorcade swept along people from all walks of life office workers hairdressers shopkeepers school children all rushed out to the street cheering waving little flags and jumping up and down was it for joy or just to get a better view

Answer pages
(For part 4: punctuation)

Apostrophes

(a) can't you've
(b) It's She's I'm John's
(c) car's It'll
(d) train's I'm he'd
(e) It's babies' What's
(f) Women's men's I'm
(g) day's we'd
(h) firm's they've Queen's
(i) Mark's dad's everyone's
(j) school's vandals' It's

Brackets

(a) Edward (his best friend) ignored Roger in the street.
(b) Mrs Crawford (a woman I have always admired) is coming to our party tomorrow.
(c) We were (still are) happy to see her settled in a regular job.
(d) No one in our house (according to my young sister) knows how to cook properly.
(e) The Royal Family (pictured left) flew to Brazil this afternoon (picture on page 3) for a state visit.
(f) His collection of wild flowers (anemones, primroses, orchids) is world famous.
(g) Precious metals (gold, silver, platinum, etc.) are best kept locked up in the bank.
(h) Edinburgh (population 450,000) is more than twice as big as Aberdeen (population 210,000) and half as big as Dublin (population 900,000).
(i) We spent 45 euros (about £30 sterling) for a trip to explore the caves.
(j) He's a complete eccentric (eats snails, it's said), so his neighbours tend to keep an eye on his movements.

Capital letters

(a) I'm reading Philip Larkin's *Collected Poems* again. It's to be returned to the library by 1 September.
(b) The English cricket team will visit Pakistan in December on their way back from Australia.
(c) Will the BBC or ITV or SkyTV cover the Arsenal v Crystal Palace game on Saturday?

(d) I'm afraid I'm no expert on French or Spanish writing. You should speak to Professor Healey. He teaches French and his wife is from Argentina, I think.

(e) They used to tell us in our geography classes that America was the Land of Opportunity, Britain was the Workshop of the World and the Nile Delta was the Breadbasket of Egypt. That's how old I am!

(f) Admiral Nelson was killed at the Battle of Trafalgar and Sir John Moore fell at Corunna.

(g) The 24 bus normally goes up Tottenham Court Road to Camden Town, but yesterday there was a diversion because of a huge TUC anti-war procession along Euston Road.

(h) The Gaelic language survives in parts of Wales, Scotland, Ireland and Brittany, but it has died out in Galicia, Cornwall and the Isle of Man.

Colons

(a) Work fascinates me: I can sit and look at it for hours.

(b) We climbed four peaks last week: Lochnagar and Broad Cairn on Friday, Ben Macdui and Cairn Gorm on Saturday.

(c) There were lots of boats in the harbour: yachts, catamarans, speed-boats, fishing boats, etc.

(d) He is exactly what people say he is: a bore and a fool.

(e) The doctor told him the worst: he was not likely to recover.

(f) The following items were stolen: a purse, a ring, a diary and some cheque cards.

(g) The view from the hilltop is splendid: the Castle, the Old Town, and the spires and monuments are all spread out before you.

(h) It has to be one of the surest signs of increasing age: you start to notice how young the police have become.

Commas

(a) The opening ceremony took place in the presence of the German economics minister, the Spanish culture minister, the mayor of Frankfurt, the president of the German Publishers' Association, and the great and good of the European book trade. Also present was a gaggle of gregarious authors, assorted literary glitterati, and – of course – the ever-watchful, omnipresent, prosperous, well-fed remainder merchants.

(b) To make cucumber soup you need one large cucumber, one onion, two ounces butter, one and a half pints white stock, seasoning, and a quarter pint of thick cream. To cook, you need to chop then toss the vegetables in the hot butter for a few minutes, taking care that they do not brown. Add the stock, a small piece of chopped cucumber peel, and a little seasoning. Simmer for twenty minutes, then emulsify in a liquidiser or sieve. Cool, then blend in the cream.

(c)   As well as Mass on Sundays, and her weekly visits to a wayside dance-hall, Bridie went shopping once every month. Cycling to the town early on a Friday afternoon, she bought things for herself, material for a dress, knitting wool, stockings, a newspaper and paperbacked Wild West novels for her father. She talked in the shops to some of the girls she'd been at school with, girls who had married shop-assistants or shop-keepers, or had become assistants themselves. Most of them had families of their own by now. They had a tired look, most of them, from pregnancies, and from their efforts to organise and control their large families.

(d)   West of the town centre at 2 De Ruyterlaan is the Natuurmuseum, with a collection of rare birds, insects, reptiles and mammals, minerals, and fossils. Nearby stands the Synagogue, topped by a somewhat oriental copper dome. It dates from 1928. East of here is the Boulevard of the Liberation, from which the Langestraat branches off on the left, leading into a street called De Klomp. On the left-hand side is the Elderinkshuis (1783), the only historic building in the town to have survived the Great Fire of 1862.

(e)   We invited John and Frances and the Macdonalds for supper, and Mary happened to drop in too. Afterwards we had a long discussion about whether to have a cup of tea, or coffee with rum in it. In the end, David took us all out for a drink. He ordered a whisky and lemonade, a gin and tonic, two dry martinis with ice, three cokes, a lager and lime, and a brandy and soda. I'm glad I wasn't footing the bill.

Dash

(a)   Walk, if you please – don't run.

(b)   Yes – oh dear, yes – the novel tells a story.

(c)   We know, Mr Weller – we who are men of the world – that a good uniform must work its way with the women, sooner or later.

(d)   Advice to persons about to marry – Don't!

(e)   The English country gentleman galloping after a fox – the unspeakable in full pursuit of the uneatable.

(f)   Go directly – see what she's doing, and tell her she mustn't.

(g)   The Common Law of England is laboriously built around a mythical figure – the 'Reasonable Man'.

(h)   It is well that war is so terrible – otherwise we would grow too fond of it.

(i)   She's the sort of woman who lives for others – you can tell the others by their haunted expression.

(j)   There is nothing – absolutely nothing – half so worth doing as messing about in boats.

Full stops

(a) The crocodile lives in the mudbanks of rivers in India and Africa. His huge body grows to a length of about ten metres. People sometimes hunt him for his leather skin. He has four short legs and can walk reasonably well. But water is his chosen element. Here he can move really fast.

(b) One night a great storm broke over the city. The thunder rolled and roared. The lightning flashed and the rain fell in torrents. Everyone stayed indoors and hid from the elements. Suddenly there was a positive eruption of noise and flashes of blinding light. The bursts came again and yet again. The huddled masses trembled in their shanties all the while.

(c) You've heard of the famous Niagara Falls. Several people have tried to go over these falls in barrels or small boats. In nearly every case the barrels were smashed to pieces against the rocks and the men in them killed or drowned. The only man who ever succeeded in going over the falls was Captain Webb. A few years later he lost his life trying to swim the rapids just below the falls.

Hyphens

(a) one-eyed

(b) mouse-to-mouse

(c) two-hundred-strong thirty-odd

(d) shock-proof corrosion-resistant anti-magnetic

(e) warm-up scrum-half stand-off mid-run hair-raising full-back's up-and-unders cul-de-sac half-time

(f) made-up off-the-peg back-of-the-envelope make-up ice-cream out-patients'

(g) vice-chancellor ex-president non-executive fund-raising two-thirds

Paragraphing

Passage 1 (from *A Cool Million*)

'I wonder who did it?' asked Steve.

'I can't imagine,' answered Lem brokenly.

'Did they get much?'

'All I had in the world . . . A little less than thirty dollars.'

'Some smart leather must have gotten it.'

'Leather?' queried our hero, not understanding the argot of the underworld with which the train boy was familiar.

'Yes, leather – pickpocket. Did anybody talk to you on the train?'

'Only Mr Wellington Mape, a rich young man. He is kin to the Mayor of New York.'

'Who told you that?'
'He did himself.'
'How was he dressed?' asked Steve, whose suspicions were aroused.

Passage 2 (from *New Grub Street*)

At eight o'clock came the doctor. He would allow only a word or two to be uttered, and his visit was brief. Reardon was chiefly anxious to have news of the child, but for this he would have to wait.

At ten Amy entered the bedroom. Reardon could not raise himself, but he stretched out his hand and took hers, and gazed eagerly at her. She must have been weeping, he felt sure of that, and there was an expression on her face such as he had never seen there.

'How is Willie?'
'Better, dear, much better.'
He still searched her face.
'Ought you to leave him?'
'Hush, you mustn't speak.' Tears broke from her eyes, and Reardon had the conviction that the child was dead.
'The truth, Amy!'
She threw herself on her knees by the bedside, and pressed her wet cheek against his hand.
'I am come to nurse you, dear husband,' she said a moment after, standing up again and kissing his forehead. 'I have only you now.'

Question marks and exclamation marks

(1) ?
(2) !
(3) ?
(4) !
(5) ?
(6 .
(7) ?
(8) ?
(9) .
(10) !
(11) !
(12) ?
(13) !
(14) !
(15) !
(16) .

Quotation marks

(a) 'Is this the road to the seashore?' asked the motorist.

(b) 'I'm not sure,' replied the young lady. 'I'm a stranger here myself.'

(c) 'I told you to buy a map,' said his wife, 'but now it's too late and all the shops are shut.'

(d) My favourite reading this year has been *District and Circle*, Seamus Heaney's new book of poems, and a very funny collection of bits and pieces called *Lost Worlds*, by Michael Bywater.

(e) 'In the end,' she said, 'we took the umbrella to the lost property office. It was too good an article to leave lying in the street,' she added by way of explanation.

(f) 'But this,' said Angela, 'is murder. We need to phone the police,' she added, her voice growing ever more shrill.

(g) 'The chances of a serious accident,' began the professor, 'are probably greater than they've ever been in history. Whoever thought kamikaze pilots would deliberately set out to crash their planes into busy office buildings?'

Semicolons

(a) This is my umbrella; that is yours.

(b) She insisted on giving us the whole story; it went on and on for ages.

(c) I don't think that's fair; you don't know the whole story.

(d) They looked everywhere, but couldn't find her; she must have left the office.

(e) The doctor did her morning round of the wards at nine; she was accompanied by two nurses, a physiotherapist and a consultant.

(f) The last chickens had gone; it seemed clear that the fox had again entered the hen-house during the night.

(g) The judge passed sentence; the defendant passed out; the press corps sprinted off to relay the verdict to a waiting world.

Answer pages
(For Part 7: check-up pages)

In many instances, the suggested answers that follow only offer one or two options. These should not invariably be regarded as the only options.

1 Number

1. We heard the noises in the trees.
2. The ships have struck rocks.

3. The ladies' hats were on the pegs.
4. The wolves are eating the rabbits.
5. The children ran to the windows to see the foxes.
6. The thieves stole valuable paintings.
7. We kept the rabbits in cages.
8. The sailors are swimming to their ships.
9. Cats – or mice – may look at kings.
10. We took knives and forks.

2 Verbs

1. looked out
2. is going
3. should have spoken
4. will be landing
5. have been rescued
6. Come; see; is finished
7. was crowded
8. has risen
9. Drink
10. fought; killed; bit

3 Phrasal verbs

1. hung up
2. get away
3. broke down
4. turned up
5. called in; break up
6. give up
7. check in
8. turn down
9. kept on
10. kept at

4 Prepositions

1. to
2. of
3. for
4. of
5. to
6. in
7. of

8. at
9. for *or* on, in
10. of; in

5 Parts of speech

1. adjective
2. transitive verb
3. adverb
4. intransitive verb
5. preposition
6. copular verb
7. conjunction
8. adverb
9. pronoun (dummy subject)
10. distributive pronoun
11. noun
12. adverb
13. interjection
14. complement
15. noun phrase, in apposition
16. indefinite pronoun
17. phrasal verb
18. question tag
19. adverbial, of degree
20. phrasal verb
21. intransitive verb, passive
22. adjective phrase, complement
23. prepositional phrase
24. phrasal verb, passive
25. indefinite pronoun, object
26. adverbial
27. adjective, superlative
28. adverb, frequency
29. pronoun, indirect object
30. verb, passive

6 Phrases, clauses and sentences

1. P
2. S
3. P
4. P
5. S

6. S
7. P
8. P
9. S
10. P
11. . . . and tried to clear my head.
12. If you start fooling about . . .
13. . . . and is hiding in the garden.
14. . . . but it still needs a second coat.
15. When I opened the door . . .
16. . . . and try to relax.
17. After we'd seen the movie . . .
18. As soon as the cat appeared . . .
19. . . . and began running towards us.
20. Although she's an excellent runner . . .
21. I like chips best and my brother likes pasta.
22. The rain came on so I put up my umbrella.
23. I offered a small donation and the secretary thanked me for it.
24. Mary went by air but the flight was delayed.
25. The ice cream looks nice but the trifle looks less than fresh.
26. They knew it was a long trip so they ate a good breakfast.
27. There was a loud peal of thunder and the children were frightened.
28. She caught a large salmon and took it home for tea.
29. The taxi was summoned but nobody left the party.
30. The college boiler broke down so the students were sent home.
31. I was angry with George because he was late.
32. How can you hear me when you're not even listening?
33. The boy who sat on my left wore a black tracksuit.
34. I arrived while you were out.
35. I can't go because it's too expensive.
36. The dog barked when he heard a noise.
37. My brother likes pasta while/whereas I like chips.
38. She waited downstairs while I got ready hurriedly.
39. The explosive, which was in a plastic bag, was found by a security man.
40. She looked very edgy and worried although her companion was quite inoffensive.
41. . . . you're sure of a big surprise.
42. . . . it didn't seem very cold.
43. . . . she soon fell fast asleep.
44. . . . the Three Bears made themselves comfortable.
45. . . . the dog barked furiously.
46. I have to rest now . . .
47. I do my homework . . .
48. He's lost his job again . . .

49. . . . he'll have to move elsewhere.
50. Offer her a promotion . . .
51. Give him some more money
52. Show me the photos
53. It's five years
54. Suddenly I understood
55. I have a dog
56. She lives in Reading; (she) works in London
57. Sally's gone to Edinburgh; Andrew's gone to Glasgow
58. we were all relieved
59. you'll see a signpost
60. I was more interested in watching the game

7 Word formation

7.1 ability admiration allowance anxiety arrival beggar behaviour choice civility/civilisation creation/creativity cruelty description enjoyment exhaustion falsity/falsehood fame fierceness fragrance growth hatred holiness injury invitation laziness life loss/loser missionary movement opposition/opponent pleasure prosperity punishment reality remembrance revival security sight service sickness simplicity speech strength thought warmth weariness width worth youth

7.2 accidental affectionate angry attractive biblical British childish continental courageous crafty critical customary destructive disastrous dutiful excessive faithful/faithless fashionable favourable forgetful gigantic gracious high informative introductory legal lovely meddlesome metallic musical neglectful northern/northerly occasional parental pitiful/pitiless proud quarrelsome reasonable silken/silky starry successful thirsty thoughtful tired/tiresome united victorious vocal watery wooden youthful

7.3 beautify encircle civilise encourage criticise darken falsify fatten fertilise fill glaze grieve enjoy enlarge lengthen magnetise imperil purify enrich sharpen simplify solve speak succeed try

7.4 ably brightly courageously critically destructively exhaustively heavily heroically joyfully/joyously justly lazily readily resentfully successfully typically vainly wearily wisely worthily wretchedly

7.5 headache/bellyache backache/backside raspberry/strawberry blacksmith/ blackberry bookworm/handbook tablecloth/altarcloth holiday/Monday doorstep/doorknob footfall/footbridge grandson/grandmother heartfelt/heartache hedgerow/hedgehog household/housemaid lifetime/ lifelong manhood/postman millwheel/windmill moonlight/honeymoon newsagent/newshound nightfall/midnight piecemeal/timepiece fencepost/postbox rainfall/rainwear seascape/undersea schoolkid/schoolroom

snowflake/snowstorm sunshine/sunflower tablecloth/birdtable watertable/
waterfall witchcraft/witchdoctor workshy/handiwork

7.6 <u>amphi</u>theatre <u>anti</u>biotic <u>arch</u>angel <u>be</u>spectacled <u>bio</u>graphy <u>chrono</u>-
meter <u>counter</u>attack <u>de</u>activate <u>demo</u>crat <u>dis</u>connect <u>down</u>size <u>eco</u>system
<u>equi</u>vocal <u>for</u>go <u>hyper</u>market <u>hypo</u>dermic <u>mega</u>lopolis <u>meta</u>morphosis
<u>milli</u>pede <u>mis</u>judge <u>para</u>sol <u>peri</u>meter <u>poly</u>gon <u>post</u>date <u>sub</u>marine
<u>sur</u>charge <u>sur</u>name <u>tele</u>printer <u>to</u>morrow <u>un</u>clear <u>uni</u>cycle <u>up</u>stream

7.7 admir<u>able</u> assist<u>ant</u> bak<u>er</u> Brazil<u>ian</u> bush<u>craft</u> computer<u>ese</u> consul-
tan<u>cy</u> cook<u>ery</u> dam<u>sel</u> digest<u>ible</u> duti<u>ful</u> farm<u>hand</u> fortun<u>ate</u> girl<u>ish</u>
gossip<u>monger</u> govern<u>ment</u> host<u>ess</u> ignit<u>ion</u> interview<u>ee</u> Japan<u>ese</u>
kibbutz<u>nik</u> letter<u>head</u> machin<u>ery</u> Marx<u>ism</u> milk<u>man</u> minor<u>ity</u> modu-
l<u>ar</u> narrat<u>or</u> not<u>ify</u> official<u>dom</u> parliament<u>arian</u> pira<u>cy</u> privat<u>eer</u>
sing<u>er</u> Span<u>ish</u> station<u>ary</u> three<u>fold</u> wash<u>able</u> witch<u>craft</u> work<u>aholic</u>
young<u>ster</u>

8 Figures of speech

1. graces
2. dried
3. nail
4. holidays
5. sundry
6. cons
7. ruin
8. limb
9. call
10. main
11. to catch a thief
12. the mice will play
13. spoil the broth
14. is another man's poison
15. and not heard
16. part of valour
17. flock together
18. gathers no moss
19. has its day
20. never won fair lady
21. took to his; stood his (or went to)
22. in your cap; on your escutcheon
23. while the iron was; let the grass grow under his feet
24. sailing; hard nut to crack
25. in both; feet

9 Confusibles

9.1 practice; practise; practice; practise; practise; practice
9.2 advise; advise; advice; Advice; advice; advise; advice
9.3 altogether; all together; all together; altogether; altogether
9.4 principal; principles; principle; principal; principles
9.5 alternate; alternative; alternative; alternate; alternative
9.6 forgo; foregoing; foregoing; forgone; foregone
9.7 practical; practicable; practical; practical; practical
9.8 lay; lay; lain; laid; laying
9.9 past; passed; past; past; passed; passed
9.10 inimitable; inimical; inimical; inimical; inimitable
9.11 course; course; coarse; coarse; course
9.12 deadly; deadly; deathly; deathly; deathly/deadly (depends on the reaction)
9.13 allowed pale coarse guerrilla grizzliest losing Ordnance plate
straight altogether advice effect restaurateur

10 Spelling

10.1 practicable accessible preventable convertible approachable incredible contemptible responsible excitable indispensable invisible negligible
advisable permissible curable irritable
10.2 wait dose cede mussel martial peek team guild suite beech bored
steak hare haul veil maze cereal soar through great stair pause
thyme right check fare
10.3 certificate battalion cigarette Christmas government medicines secretary commemorate bronchial terrific
10.4 wondrous remembrance sculptress proprietress wintry disastrous
encumbrance vigorous entrance waitress laborious administration
vaporise exclamation carpentry glamorous registrar enchantress
curiosity hindrance monstrous pronunciation repetition deodorant

11 Punctuation

11.1 **Full stops**

(a) My cousin Lucy is at the University of Sussex. She is finding she has
to work very hard.

(b) Mrs Pitman has gone to the garage. She'll be back in an hour's time.
I'll tell her you called.

(c) Jackdaws look rather like rooks. They are sometimes kept as pets.
With patience they can be taught to mimic human speech. But don't
forget that jackdaws are mischievous birds. They carry off and hide
any small, glittering object.

(d) There are three ways to get a job done. The best way is to do it yourself. Then you can pay someone to do it for you. The third way is to
tell your children not to do it under any circumstances.

11.2 Exclamation marks and question marks

(a) A fine lot of good that will do us!
(b) I am asking all of you if you will subscribe a pound to the cause.
(c) If only this toothache would stop!
(d) How often do you make the round trip to London nowadays?
(e) I wonder how that trick is done.
(f) Tom and Barbara are coming with us, aren't they?
(g) Tell me why you asked that question.
(h) Get out, stay out, and don't come back! (*or*) Get out! Stay out! And
don't come back!
(i) Question: What do you call a budgie that's been run over by a lawn
mower? Answer: Shredded tweet!

11.3 Commas

(a) I will not detain you, ladies and gentlemen, any longer than necessary.
(b) Beethoven, one of the world's greatest composers, was stone deaf towards the end of his life.
(c) Fill all the cracks with plaster, rub down with fine sandpaper, apply a
first coat of size, allow to dry before rubbing down again if necessary,
and then apply the first coat of paint.
(d) After what seemed like ages, we found an area of flattish ground,
unloaded our gear from the car, and began to erect our tent in pitch
darkness.
(e) He told me frankly that he had telephoned the police, and that he
didn't care when I went, where I went, or how I went, so long as I left
his premises at once.
(f) According to tradition, a bride should carry or wear something old,
something new, something borrowed, something blue.
(g) They say the unexpected doesn't always happen, but when it does, it
generally happens when you are least expecting it.

11.4 Semicolons

(a) Swallows migrate vast distances; a thousand-mile journey is nothing
to these amazing little birds.
(b) Like alligators, crocodiles lay eggs; snakes also reproduce themselves
in this manner.
(c) 'Friends, Romans, countrymen, lend me your ears; I come to bury
Caesar, not to praise him.'
(d) The sun sets; night falls very suddenly; and after the great heat of the
day, the desert quickly becomes cold. This causes the rocks to split
and crumble.

(e) A gossip talks to you about others; a bore talks to you about himself; a brilliant speaker talks to you about you.

(f) The items which were found on the beach consisted of a particularly grubby, tattered old shirt you wouldn't be seen dead in; a pair of old shoes made out of rope, string, and bits of old tyres; and finally, a torn and grease-stained pair of overalls.

11.5 Colons

(a) We visited many interesting places during our trip to Paris: the Eiffel Tower, the Champs Elysées, the Louvre, the Pantheon, and the cemetery at Père Lachaise.

(b) 'This is Captain Steadman speaking. First I'll give you the good news: the flight-time is a world record. Now the bad news: because of fog at Frankfurt, we are having to divert to Amsterdam.'

(c) There is only one way to win wars: make certain they never happen.

(d) We had quite a shock when we reached home: the house had been burgled.

(e) Take care of the pennies: the pounds take care of themselves.

(f) Richard II said: 'Not all the water in the rough-rude sea can wash the balm from an anointed king.'

11.6 Apostrophes

(a) ALL TODAY'S TENNIS RESULTS

(b) NEW ROUTES FOR LONDON'S BUSES

(c) FIRE DESTROYS NURSES' FLATS

(d) LORRY'S BRAKES FAIL ON HILL

(e) SHIP'S CREW ADRIFT IN DINGHIES

(f) PENSIONS FOR SOLDIERS' WIDOWS

(g) CITY GALLERIES' FINANCIAL PROBLEMS

(h) THREE MONTHS' RAIN IN TWO WEEKS

(i) CABINET MINISTERS AT ST PAUL'S

(j) A smile's the way to start the day: that's what I'd say.

(k) I'm sorry, but you've got the wrong number. There's no Mike here.

(l) She was in the '95 hockey team when I last saw her. She's changed a bit since then, of course.

(m) My cousin's hands were badly hurt.

(n) John's watch is five minutes slower than Andrew's.

(o) The ladies' cloakroom is on the left, opposite the men's.

(p) The children's books were all left at Uncle Colin's house.

(q) There were displays of babies' clothes in the shop windows.

11.7 Capital letters

(a) I bought a copy of the *Daily Mail* at Edgware Road and read it on the underground to King's Cross.

(b) Mr Briggs, who is Irish, teaches French and German at St Paul's School in Hammersmith.

(c) Camilla Duchess of Cornwall inspected the guard of honour at St James's Palace, before going on to the Haymarket Theatre to see an afternoon performance of *The Cocktail Party*, by T S Eliot.

(d) Julius Caesar conquered North Africa; he conquered Gaul; he conquered Britain; but before he could take Ireland, he ran out of conkers.

(e) Dr Barbara Holland, consultant at the Royal Hospital for Sick Children in Glasgow, is seen in our picture caring for Scott, Stephanie and Karen, a set of very premature triplets from Paisley.

(f) This term our English class is studying the poetry of John Milton. Last week we read 'Lycidas' and for next week we have to study the poem called 'On His Blindness'.

11.8 **Hyphens**

(a) The idea of inter-continental air travel would have been considered far-fetched three-quarters of a century ago.

(b) Telling a hair-raising story to a bald-headed man is a good example of time-wasting.

(c) There are twenty-seven people in my French class at the Franco-British Institute.

(d) He had one of those insufferable I'm-better-than-you-and-you-know-it expressions on his silly, pompous face.

(e) There was a thirty-gallon tank in the attic full of the most evil-smelling liquid.

(f) A three-ton lorry with a top-heavy load bumped into a two-door sports car at the crossroads.

(g) They were hiding in a bomb-proof shelter in the cellar of that prison-like building beside the palace.

(h) second version: Our reporter John Walsh sends us this on-the-spot report.

(i) first version: It was a never-to-be-forgotten cup final.

(j) first version: The first-night audience gave the show a good reception.

(k) second version: This is an out-of-date timetable, and not to be trusted.

(l) second version: Things have settled down since the last balance-of-payments crisis.

(m) second version: He is a good, common-sense person.

11.9 **Quotation marks**

(a) The young man asked, 'Have you seen my chisel?'
'Yes,' replied my brother. 'You left it on the kitchen table.'

(b) 'Oh no!' cried the boy. 'I don't believe in that sort of thing any more.'

(c) 'I hope,' said the child to her father, 'that you will tell me the story of the African pirate king.'
'Well,' smiled her father, 'I may do that – but not until you've finished your homework.'

(d) 'I believe he's gone to the police station,' said the young lady to the inspector, in a very quiet voice.

'I'm afraid I shall have to ask you too for a statement,' said the inspector, taking out his notebook.

(e) I asked John if he was angry and he answered, 'Not really, I'm more annoyed than angry.'

(f) 'This,' said Miss Johnstone looking out of the window, 'is the most important day of my life.'

(g) 'If I see anyone move,' said Elizabeth, 'am I to fire at them?'

(h)) 'Do you know a poem called "The Raven"?' I asked my mother.

'Oh yes, I think I do,' she said. 'It was one of those things we had to learn by heart at school. It's by Edgar Allan Poe, isn't it?'

'I haven't the faintest,' I admitted, 'but it's a clue in today's *Telegraph* crossword. Do you remember how it went?'

'Erm . . . "Once upon a midnight dreary, while I pondered, weak and weary" . . .' began my mother, with a weary, pondering look on her face.

'That's it!' I interrupted her. 'I've got it now. Thanks.'

11.10 **Parenthesis**

(a) Now and then, as though dreaming, she smiled in her sleep.

(b) I shall need a rucksack – a really big one – for all that gear.

(c) Roger tells me – I hope he is right – that admission to the castle is free.

(d) The following day (Bank Holiday Monday), we all went down to Brighton to see the sea.

(e) It was at the nearby town (Saumur) that we had planned our rendezvous with John.

(f) The officer searched the drawers – all the cupboards were locked – and he unearthed some useful clues.

(g) I have reached the conclusion, having considered all the evidence thoroughly, that this young man is innocent.

(h) Fife District (area 507 sq m) has a population of 350,000 (Local Authority Statistics 2001).

(i) Abou Ben Adhem (may his tribe increase!) awoke one night from a deep dream of peace.

(j) People, like peaches and pears, grow sweet shortly before they begin to decay.

11.11 **A final punctuation check-up**

(a) 'Where's the car?' asked the mechanic.

(b) Her uncle said, 'Here's a cup of tea.'

(c) Mrs Jones exclaimed, 'What a dreadful storm!'

(d) 'He's gone to the police station,' said James in a quiet voice.

(e) The girl suddenly shouted, 'Look!'

(f) 'Oh!' cried the child, 'I've got no money for the bus!'

(g) 'Come here,' said the teacher. 'Coming,' replied George.

(h) The gardener asked, 'Have you seen my rake?'
    'Yes,' replied his mate, 'I put it back in the shed.'

(i) John asked, 'Have you time for a coffee?'
    'Sorry, not tonight,' I replied. 'I'm late for my train.'

(j) 'When we get home,' said her father, 'I'll tell you the story of the
    pirate king.'
    'Oh good,' she replied. 'Are we nearly there?'

(k) Let's make a list of the places we want to visit. First, Carthage; second,
    Tunis; third, Kairouan. We're going to need a good long holiday.

(l) He said that Andrew, who usually went fishing at weekends, had gone
    to London instead.

(m) A tall woman walked into the shop, removed her hood, laid down her
    umbrella and handbag on a chair, and drummed her fingers on the
    counter. 'I'd like to buy a pair of black flat-heeled shoes,' she announced
    to the shop at large, glancing round briskly for an assistant.

(n) In a climate like ours, blue – comparatively speaking – is one of the
    coldest, most unfriendly colours one can use to decorate a room. Or
    at least that is my opinion.

(o) As the presidential motorcade swept along, people from all walks of
    life – office workers, hairdressers, shopkeepers, school children – all
    rushed out to the street cheering, waving little flags, and jumping up
    and down. Was it for joy, or just to get a better view?

Index

Bold type indicates the main reference for a topic. *Italic* type indicates an exercise on that topic in the check-up pages at the end of the book.